W9-BKT-082

Popular Mechanics

MONEYSMART MAKEOVERS

LIVING SPACES

RICK PETERS

HEARST BOOKS
A Division of Sterling Publishing Co., Inc.
New York

Note: The safety guards were removed for clarity in many of the photographs in this book. Make sure to always use all safety devices according to the manufacturers' instructions.

Produced by How-2 Media Inc.
Design: Triad Design Group
Photography: Christopher J. Vendetta
Contributing Writer: Cheryl A. Romano
Cover Photo: Christopher J. Vendetta
Illustrations: Triad Design Group
Copy Editor: Barbara McIntosh Webb
Page Layout: Triad Design Group
Index: Nan Badgett

Library of Congress Cataloging-in-Publication Data available.

Published by Hearst Books
A Division of Sterling Publishing Co., Inc.
387 Park Avenue South, New York, NY 10016

www.popularmechanics.com

For information about custom editions, special sales, premium and corporate purchases, please contact Sterling Special Sales Department at 800-805-5489 or specialsales@sterlingpub.com.

Distributed in Canada by Sterling Publishing
c/o Canadian Manda Group, 165 Dufferin Street
Toronto, Ontario, Canada M6K 3H6

Distributed in Australia by Capricorn Link (Australia) Pty. Ltd.
P.O. Box 704, Windsor, NSW 2756 Australia

Manufactured in China

ISBN 1-58816-395-4

Acknowledgments

For all their help, advice, and support, I offer special thanks to:

Connie Edwards, CKD, CKB, Director of Design at Timberlake Cabinet Company, for designing the gorgeous built-in entertainment center featured in the high-end living room makeover and for supplying the cabinets to build it.

Randy Hicks, National Sales Manager for Quality Doors, for the materials used for refacing the cabinets in the mid-range dining room makeover.

Brad Ries from Pergo for providing technical assistance and their handsome and highly durable laminate flooring used in the mid-range dining room makeover.

The folks at Armstrong Flooring for providing good-looking and easy-to-install sheet vinyl tile used in the economy dining room makeover and the laminate flooring used in the mid-range bedroom makeover.

Cori Schleger from Mohawk Industries for supplying the lush carpeting used for the high-end bedroom makeover.

Kathy Ziprick with Style Solutions for supplying lightweight and easy-to-install urethane foam moldings used in the high-end dining room and high-end bedroom makeovers.

Rob Glenn from Armstrong Cabinets for providing the beautiful and well-made cabinets and hardware used in the high-end dining room makeover.

Gary Feder from Hunter Fan for supplying their quiet, quality-crafted ceiling fan used in the high-end living room makeover.

Kathy Ziprick and Gary Good from Hy-Lite Products for technical assistance and supplying the lightweight acrylic block products used in the high-end dining room makeover.

Hackettstown Carpet for supplying the area rug used in the economy bedroom makeover and for installing the carpeting in the high-end bedroom makeover.

Armstrong/Bruce Flooring for providing the prefinished hardwood strip flooring used in the mid-range living room makeover.

Elina Gorlenkova with Armstrong Ceilings for providing their Easy-Up grid system and ceiling paneling used in the high-end living room makeover.

Christopher Vendetta, for taking great photographs under less-than-desirable conditions.

Rob Lembo and the crew at Triad Design Group, for superb illustrations and page layout skills that are evident on every page of this book.

Barb Webb, copyediting whiz, for ferreting out mistakes and gently suggesting corrections.

Heartfelt thanks to my constant inspiration: Cheryl, Lynne, Will, and Beth.

Contents

Introduction

Living spaces? Of course, your entire home is living space; but we're not talking about kitchens or baths, which have complex plumbing and electrical systems to accommodate in a makeover. In *MoneySmart Makeovers: Living Spaces,* we're looking at comparatively easier rooms: living rooms, dining rooms, bedrooms—the places we sleep, eat, relax, and entertain in.

As we emphasize in the entire MoneySmart Makeovers series, our makeovers aren't staged in a studio. Our real-life transformations are done in real homes, lived in by real people. This time out, we offer no fewer than nine makeovers for your consideration.

In these pages, you'll see how we took an actual living room, bedroom, and dining room, and made each over three times. This novel approach shows you just what kinds of upgrades and renovations you can make at three spending levels: economy, mid-range, and high-end. Whatever your own makeover plans, we hope you can find a compatible style and project in these pages...something that makes you say, "That's what I want!"

To help you reach your makeover goals, the book is divided into three parts. The "Planning Your Makeover" section includes the fundamentals on which you'll base your new look. In "Real Makeover Examples," you'll see the real-life rooms (living, dining, and bed), and the three makeovers in each to demonstrate the effect of three budget levels. And in "Creating Your New Look," you'll go step-by-step through the basics that let you actually do the projects yourself.

We hope you find your new living space right here within these pages.

—James Meigs
Editor-in-Chief, *Popular Mechanics*

PART 1

Planning Your Makeover

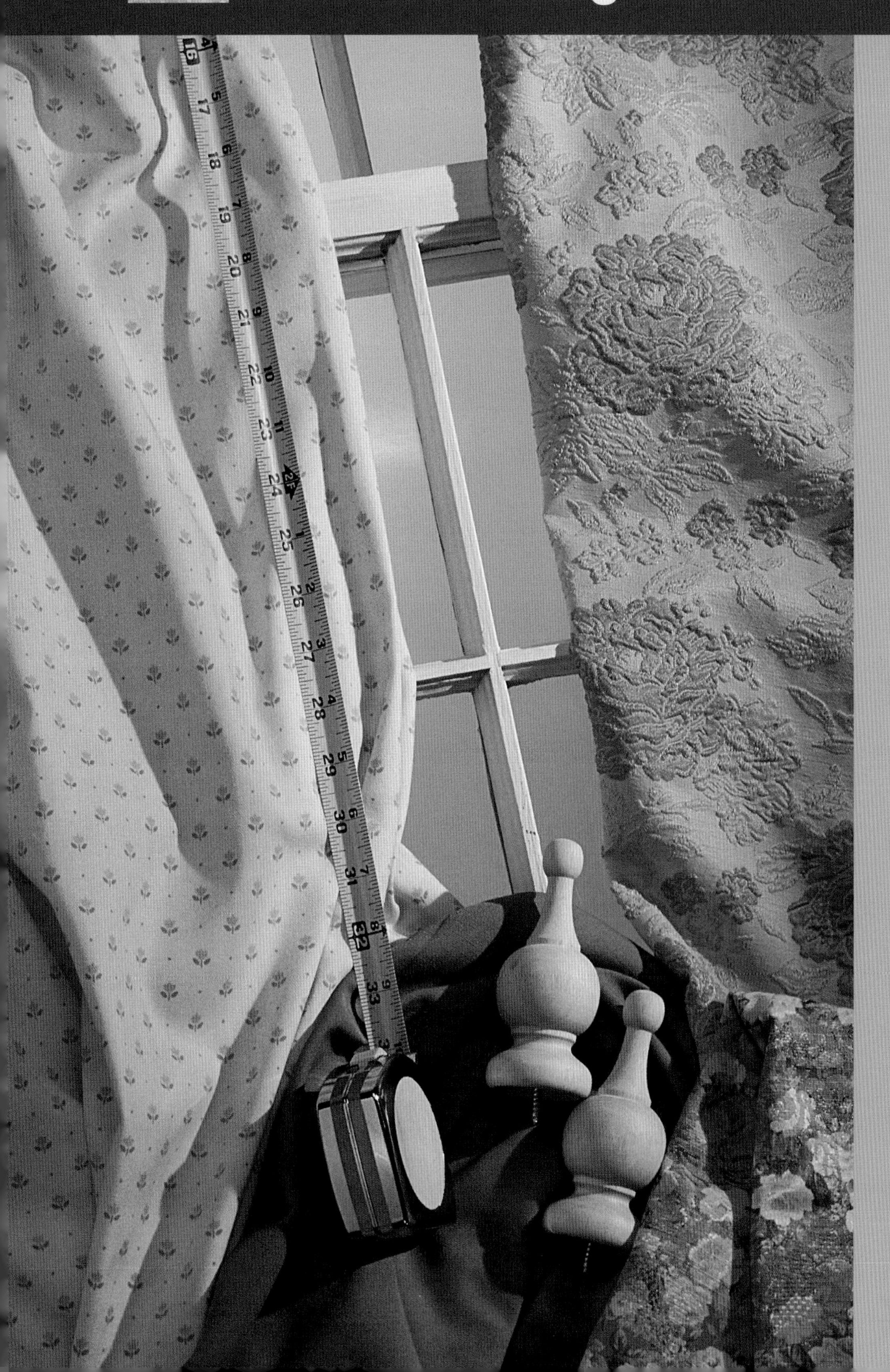

Your living room looks dated. Your bedroom is bland. Your dining room is a dud. If one or more of those descriptions apply, you've already decided that a makeover is in order. Now what? This isn't the part where you run out and buy things; this is the part where you first plan what needs to be done, then plan how to accomplish that, and then run out and buy things. Planning is the point of this section.

We'll break it down step by step, discussing the basics you need to know in the most important areas: room design, choosing materials, and systems (electrical and framing). Want a top-to-bottom redo? You'll find out how to do it yourself, from installing ceiling paneling to applying wallpaper to refinishing a hardwood floor. If you just want to brush up on the basics of painting, or learn how to install a dimmer switch, we'll cover those, too.

Whether your living space needs a little work or a lot of help, you'll find the money-smart ways to make it happen here.

DESIGN GUIDELINES

Every room in your home is a living space, of course, but we use the term to focus on living rooms, dining rooms, and bedrooms—basically, the non-kitchen, non-bath areas that most people want to improve. And that's the good news for these makeovers: Because complex plumbing and electrical systems are usually not involved, the costs can be minimal—and ditto the skills needed to do the projects.

Something as basic as a fresh coat of paint may be all you'll need to produce a fresh new look—but why stop there when there are so many other moneysmart upgrades you can bring to your home? To help you make smart choices about the projects that will bring new life (and usability) to your living spaces, this section will help you plan what you want to do—and estimate what it will cost. Then, you'll be set to start your own makeover.

LIVING ROOM STYLES

In the days of formal parlors, there was basically one style: formal. But today's living rooms put the emphasis on living, so every style has room around the edges for personal touches and preferences. And the styles themselves are fairly fluid: A traditional look might have Asian influences, or you could see a country flair in a contemporary setting.

The important thing about style is that it's ultimately personal, and a makeover is all about what you want in your home. Still, it may help to see some of the major style groups and put a name with a look to help you identify your own special style.

Contemporary. Bold, angular lines and natural materials (or lookalikes) are the hallmark of this style (above). Note the stone-look vinyl flooring, the nubby cotton upholstery, and the metallic elements in furniture legs. Almost no bold color, just calming neutrals that harmonize.

Contemporary/Casual. Strong horizontal elements and clean lines characterize contemporary, while casual is just that (left). The warmth of the wood above and below can be any style; so coupled with the inviting furniture, this room is both up-to-date and everyday.

Transitional. The metal in the coffee table (left) says modern or contemporary, while the furnishings vary from classic Queen Anne to traditional, so you have an eclectic look that observes no style boundaries—it transitions among several. Change the furniture, and the room could be any style at all.

Traditional. Familiar, timeless, and flexible, this is the look that's at home with much of America (above). The furniture features classic shapes and fabrics, walls and wallpaper tend toward muted tones, and accent pieces can borrow from almost any style.

Modern. Punchy, bold color and the strong linear profiles (left) put this room squarely in modern mode. It's a clean look that never really ebbs, plus it's versatile: Repaint the walls and change some of the accent pillows, and you have a whole new mood.

Living Room Layouts

Although there are almost endless ways to lay out a living room, there are three common methods that pop up more often than others. They all center on how you enter the room: direct entry, small attached foyer or entryway, and separate foyer.

Direct entry. The direct entry layout is the least expensive way to lay out a living room and so is common on less-expensive tract housing. The big disadvantage to this layout is that there's no entryway to block the elements when someone enters the room. This is especially bothersome in bad weather, when rain or snow can blow directly into the room. In addition, this layout usually makes no provisions for any kind of closet to store coats and jackets.

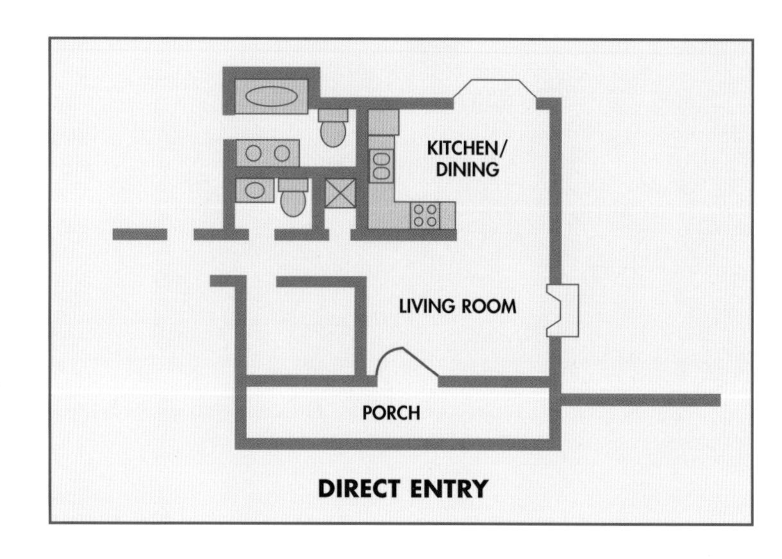

DIRECT ENTRY

LIVING
ROOM
MASTER
FOYER
PORCH
BR
BR

SMALL FOYER

Small attached foyer. The next step up in living room layouts is to add a small, attached foyer to the living room. This calls for additional framing—and therefore additional costs—but most homeowners think it's worth the extra money. Just the addition of a short hallway provides some buffer against the elements. Creative home designers can usually work in a closet nearby, as well.

Separate foyer. Perhaps the most enjoyable living room layout is the result of having a foyer or entryway that's completely separate from the living room. Keeping the living room separate from the entryway prevents both people and the weather from invading your space—at least directly. Separate foyers aren't for everyone, since some folks like to be able to see who is coming and going without having to get up. A separate foyer requires much more additional framing than the small attached foyer and therefore is correspondingly more expensive.

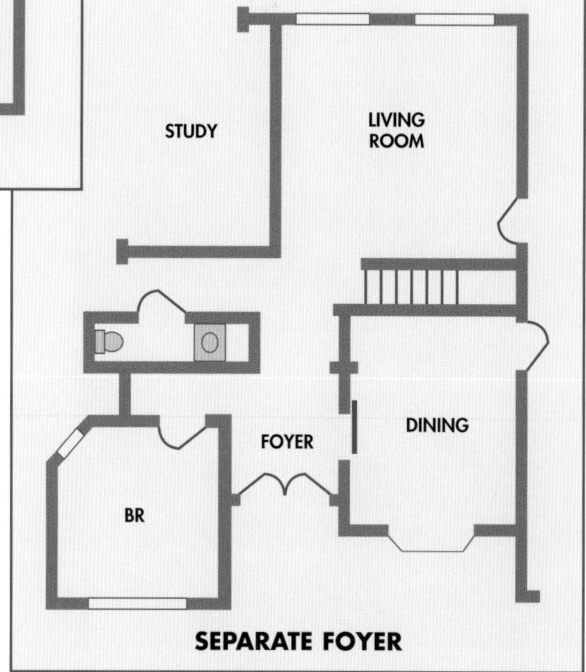

SEPARATE FOYER

Dining Room Styles

Whether you dine in a grand room or a modest area off another space, you're bound to have a table and chairs. As the dominant elements in the room, they really determine the overall style. So, you can use wall coverings, flooring, lighting, window treatments, and decorative accessories to underscore that style.

Since dining furniture is usually the priciest element in the room, you'll need to either work with what you already have, or choose something that you won't tire of in a few years. After all, it's easy enough to repaint, repaper, or buy an area rug to update your furniture. Update some accent pieces and you have a makeover.

Contemporary/casual. Add the cool tones of the walls (left) to the bright colors in the rug and accents, center around a clean-lined dining set of light maple, and you have...a mix. Casual without looking slapdash, contemporary without feeling "cold"—dinner's ready.

Country. Note the sturdy oak table that doesn't match the chairs (below left), and a sideboard that doesn't match anything: That's a hallmark of country style. The table sets the tone, aided by the fruit-patterned wallpaper and simple accents. There are no "mistakes" with this graceful mix-and-match.

Colonial. Early American is another name for this history-steeped style (right). Dark woods, the curves-and-spindles of the chairs, and the hefty majesty of the hutch carry almost the entire decorating message. Accents and colors are downplayed; the rug offers soft texture and low-key impact.

DINING ROOM STYLES
continued

French country. Light, bright, yellow and blue (top right): This is country with a French accent, from the creamy-white furniture to the needlepoint rug, from the rustic iron chandelier to the daffodil-hued walls. Is it informal? Dressed up? Charming? Impressive? Yes.

French Provincial. The shapes are delicate and feminine (above left), the tones softly neutral, the feeling more formal than not. A crystal chandelier is perfectly at home with this dressy (but not too fussy) style, the perfect backdrop for fine china, sparkling stemware, and gracious company.

Contemporary. Pared down and sleek (bottom right), a mix of nature and metal, this room is a "Wow!" for those who favor the look. Over wood-lookalike laminate flooring, a dining set of spare wood and steel carries the eye directly to the single piece of vivid artwork.

Dining Room Layouts

How a dining room is positioned in relation to the other rooms in the home will depend much on the homeowner's tastes—particularly when it comes to entertaining. The three most common layouts for dining rooms are: kitchen and dining room combined, living and dining rooms combined, and a separate dining room.

Kitchen/dining room combined. Many smaller homes don't have a separate dining room. In fact, what they really have is an eating area next to the kitchen This is fine for informal family meals, but lacks the separation from the kitchen that most homeowners want when entertaining.

KITCHEN/DINING ROOM COMBINED

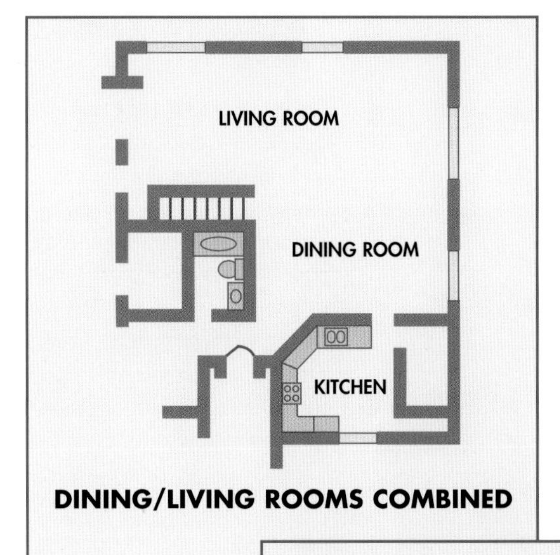

DINING/LIVING ROOMS COMBINED

Dining room/living room combined. One layout that's continuing to gain popularity is the combined dining and living room, commonly known as a great room. Here, the kitchen is still separate from the eating area; but because the dining area is connected to the living room, the atmosphere is casual.

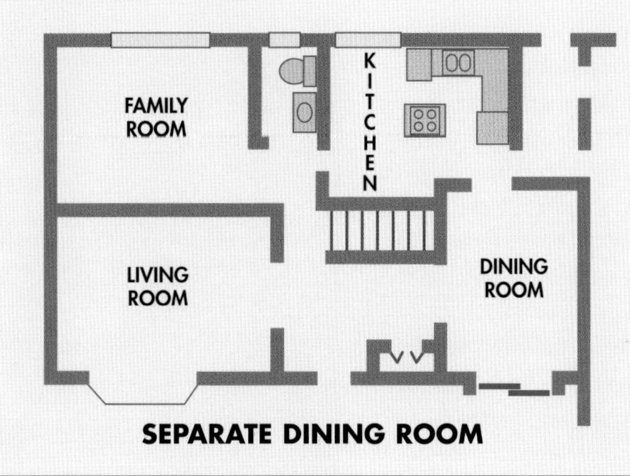

SEPARATE DINING ROOM

Separate dining room. For the homeowner who enjoys more formal entertaining, nothing will do but a separate dining room. With this type of layout, the kitchen is usually directly off one side of the dining room to make meal serving easy. With this setup, you're in a room designed for leisurely eating, and lengthy conversations over coffee and dessert.

Bedroom Styles

Perhaps the most intensely personal room in the home, the bedroom has morphed into the sleeping/lounging/reading/TV-watching/office room. But its fundamental purpose is still to house your bed, you, and your bunny slippers. So whether it's a satin boudoir or a rustic cabin retreat, it should reflect your taste—and maybe the private self that's off-limits to others.

In this living space, almost always separate from common areas, your personal preferences are paramount: Few if any others may share the space, so you (and your partner, if you have one) will need to create a room that says "Mine."

Country. Frilly? Look again—not one frill or lacy flutter is here (above right). The color and scale are what make this room seem delicate: lavender, white, and cream, with modest, seafoam green accents and a bordered wall-paper. Sweet dreams.

Contemporary. Tone, color, and clean lines (left) say it all in this airy, appealing room. The canopy-free four-poster keeps the space open, while light maple woods and a moderately colorful rug give a sense of comfort and light.

Traditional. As in most living spaces, in the bedroom this term calls up timeless, familiar style (bottom right). Solid-looking furnishings contrast with the satin coverlet and faux-fur throw, while the neutral walls and floor covering could take on any design scheme.

Children's. Color and textiles define kids' rooms (right), as in this inviting space set off by patterned wallpaper. A headboard fit for a super-child oversees a playful spread, wall accents, and a throw rug. Come teenage time, just a few changes will help this room mature.

Colonial. Curved wood and carved spindles (left) are the furniture hall-mark of this style, which evokes early American times (hence the alternate name). Dominated by the four-poster bed, the room is softened by printed fabric, the patterned rug, and soft-yellow walls.

Bedroom Layouts

The bedrooms in most homes are usually configured in one of three ways: cluster, split, and second-level. Each has its advantages and disadvantages.

Cluster bedrooms. When bedrooms are arranged in a cluster formation, walls are typically shared among the rooms. This makes for a lot of sleeping space in a small area, but also can be the loudest arrangement because of the common walls. Many young families prefer this layout since they can see and hear activity in the kids' bedrooms. Usually, the master bedroom has its own bathroom and the remaining bedrooms share a bath.

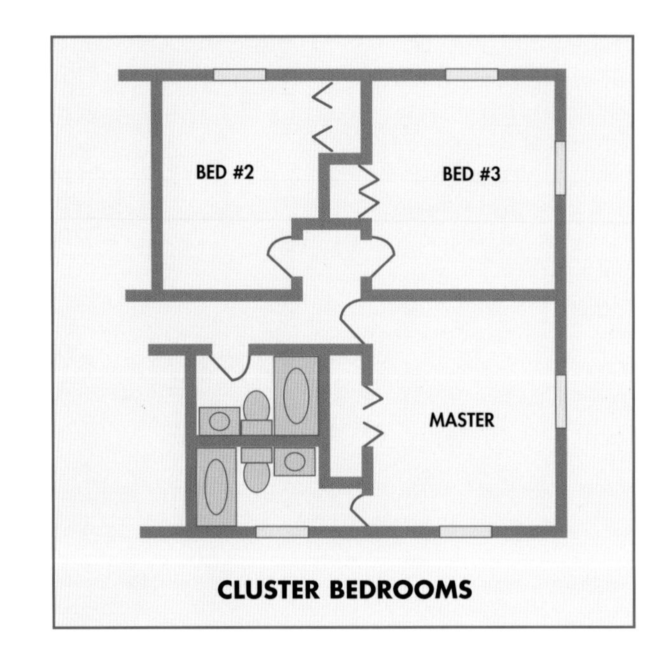

CLUSTER BEDROOMS

Split bedrooms. When the kids get older, some parents are looking for a little peace and quiet. At least at night they can get this in a home with a split-bedroom layout. Here, the master bedroom and bath are located on the opposite end of the house from the other bedrooms and bath. This is great for quiet, but can pose a supervising problem with younger children.

SPLIT BEDROOMS
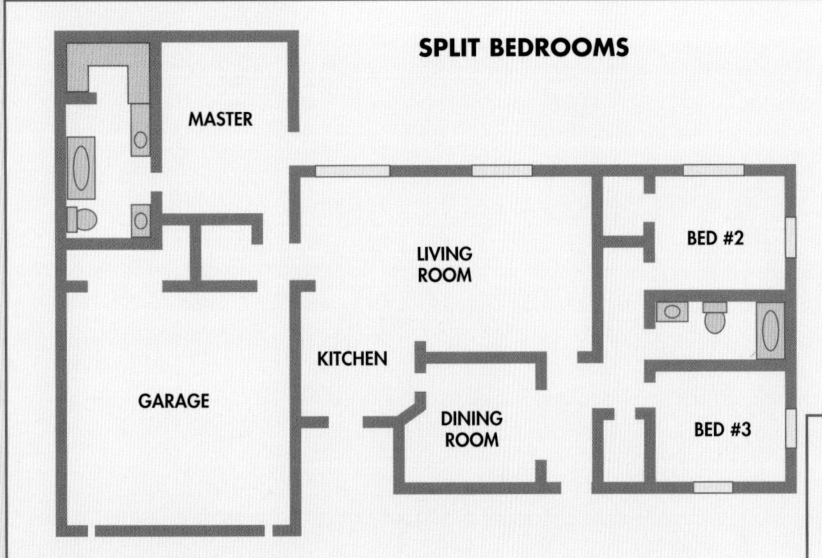

Second-level bedrooms. A different version of split bedrooms, but with the same idea, is placing bedrooms on the second floor. With this layout, the master bedroom and bath are still separated from the other bedrooms, but not by as great a distance. This affords some privacy, but still keeps parents within earshot of the children. Alternatively, the master or guest bedroom can be located on the main floor, with the remaining bedrooms upstairs.

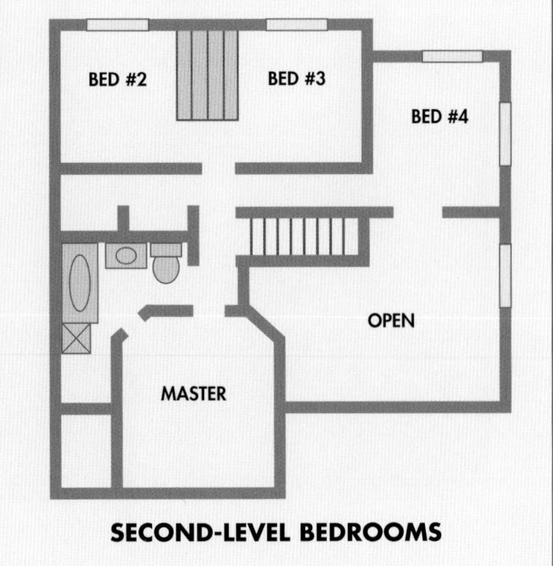

SECOND-LEVEL BEDROOMS

LIVING SPACE CLEARANCES

Housing standards recommend that certain clearances be maintained throughout a home. The standard width of doorways is 32" wide with the standard width of all hallways 36" wide; see the drawing below. Realize that these are minimums and that many designers try to make doorways and hallways as wide as possible. The proponents of universal or barrier-free design—where spaces are designed to be usable by all people—recommend doorways be a minimum of 36" wide and hallways be a minimum of 42" wide.

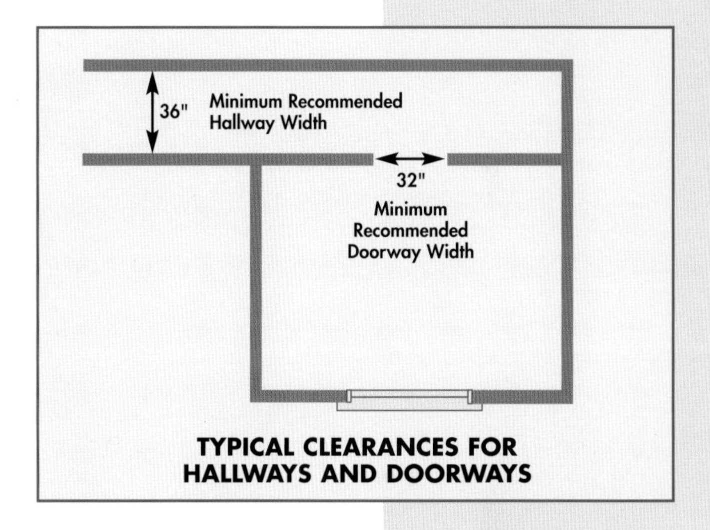

TYPICAL CLEARANCES FOR HALLWAYS AND DOORWAYS

RECOMMENDED ROOM SIZES

Area	Minimum size	Recommended size
Bedroom (1 twin bed)	9' × 10' or 7' × 12'	9' × 12'
Bedroom (double bed)	10' × 12'	11' × 12'
Bedroom (2 twin beds)	12' × 12' or 10' × 14'	14' × 14'
Bedroom (Queen bed)	11' × 12'	12' × 13'
Bedroom (King bed)	12' × 12'	12' × 14'
Living room (small)	12' × 16'	14' × 18'
Living room (large)	14' × 18'	16' × 20'
Dining room	Size of dining table + 36" between table and walls	Size of dining table + 42" between table and walls

Room sizes. The chart at left identifies minimum room sizes throughout the home and lists recommended sizes when applicable. These standards are particularly useful if you're planning to move a wall or two as part of a makeover.

Working With a Designer

Have you thought about bringing in a design professional—but wondered about the cost versus the benefits? Certainly, hiring an interior designer or interior decorator increases your budget. But, it might be a smart move that could actually save you money and help deliver results that you'll be happy to live with.

In most cases, designers and decorators have access to materials and products that are available "to the trade only"—not to the public. So, they can obtain goods that you're not likely to see in your neighbor's house. And in working with these goods, professionals gain experience with style, color, and pattern that can help avoid an unfortunate selection.

Here's where professionals really shine: They're better than most of us at seeing the big picture. For instance, a designer might find an elegant solution to traffic-flow jams or cramped spaces by recommending that you move a wall—something the average homeowner may not consider.

Working with a design professional doesn't have to mean hiring her or him to do your entire makeover—you might engage someone on an à la carte basis to help select a theme or color scheme. On the nuts-and-bolts side, a decorator or designer can help you source contractors if you need them.

If you do work with a professional, be sure to check their references, and get a written quote for their work. Make sure both of you understand, in writing, exactly what services will be provided.

Windows and Doors

It's easy to overlook the windows and doors in a home—until you upgrade them. Then, it's easy to see what an enormous impact they can have on the look, feel, and livability of a room.

If you've flipped through home magazines or strolled the home center aisles, you have an idea of the array of styles, finishes, and formats available today—and that's just the stock items. Add in custom-order solutions to solve a problem or match a theme, and it opens up a new level of makeover possibilities.

Textiles and treatments on the windows themselves, of course, can also revamp a look: Swap out nylon sheers for tab-top insulated drapes, or upgrade your old shades with pleated pastel versions, and the change can be dramatic.

Consumer options in windows and doors are real bright spots in makeover plans. Frosted glass panels add beauty while preserving privacy... would you like them in a beveled, floral, or abstract design? Acrylic block windows are durable and lighter than glass—would you care for a whole wall, or just a partition? The doors, too, open up more choices—steel security doors now mimic fine woods, or come in shades to match your shutters. The point is, like everything else for today's home, windows and doors give you choices. And that's a good thing.

Storage

It's the one thing no one ever seems to have enough of: storage space. The question is, how can you add more without trashing your decor? Find three answers in the handsome solutions on this page: a country-style entry unit that serves many useful functions; a plush window seat with lots of room underneath; and a bedroom built-in that gives a custom look from stock cabinets.

Entryway storage. Don't touch that kitchen sink—but just about everything else can get stashed here (top photo): hooks to hold hats, jackets, keys, and more; a padded bench for putting on boots; and underneath it all, two generous cabinets for whatever else needs storing.

Using stock cabinets for built-ins. "Go custom" used to be the stock answer for built-in cabinetry, but you don't have to. These good-looking units (middle photo) are stock cabinets that take modest skills to install almost anywhere.

Window seat. This handsome window seat (bottom photo) invites you to rest, read, put your feet up, and know that the double cabinets underneath, storing your old video collection, still have room for CDs and books.

Lighting

Science tells us that bringing in light helps brighten people's moods, so bring it on. In addition to working as a mood-enhancer and letting us literally see what we're doing, lighting does more than merely illuminate: It spotlights the high points of a room and puts the low points in shadow. It sets a mood—romantic, cozy, welcoming, bustling. And it comes in basically two types: natural and artificial.

Natural light, of course, is what we see between sunrise and sunset. Photographers and painters swear by it, and as a species we've been devising new ways to let it into our homes for thousands of years. Artificial light is a relative newcomer, and is classed in three categories: general, like a ceiling fixture in a dining room; task, such as a reading light on an end table; or accent, as when a recessed light showcases a piece of art.

Natural light. The more natural light you can get into a room, the more open and spacious it will feel. If the budget allows, consider giving up wall space for larger windows. Alternatively, think about skylights (top left); they can bring in abundant light without touching an inch of living space.

General lighting. General lighting lets you use and move around a room safely. In days past, general lighting consisted of an incandescent or fluorescent overhead. Today, the trend is toward recessed lighting. Pendant lights like the chandelier shown here are still extremely popular over dining tables (and how about a dimmer for those grown-ups-only meals?).

Task lighting. Task lighting puts light where you need it to perform tasks, like dining at a table in this high-ceilinged room. Recessed lights mounted over a countertop are another example of task lighting. Such under-cabinet lights are usually either strip or single "puck" halogen lights. They're often low-voltage and can be installed with ease (see pages 186–187).

Accent lighting. Decorative or accent lighting is designed to show off a room feature. Whether you want to spotlight a pottery collection with under-shelf lighting or emphasize artwork with a pair of wall sconces (as shown at far left), you can create a completely different look or mood simply by flipping a switch.

COLOR

Color can stimulate the appetite, soothe the frenzied soul, cheer the pensive, encourage the childlike—about the only thing color can't do is apply itself, and that's where you come in. Color…tone…hue…whatever the nuance, you can use it to your advantage in making your makeover a success.

A note of caution: When you go bold or trendy with color on a high-ticket item, such as furniture or floor covering, be aware that a few seasons from now, it may look dated, or you may just have outgrown it. It's safer—and more cost-effective—to express yourself with paint, wallpaper, and textiles. There's so much available in these materials that you could live several lifetimes and still not come near to exhausting the possibilities. Here are some examples of how color can, well, color a room.

Fabrics. Fabrics (above left) are an easy and relatively inexpensive way to change color or add color to almost any living space. Bedding and coordinating window treatments, like this soothing, pale green, help make a bedroom a calming oasis. Don't forget area rugs, throw pillows, and upholstery as other color targets.

Wall treatments. The zippy, all-American red, white, and blue of this wallpaper theme (bottom right) brings high energy to a child's room. The sisal rug is a calm foundation for the bright tones, and holds up well under little, pounding feet.

Furniture. If red is you, and has been for years, go ahead: Jump into vivid upholstered pieces like those shown in the top center photo. Yes, you'll probably have them for years (unless the inheritance kicks in), but that's okay—by painting or wallpapering the walls and changing the area rug, you could change the look of the room.

What color is your makeover? Before you answer that, it's helpful to review some color basics. As you probably remember from grade school, the three primary colors are red, yellow, and blue; these are used to mix all of the other colors. The secondary colors are orange, green, and violet; they are mixed from equal parts of two primaries. In between? There's an array of what are called intermediate colors; see the color wheel at right. If you want to select a contrast color (as a trim accent, let's say), choose a color that's opposite it on the color wheel. For example, a contrast to blue is orange. On the other hand, to find colors that will blend well, choose adjacent colors (such as yellow-green and green). Soft pastel shades are the result of mixing white with one of these pure colors.

Another consideration that makes a difference: Colors look different in different types of light. Incandescents, the familiar stuff of lightbulbs, emphasize reds and yellows. Fluorescents, though, highlight blues. That's why it's so important to examine paint chips and wallpaper samples in your home to see how they look in a target room before deciding on a color; never choose these at the home center. Consider, too, how much of a color you'll be using—this affects how you'll see it. Lime green may make a great trim paint accent, but may be overpowering on an entire wall.

One last thing: Color is affected by all the colors around it. That's why you should hold chips and samples next to each other before making final selections.

So: Ready to choose your color scheme? Not quite—you'll make your best choice when you also know the three kinds of color schemes: monochromatic, analogous, and complementary (it sounds harder than it is). A monochromatic scheme uses shades, tints, and intensities of a single color, say, blue. An analogous theme combines variations of colors that are close to each other on the color wheel such as yellow, yellow-orange, and orange. A complementary theme uses combinations of complementary colors such as red and green or violet and yellow.

Since colors create moods, as you know, it's often best to begin by picking the primary "mood" you're after, and its corresponding color. Want a warm "feel"? Reds, pinks, oranges, and yellows will do the job. For a cool, peaceful effect, choose soft greens and blues. To go bold and flashy, choose contrasting colors. If it all seems overwhelming, go to the paint aisle and say "Help!" Paint companies provide hundreds of professionally selected color palettes to help guide your choices. They'll get you off to an excellent start.

Flooring. An expanse of blue sheet vinyl (above) partners cheerfully with yellow in a kids' play room that says "let's play!" as soon as you enter. Accents that echo the blue—pillows and chairs—could be part of a future makeover. Paper or paint the walls in another shade entirely, change the furnishings and accents, and you could have an office, hobby room, or—?

CHOOSING MATERIALS

Being moneysmart about your makeover doesn't necessarily mean buying the least expensive products and materials. There are certainly times and places where a less costly lookalike will serve as well as a high-end item (a laminate floor instead of hardwood, for example), and we'll be sure to point these out.

But sometimes it's worth it in the long run to invest a little more for that special look you love—or the durability you want (think how quickly you'd tire of a cheap cabinet shelf that cracked right away, or how good you'd feel waking up every day to wallpaper that wears and wears and wears).

How can you know when to spend, and when to spend less? It takes product knowledge: what features signal quality, what materials are time-tested, and basically what's worth your makeover investment in time and money. When you're choosing materials, it feels good to know that you're making a great choice.

FLOORING

For the floor in your living space makeover, the sky's pretty much the limit: Without the water concerns of a kitchen or bathroom floor, the choices are wide open. You can opt for the wall-to-wall softness of carpet; get a great tile, stone, or wood look in laminate; go for real wood; or let sheet vinyl be your low-maintenance material. Here's what you need to know to choose the type that's best for you.

You already know that carpet is offered in a dizzying variety of colors and patterns (left). But do you know about the different types of carpeting available? The four most common are: cushion-backed carpet, where the carpet has a foam backing bonded to it; loop-pile carpet, which provides a textured look resulting from the uncut loops of yarn; plush carpet, with the pile trimmed at a bevel to give it a speckled appearance; and velvet-cut pile carpet, which offers the densest pile of all.

When most folks think of laminate flooring (top right), they envision boards or panels that imitate hardwood strip flooring. But laminate flooring is available in a great many more colors, patterns, and textures. In fact, you can find laminate flooring that mimics almost every other flooring type except carpet. Once you've decided on a style, be wary of inexpensive imitations that look good but won't last long. The primary difference between cheap and quality laminate flooring is the thickness of the top laminate. Quality flooring from a reputable dealer or contractor will have a thick top laminate that will hold up better over the years.

Regardless of the color, pattern, or texture, all sheet vinyl (below right) is one of two types: full-spread or perimeter-bond. Full-spread flooring has a felt paper backing and is designed for the entire surface to be glued to the underlayment with flooring adhesive. Perimeter-bond flooring has a smooth, white PVC backing that is secured to the floor only at the perimeter with staples. Because it has no backing, perimeter-bond flooring has some give-and-take, so it can be stretched slightly during installation.

Hardwood flooring (middle right) is available in a multitude of woods, widths, and grades. The most common wood used for flooring is red oak. But often you can purchase other types from a flooring dealer or contractor. Hard maple, beech, birch, ash, sycamore, even pine flooring are some of the more common types. Most strip flooring is 3/4" thick and can be bought in 1 1/2", 1 3/4", 2 1/4" (the most common), and 2 3/4". Strip flooring is manufactured with tongues and grooves along its edges and ends.

ONE ROOM, FOUR DIFFERENT FLOORS

Is a floor just a floor? Are you skeptical about the difference that different materials can make in the look and feel of a room? Then take a look at these four photos, courtesy of the flooring experts at Mohawk Industries. One elegant room has been done over four times with four different flooring materials: ceramic tile, hardwood, carpet, and sheet vinyl. If you had any doubts about flooring's impact, they should be gone now.

Ceramic tile. Beautiful, durable ceramic tile gives a cool grace to the room. And yes, you can install it yourself with a little time and care.

Hardwood. A gleaming hardwood floor says "high end" almost anywhere, with cost on the higher side, too. Its warmth and appeal will last for years.

Carpet. For softness underfoot and a "Shhhh!" effect on noise, carpeting rules, here in a neutral that lets the room and its furnishings be the stars.

Sheet vinyl. Geometric accents give this sheet vinyl visual interest—and with so many colors and patterns offered, it's tough to pick just one.

CABINETS

If a room makeover calls for removing, replacing, or installing new cabinets, it's important to understand how cabinets are made (and it's potentially costly if you don't). While it may be tempting to shop for style first, you should define what type of cabinets you're after and use this to narrow the choices for style. It's easy to fall in love with your dream cabinets, only to find out that they won't meet your needs. Cabinets are constructed in one of three ways: They're built on site, or they're built individually either with or without face frames.

Site-built cabinets. Site-built cabinets (above right) are common in older homes. As the name implies, these were actually constructed on site. The carpenter may have cut parts to size in the shop, but the cabinets themselves were assembled in the kitchen. You can usually identify a site-built cabinet by looking closely at the dividers between the cabinets and at the backs of the cabinets. If there is no back and the dividers are a single thickness of plywood or particleboard, the cabinet was built on site.

This type of construction did save on materials, but site-built cabinets are a pain to work on. Say, for example, you want to replace just the countertop. You can't simply pry it off, because you'll risk damaging the cabinets—especially if the plywood was secured with screws. Also, to remove the cabinets, you basically have to disassemble them in the reverse order they were constructed. Any of these tasks requires patience, along with knowledge of how the units were made.

Face-frame. Cabinet manufacturers quickly realized it would be faster for an installer to assemble premade cabinets than to build cabinets to fit. The standard cabinet they developed is still widely used today: the face-frame cabinet.

The sides, back, top, and bottom are made of thin material joined together with glue and staples. The cabinet strength comes from a solid-wood frame that's attached to the front of the cabinet; see the drawing on the opposite page. Doors and drawers are then cut to fit the openings. Because the face frame reduces the size of the openings, there is less interior storage space—especially for drawers. On the plus side, face-frame cabinets are the easiest to install because any gaps can be filled with filler strips (see page 107 for more on these).

The face frames are typically 1¼"- to 1½"-wide, ¾"-thick hardwood. On quality cabinets the frame parts are joined with mortises and tenons, or at the very least dowels. The sides and bottom can range anywhere from ¼" to ¾" particleboard or plywood; ¾"-thick plywood is the sturdiest. Back panels are usually ⅛"-thick hardboard. The back and bottom typically fit in dadoes or grooves in the sides. Corner brackets help hold the parts together and also provide a means for securing the countertop.

Frameless. Frameless cabinets have been popular in Europe for years. This method uses fewer materials than face-frame cabinets and offers a clean, contemporary look. Frameless cabinets are often called 32mm cabinets because this is the increment which all holes, hinge fittings, cabinet joints, and mountings are set apart. Since this method originated in Europe, the metric system was used throughout.

The sides, top, and bottom are typically manufactured from 3/4"-thick particleboard. Because of this added thickness, the cabinet parts when assembled are sufficiently strong and do not need a face frame to provide support. This opens up the full interior space for storage. Doors are mounted via fully adjustable hinges that attach to the inside of the cabinet.

Since the cabinets don't have face frames, extreme care must be taken in ordering and installing these, as any filler strip used will be painfully obvious. Also, there are some concerns about the stability of the cabinets over time: They can exhibit a tendency to "rack" or twist out of shape and alignment, since there's no face frame to prevent this.

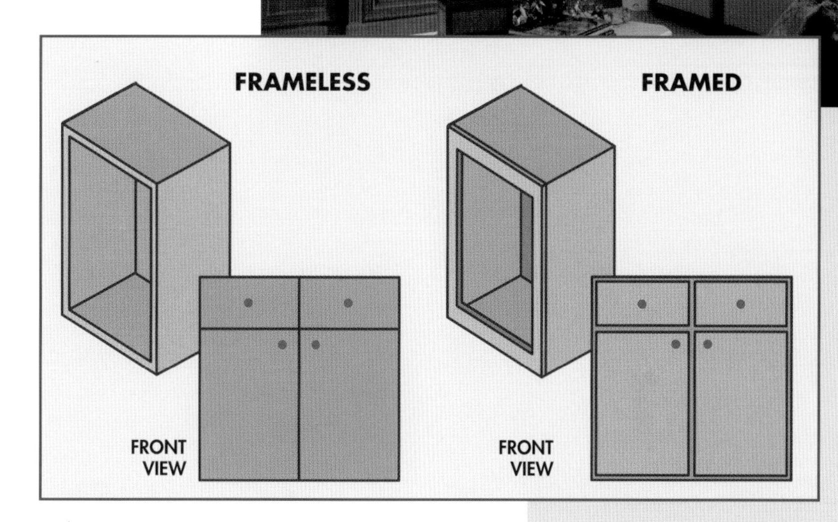

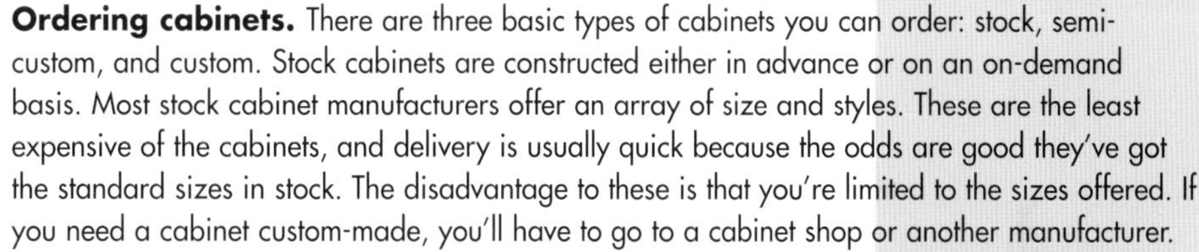

Ordering cabinets. There are three basic types of cabinets you can order: stock, semi-custom, and custom. Stock cabinets are constructed either in advance or on an on-demand basis. Most stock cabinet manufacturers offer an array of size and styles. These are the least expensive of the cabinets, and delivery is usually quick because the odds are good they've got the standard sizes in stock. The disadvantage to these is that you're limited to the sizes offered. If you need a cabinet custom-made, you'll have to go to a cabinet shop or another manufacturer.

Semi-custom cabinets are the next step up from stock cabinets. Semi-custom manufacturers do make some stock cabinets, but most are made on an on-demand basis. You'll find a wider choice of cabinet sizes and styles, along with greater offerings in terms of accessories such as interior fittings. Some true custom sizes and fittings are possible, but at a substantial cost.

Custom cabinets are all made to order. Although custom cabinet manufacturers tend to stick with the 3"-increment units, fully custom sizes are possible. Since these are all custom-made, there is no warehouse full of stock cabinets. This usually means a significant wait between the order and delivery. But custom cabinetmakers often offer the latest and greatest accessories, as well as superior materials and construction methods. Drawers are assembled with dovetails, and doors with mortise-and-tenons. Custom finishes are also possible—all it takes is money.

Regardless of the construction method you choose, the overall appearance of the cabinet will depend primarily on the door and drawer style. Your choices range from a simple full-overlay door to highly sculpted doors. Most designers will specify the more ornate doors (like cathedral) for wall cabinets only; since base cabinets are less visible, they're typically fitted with plain doors in the same style. Common woods for doors and drawer fronts include oak, maple, cherry, hickory, and pecan.

WINDOWS

When it comes to buying new or replacement windows, you need to know about the different types before you can make an intelligent purchase decision. The most common types are: single- and double-hung, casement, bay, bow, awning, and decorative.

Single- or double-hung. In terms of appearance, there's little difference between a single-hung and a double-hung window. What is different is whether both the upper and lower sashes have the ability to move. On a single-hung window, only the lower sash can be raised or lowered. With the double-hung window, both sashes can move (this movement also applies to tilting-sash windows). Only the lower sash on a single-hung window tilts in for easy cleaning. Both sashes on a double-hung window can be raised or lowered independently of each other. On older windows, the weight of the sash is counterbalanced by sash weights suspended on sash cords. The weights move up and down inside a cavity next to the side jambs. As this system is bulky and prone to problems, it has been replaced over the years with either a spiral balance (basically an adjustable spring) or a block-and-tackle balance that operates much like a retractable tape measure.

Casement. A casement window is any window where the sash is hinged on the side to allow the sash to pivot inward and outward like a door. Most casement windows project outward and therefore provide significantly better ventilation than sliding windows of equal size. Another reason casement windows provide better ventilation over a sliding window is that virtually the entire window area can be opened. On sliding windows, only about one-half of the available window space can be open.

Awning. Awning windows are hinged at the top and swing open at the bottom. Just like casement windows, awning windows provide greater ventilation than sliding windows, since practically the entire window area can be opened to catch a breeze. Awning windows can be installed so that the sash opens outward (such as in a garage or workshop), or inward in the case of a basement window.

Bay. A bay window protrudes out from an exterior wall to make a room feel larger without requiring expensive structural changes. They are typically made up of three or more windows that project out from the house at 30, 45, or 90 degrees. The center section is usually parallel with the

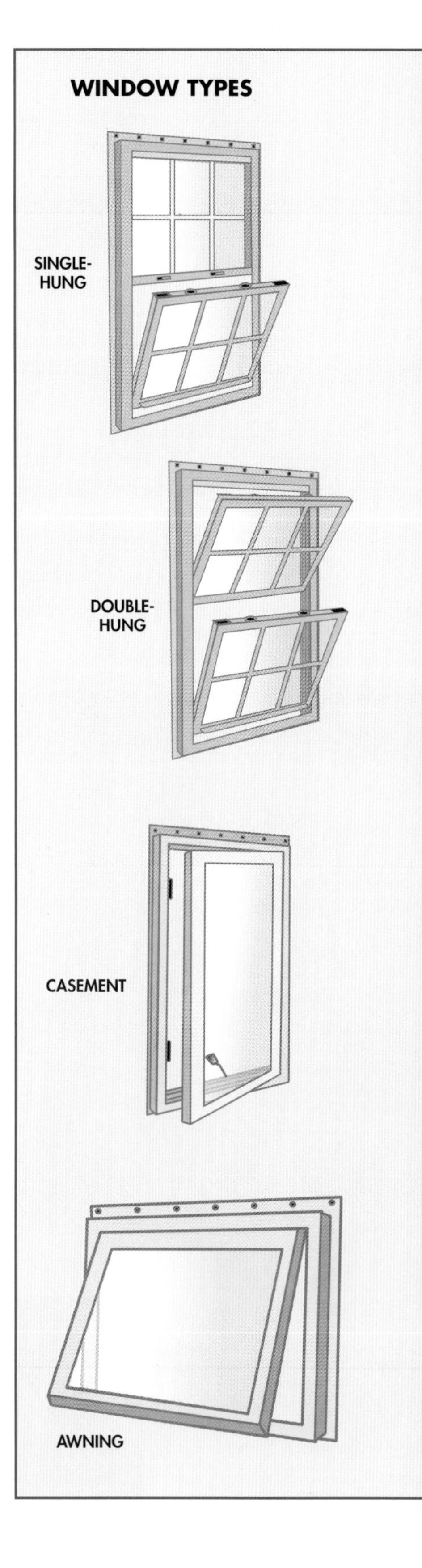

exterior wall and is made up of one or two units. Each of the window units can be fixed, operating, or a combination of both. Since bay window units are fairly heavy, care must be taken to fully support the unit during and after installation.

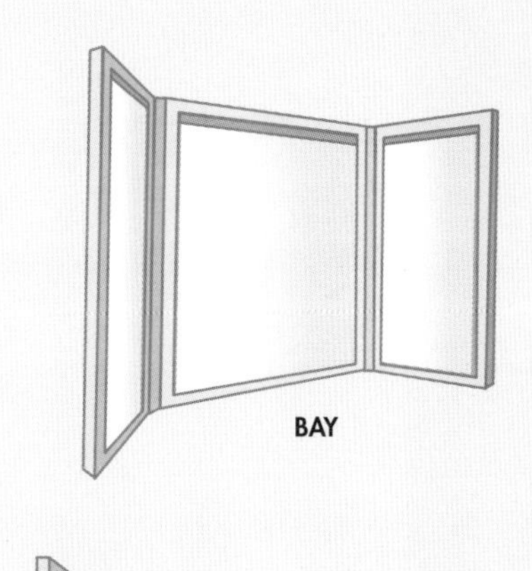

Bow. Bow windows are often confused with bay windows because they appear somewhat similar. The main difference between the two is that a bow window typically has four or five sections that are formed into a graceful curve or bow. Like the bay window, the sections of a

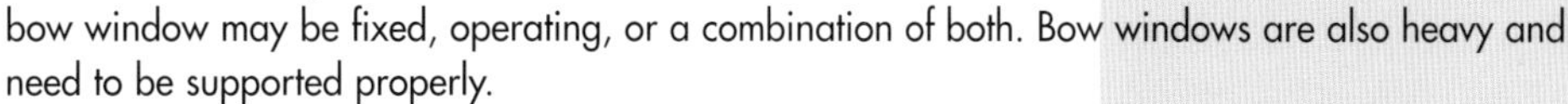

bow window may be fixed, operating, or a combination of both. Bow windows are also heavy and need to be supported properly.

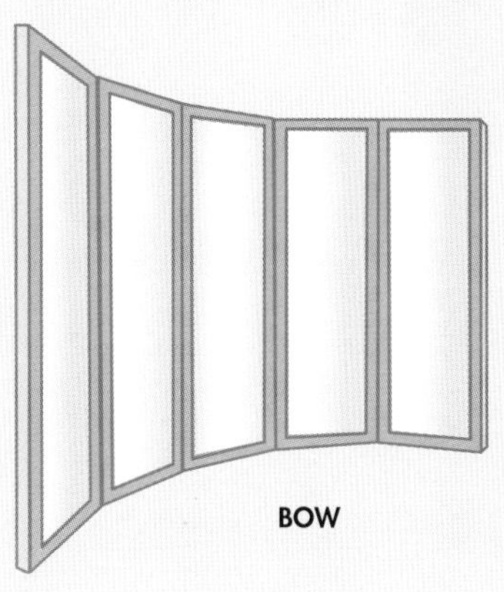

Decorative. Common decorative window shapes are octagon, triangle, trapezoid, pentagon with a flat top, pentagon, hexagon with a flat top, quarter circle, half circle (shown here), oval, half ellipse, half cloverleaf, gothic arch, arch top, and full circle—to name just a few. Because of their shape, most decorative windows are fixed, though some can be opened.

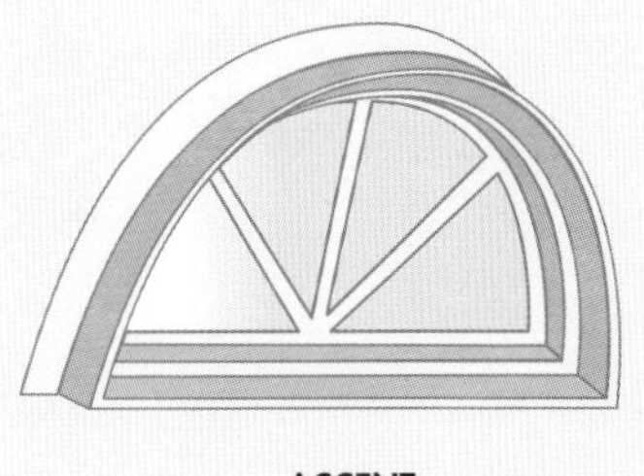

Single-pane. The least energy-efficient window is the single-pane variety; see the drawing below. Common in older homes, this type of window is suitable only in mild climates. A better choice is double- or triple-pane windows; see below. One option that can help with a single-pane window is to have a low-E coating applied to the pane. This coating filters out UV rays to protect furnishings while also helping to insulate the home in winter and summer.

Double-pane. A double-pane window has two panes of glass separated by an airspace. When sealed properly, this airspace provides insulation from both summer heat and winter cold. To further increase the insulating properties of the window, some manufacturers inject a safe, colorless gas (such as argon) into this space. A quality gas-filled double-pane window with low-E coatings will typically provide an R-value of around 4 to 5.

Triple-pane. The ultimate in insulated windows is the triple-pane; see the drawing below left. Three panes of glass offer two separate insulating spaces. Here again, these spaces can be filled with argon or other gas to increase the insulting properties. R-values around 10 are common with triple-pane windows. A side benefit of both double- and triple-pane windows is that they also significantly reduce noise transmission. The drawback to both of these is that they're more expensive than single-pane windows.

Space between panels may be filled with gas to increase insulating properties.

SINGLE

DOUBLE

TRIPLE

TYPES OF GLAZING

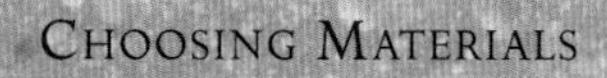

Doors

When shopping for a new or replacement door, start by identifying the type of material you want it made from. For doors exposed to the elements, choose either metal or wood. Because interior doors don't come in contact with the weather, they are typically made of wood: either solid wood or with a hollow core.

Solid-wood. A door made of solid wood is still a common choice for many homeowners. That's because the natural beauty and strength of wood is a welcoming touch to any home. Most solid-wood doors feature mortise-and-tenon construction and have raised panels that "float" in grooves in the door frame. This allows the panels to move with seasonal changes in humidity without causing the door to bind. (Note: Even the best-made door will swell in the summer and shrink a bit in the winter.)

Metal. Metal doors have a number of advantages over solid-wood doors. First, since they're metal, they won't swell or contract with seasonal changes in humidity like a wood door does. Second, the hollow core of the door can be filled with foam to provide insulation. Third, metal doors are tough—they stand up extremely well to regular use (and abuse). Metal doors are available in a multitude of shapes and sizes and can even be found covered with a wood veneer to give the appearance of solid wood.

Hollow-core. Hollow-core doors are designed for interior use, as they're not heavy-duty enough for exteriors, nor do they offer the insulating properties that solid-wood or metal doors do.

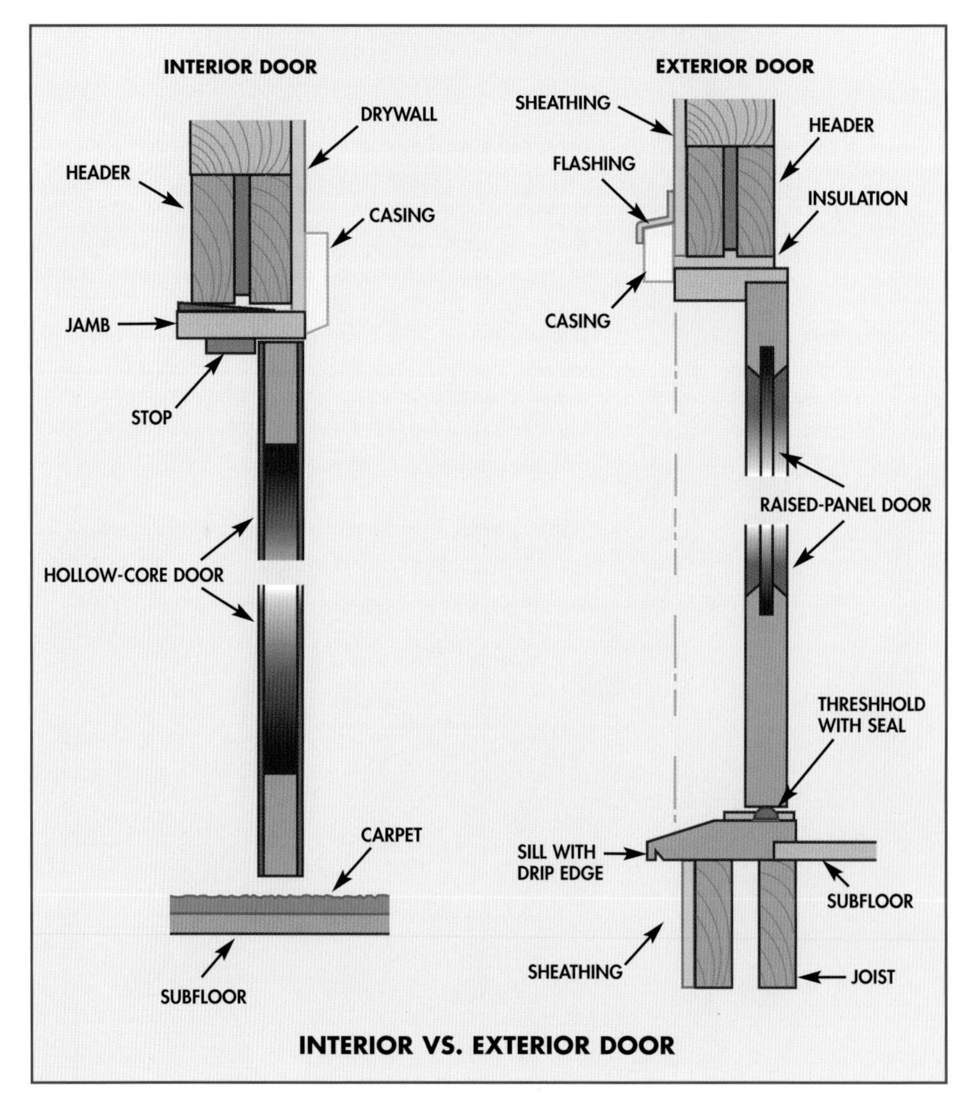

INTERIOR VS. EXTERIOR DOOR

Hollow-core doors are made by covering a wood frame with two sheets or "skins" of wood veneer, typically lauan, birch, or oak. Although you'd assume the core (the space) between the skins is empty, it's not. Instead, there are strips of corrugated cardboard on edge, glued to the skins in an X pattern. This does a surprisingly good job of supporting the skins and prevents them from bowing in.

Interior doors. Interior doors range from simple to decorative. The most common type of interior door is a flush door that's comprised of a wood frame covered with a plywood or solid-wood veneer—typically in oak, birch, or lauan. The core of the door can be solid wood, particleboard, or hollow. More decorative doors are constructed with a wood frame that holds "floating" wood panels (or glass) that can expand and contract with changes in humidity without affecting the door's dimensions.

Exterior doors. Of all the types of doors you can buy, exterior doors come in the greatest variety. That's because many homeowners want to make a personal statement with their front or entrance door—they want a door that's unique like they are. Hence, the huge variety available. Exterior doors are usually constructed out of solid wood or else metal that's filled with insulation. Solid-wood doors offer natural beauty and can easily be stained or painted to suit your tastes. Metal insulated doors offer better insulation properties than a solid-wood door, won't expand and contract with seasonal changes in humidity, and are considerably tougher than wood doors.

If you're replacing a door, or are installing a new one and the rough opening is a standard dimension, go with a pre-hung door—they're just so much easier to install; see the sidebar below. Regardless of the type you choose, look for quality construction and as high an insulation value as you can find (here's one area where metal insulated doors really shine).

PRE-HUNG DOORS

Whenever the job is installing a new door, it's easier using a pre-hung type. There are no mortises to cut, hinges to install, or holes to drill. All you need to do is slip the door into the rough opening, shim it so that it's plumb and level, and nail it to the framing members. If it's so easy, why would you ever want to install a standard door? Standard doors are useful for odd-sized doors that need to be trimmed to fit, and when you just can't find the style of door you're looking for in a pre-hung.

CEILINGS

Quick: Without looking up, describe the ceiling over your head. You probably can't, and it probably isn't because you failed to notice. In the room you're in, as in most spaces, the ceiling is most likely white or off-white, with a flat surface or with the familiar textured popcorn finish. No wonder ceilings go unnoticed.

But, as you can instantly see from the photos here, ceilings can be great makeover subjects, too (take that, floors and walls). At the very least, you can use a paint other than white to accent your room colors or set a mood. The cost is minimal and the results can be surprisingly dramatic. More ambitious? Look into the ceiling coverings offered by manufacturers, and you'll be amazed by today's market in acoustical tile, suspended ceilings, and ceiling paneling.

With a modest investment and not very much time, you can add charm, warmth, and interest to any room—while hiding a boring or damaged ceiling. You might say that when it comes to making over a ceiling, things are really looking up.

Paint. It's true: Many designers will tell you the only color for a ceiling is white because it tends to draw the eyes up and help make the room appear larger. But it's also true that you can effectively change a room's appearance for the better with a little color. Subtle pastels like light yellow and pale green can soften the feel of a room to create a more inviting or calmer environment. Alternatively, you can make a bold statement with color.

Textured paint. Often called popcorn ceilings, this type of ceiling is common in inexpensive homes where the builder needed a quick way to conceal bad taping or drywalling on the ceiling. The texture is sprayed on with a special machine that mixes the paint with the filler—typically gypsum. Although these do a fair job of hiding problems, they can also obscure future problems in the form of leaks or stains. If you have a popcorn ceiling and want it to go away, you have two options: You can either conceal it with acoustical tile or paneling, or remove it by wetting it and then scraping it off—a messy and unpleasant job.

Ceiling paneling. Ceiling paneling has recently become popular, thanks to some of the new installation methods that manufacturers have designed. With a snap-in-place system, the panels go up in an afternoon. The only challenge is getting the grid system in place so that the tracks are parallel and equally spaced. This is not a problem if you have patience and take your time.

Most ceiling paneling is covered with long-lasting laminate, so it doesn't require any special care. This is basically the same material used for laminate flooring, but thinner. These panels are a great choice for adding flair to a room, whether they're colored a warm wood tone, a whitewashed effect, or something in between. Once installed, they may make the ceiling the first thing people notice on entering the room—instead of not being noticed at all.

Acoustical tile. Acoustical tile goes up in manner similar to ceiling paneling and also does a great job of concealing a bad ceiling. Acoustical tile comes in many patterns and almost always in white. It is available in 12" square tiles that can be fastened to furring strips attached to ceiling joists. Alternatively, if you have plenty of ceiling height, you can purchase larger tiles (2' square or 2' × 4') and drop these into a grid that's suspended from the ceiling. Installing the grid for a suspended ceiling can take quite a bit of time, since it's often a challenge to get all the grid parts leveled.

Tin-look. A special form of acoustical tile is patterned to look like an old-fashioned tin ceiling. Like standard acoustical tile, these tiles come in white, but can be easily painted with metallic paint to mimic copper, tin, or gilded ceiling panels. If you're simply after texture, you can use the tile in its white shade or paint it to match the design scheme of the room.

Storage

With a little ingenuity and some stock cabinets, you can create loads of storage in any room, using one of two construction types: freestanding or built-in.

Freestanding storage. Most homeowners think of cabinets only in terms of a kitchen. That's too bad, because the possibilities that stock cabinets offer are limitless. If you let your imagination run free, you can come up with interesting combinations to create almost any kind of custom furniture look.

Puppet theater. Okay, not everyone needs (or wants) a puppet theater in the house, but we've shown this as an example of how easy it is to make a custom piece of furniture from stock cabinets (top right photo). With a little imagination and a stock cabinet catalog, you can quickly add custom furniture throughout your home.

Bedroom suite. Who doesn't need storage in a bedroom? Imagine how much closet space would be freed up by making a headboard and bed frame out of cabinets, and then filling all that new storage space. Even the packrat of the house would be pleased. Add a few more stacked cabinets, and you've got a matching bookcase and desk like those shown in the left middle photo.

Armoire or entertainment center. Stack a couple of cabinets on top of each other, add some matching side panels and crown molding, and you've got a beautiful armoire like the one shown in the bottom right photo. The finishing touches are a set of bun feet and antique paint. For an entertainment center, many cabinet manufacturers offer hardware to convert standard doors into pocket doors. Pocket doors open wide and then slide back into the cabinet to expose a television or stereo system.

Built-in storage. Built-in storage is generally less expensive than freestanding storage: The cabinets usually fit in a recess and you don't need to cover the ends with matching panels. You also don't need to finish the back or add feet. With the wide array of shapes and sizes available from hundreds of cabinet manufacturers, odds are you'll be able to find just the right stock cabinets for your needs. Filler strips (see page 107) allow you to fit stock cabinets into almost any space.

Staircase desk. It's amazing where you can shoehorn a little storage and workspace with the right combination of cabinets and accessories. The small but useful desk shown in the top left photo is carefully tucked under the staircase to take advantage of unused space.

Bookcase. Most cabinet manufacturers make some kind of open shelving units that are easy to convert into a bookcase, like the one shown in the top right photo. A little crown molding along the top edge and you have a custom-made piece for a non-custom price.

Curio cabinet. A couple of wall cabinets with glass doors on both sides is all it takes to create a distinctive see-through curio cabinet, like the one in the bottom left photo. The cabinet top can be wood, but for an elegant touch consider an alternative material like marble (as shown here), granite, or solid-surface material.

Buffet. Whether in the dining or living room, storage space can be added by fitting a set of base cabinets between the walls of a recess, like that shown in the bottom right photo. Notice the combination of different-width base units that were used to almost perfectly fit the space.

Wall and Window Treatments

What's used to cover walls and windows is a major design element for living spaces. This is in contrast to kitchens and baths, where perhaps one or two windows and a modest stretch of wall get some attention. In a living room, bedroom, dining room, or family room, there might be several expanses of glass—and they all take shades, blinds, and/or fabric. And, there's usually much more wall real estate to cover.

Windows. For bedrooms, you can purchase "ensembles" of coordinated comforters, drapes, pillows, and table covers. This way, all your textiles go together, guaranteed. For any living space, you can often find wallpaper coordinates (drapes and pillows) to match your paper. Of course, you can just choose a drape of fabric to complement your style and be done with it—almost. Bear in mind that you can do a lot of eye-fooling with curtains and drapes. To make a tiny window look bigger, don't hang drapes right at the edges of the window—place rods and brackets so they extend outside the window boundaries. The end result will be a much bigger-looking window.

Paint. It's probably the easiest, fastest way to make over walls. For living spaces, a flat latex finish is usually best (try eggshell in kids' areas). Some specialty paints provide texture such as suede, and faux finishes like ragging or sponging help bring a richer, more interesting texture to any painted surface.

Wallpaper. A bit more challenging to use than paint, wallpaper offers the advantage of thousands of patterns, textures, and shades (you'll find stacks of wallpaper sample books at home and decorating centers). Want your walls to look like bamboo, woven cloth, or even metal? Paper is the way to go, but be sure to choose the strippable kind—it's much easier to remove when it's time for another fresh look.

LIGHTING

In most older homes and many new homes, general room lighting typically comes from a single overhead fixture, either incandescent or fluorescent. Modern homes usually use a combination of natural light from windows and recessed cans in the ceiling. Task lighting—lighting designed to illuminate a specific area—is usually under-cabinet lights in the form of strips or "pucks." Accent lighting can be anything from interior cabinet lights to pendants to wall sconces.

Pendant. Pendant lights are perfect for lighting eating areas. There are two basic versions of a pendant light: one where the light is suspended simply by its electrical cord, or, like the one shown in the top left photo, where the light is suspended via a metal rod that hides the electrical cord.

Under-cabinet. Under-cabinet lighting (right) comes in a variety of shapes and configurations, with strip lights and individual "pucks" being the most common. When choosing under-cabinet lighting, go with halogen—it creates a light more natural than fluorescents (inset), which tend to cast a greenish tint on surfaces.

Recessed. Some recessed lights attach to the ceiling via a set of clips; others attach directly to ceiling joists or electrical boxes attached to them. Alternatively, the light can attach to a pair of sliding brackets that are fastened to the ceiling joists. When selecting recessed cans, make sure to choose the type that's rated for insulation contact. You can install these lights in the ceiling without having to move the insulation out of the way (which would create an unwanted path for warm air to leak out of your kitchen). For the ultimate in flexibility, choose cans that have pivoting lenses (like those shown in the bottom left photo) so you can direct the light where you need it most.

LIVING SPACE SYSTEMS

Unlike the kitchen and bathroom, the mechanical systems of the other rooms in your home are fairly simple. Although all will have an electrical system, this will primarily consist of wall receptacles, light switches, and lighting fixtures. Very few of these rooms have any plumbing, and when they do, it's often something straightforward like a wet bar. Each of the living spaces in your home will have some sort of heating and/or cooling, except for porch-like spaces that provide seasonal use.

The one system that may come into play during a living space makeover is the structural framing system of the home. It's important to be able to identify which walls in your home are load-bearing, and which aren't. It's also useful to know how a typical wall is framed, in case you need to modify it. Now we'll see how various systems may affect your makeover plans.

PLUMBING SYSTEMS

Most living spaces in your home other than the kitchen and bathroom will not have any plumbing. When plumbing does exist in one of these rooms, it's typically for a wet bar; see the drawing below right. Any plumbing system commonly consists of three types of lines: supply, waste, and vent.

Supply lines direct pressurized water to the plumbing fixtures. Fresh water enters the home via a local water utility or from a private well; the pressure comes from the city's pumping stations or from the well pump, respectively. Regardless of the source, the water flows through a main shut-off valve (and a water meter if supplied by a utility), and then to the hot water heater. From there, both hot and cold water branch out to various parts of the home. All lines terminate in some sort of valve that, when opened, will allow water to flow. Valves such as sink faucets are operated manually; other valves like those in refrigerator icemakers are automatic.

Solid and liquid wastes are transported out of your home by the waste lines. These rely on gravity to move the waste water from sinks out of the fixture and into a line (often called the soil stack) that empties into the municipal sewer or a private septic tank. In between every fixture and the waste line is a trap—basically a curved section of pipe that captures or "traps" water. The trap fills with sufficient water to form an airtight seal to prevent sewer gas from entering the home.

A vent line allows the waste water in the drain line to flow freely. It also prevents siphoning, which can pull the water out of traps, allowing sewer gas into the home. In both cases, a vent line does its job by allowing fresh air to flow into the drain line the same way the second hole (or vent) in a gas can allows the gas to flow out freely. Vents are connected along each fixture's drain line past the trap. In addition to allowing fresh air in, vents also allow sewer gas to flow out of the home and harmlessly up through a roof vent.

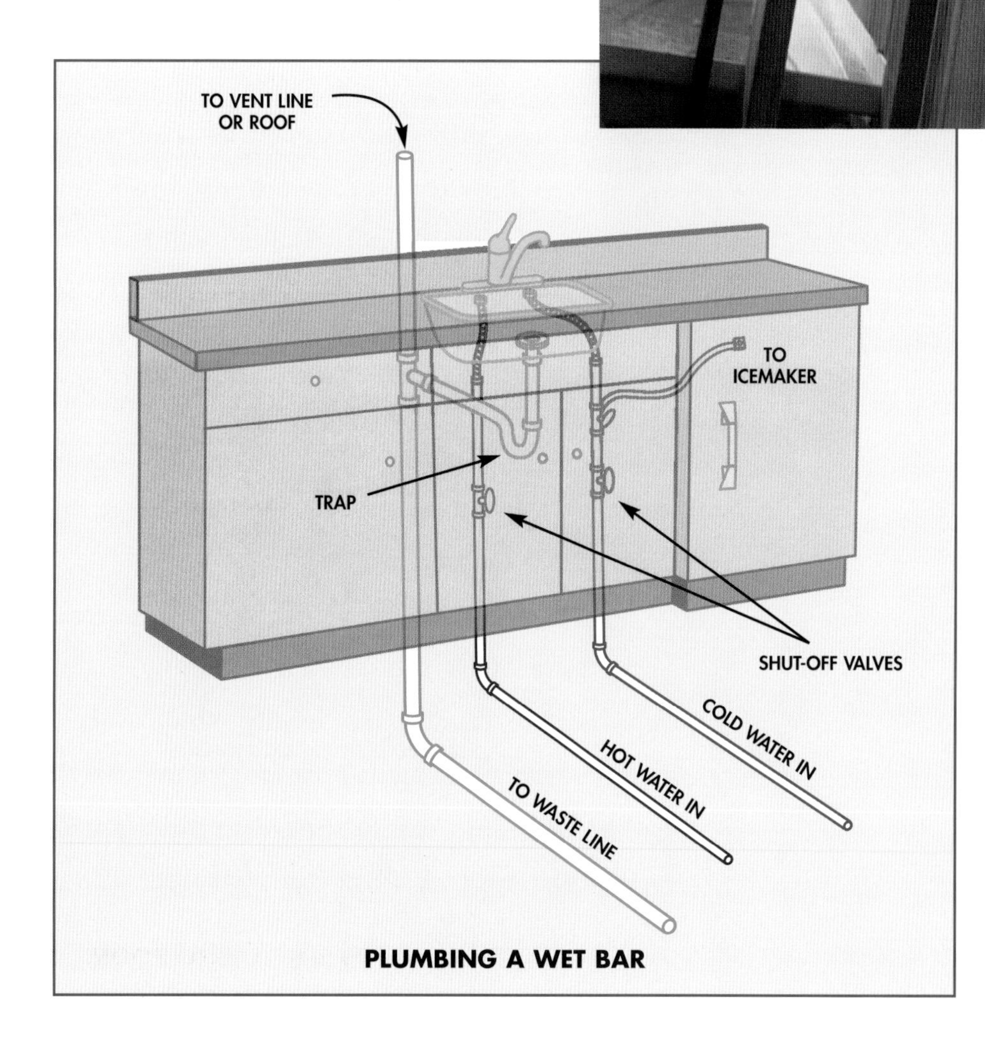

PLUMBING A WET BAR

ELECTRICAL SYSTEMS

The electrical system in rooms other than the kitchen and bathroom are uncomplicated, generally consisting only of receptacles, switches, and light fixtures. Unless you're using electric heat, odds are that you'll have only 110-volt circuits in these rooms.

Electricity is distributed throughout your home via individual circuits, each protected by either a fuse or a breaker. Individual circuits are connected to the home's service panel by way of a cable, or separate conductors protected by conduit. Current flows to the device through the "hot" or black wires. Then it returns to the source via the "neutral" or white wires. Control devices, like switches, are always installed in the "hot" leg of the circuit.

Switches control the "hot" leg of the circuit. A single-pole switch controls a light fixture from a single location; three-way switches control a light fixture from two locations. Receptacles, or outlets, allow quick and safe access to the power system via any plug-in device; a series of these generally form a circuit that's protected by a fuse or breaker.

Most light fixtures attach directly to electrical boxes—the fixture wires are joined to the circuit and stored within the box. Other fixtures, such as recessed lights, don't require an electrical box for mounting—but they do need one nearby to encase the connections to the electrical circuit.

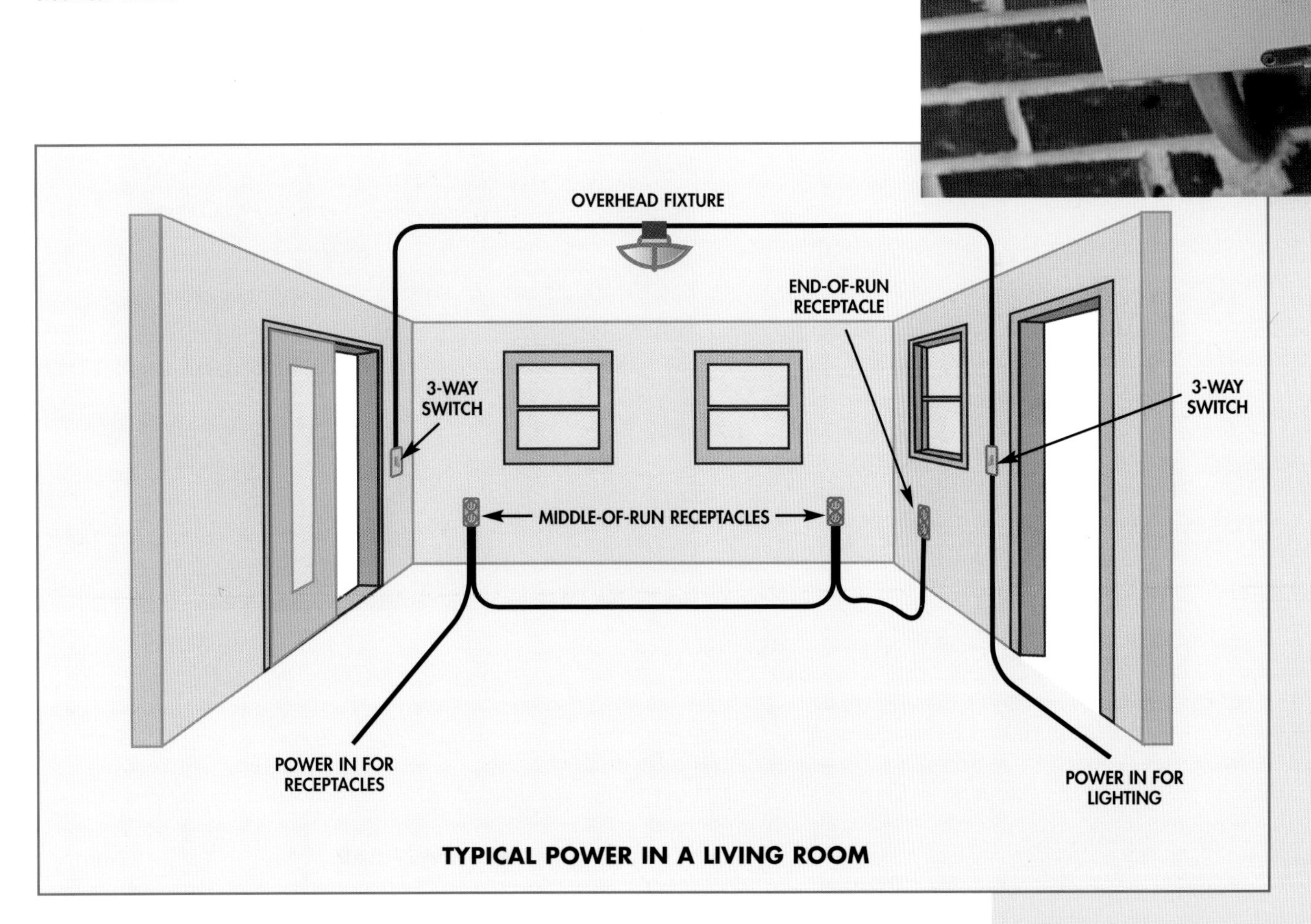

TYPICAL POWER IN A LIVING ROOM

Heating and Cooling Systems

There are three types of heating systems common to most homes: forced air, hot-water radiators, and electric baseboard. Each has its advantages and disadvantages; see page 45 for more on these. Common cooling systems include central air, window air conditioners, and evaporative coolers (in dry climates like the southwest).

Central air conditioning units are typically mounted on the side of the house or on the roof. When mounted on the roof, they are usually combined with heating and are often referred to as "heat packs." With central air conditioning, cooled air is forced through metal ducting to various points in the home. Each room may have its own return duct, but it's more common to have only one or two strategically placed throughout the home. These systems do the best job of cooling a house, but at a cost. Summer cooling bills can be quite expensive.

Individual room air conditioners, if sized correctly to match the square footage of the room, do a fair job of cooling. However, they are noisy and can also be quite expensive, depending on use. The advantage of these units is their portability: You can move them as needed to cool different areas of the home, and you can take them with you if you move.

Evaporative coolers are the least expensive form of whole-house cooling, but work only in arid climates where humidity is low. These consist of a large fan that blows air through a wet filter, thereby producing cooled but moist air. This air is distributed throughout the house, either through a large single vent or via metal ducting.

Most homes are heated via a forced-air furnace, heated-water radiators, or electric baseboards.

Forced air. Forced-air systems do the best job of distributing heated air throughout a home. Warm air travels through metal ducting. Since the air is forced into a room, it tends to mix with the air in the room better to warm the room more evenly. Returns may be in every room or spaced evenly throughout the house. The expense of forced-air heat depends on how the hot air is generated. Natural gas and oil-burning furnaces tend to be less expensive than propane furnaces and other units that use electricity to heat the air. One of the disadvantages of forced air is that it tends to redistribute dust around the house as well. This can be largely prevented, though, by changing the intake filters of the furnace regularly.

Radiators. Instead of using warm air to create heat, radiators use heated water. Water is warmed in the furnace and then pumped through piping to the radiators in the room. As the heated water passes through the radiator, fins attached to the piping siphon off the heat, and gravity moves the heated air between the fins up and into the room. As with forced-air heat, the cost of heating a room depends on how the water is heated. Also, because these systems are constantly heating up and then cooling down, the pipes and fins tend to make ticking noises that some homeowners find annoying. An advantage of radiator heat is that air is not blown in and out of the rooms, so they do not distribute dust as a forced-air unit does.

Electric baseboards. Like their water-based radiator cousins, electric baseboards do not rely on forced air to distribute heat. Unfortunately, creating heat with electricity is the most expensive way to heat a room, so electric baseboard heat is costly. One advantage to this type of system is that it usually has individual room controls instead of multiple zones, which is common with forced air and radiators. This lets you turn off or lower the heat in rooms that aren't being used. It's also important to note that most electric baseboards run on 220 volts; your service panel must be able to handle the additional load that these heaters produce.

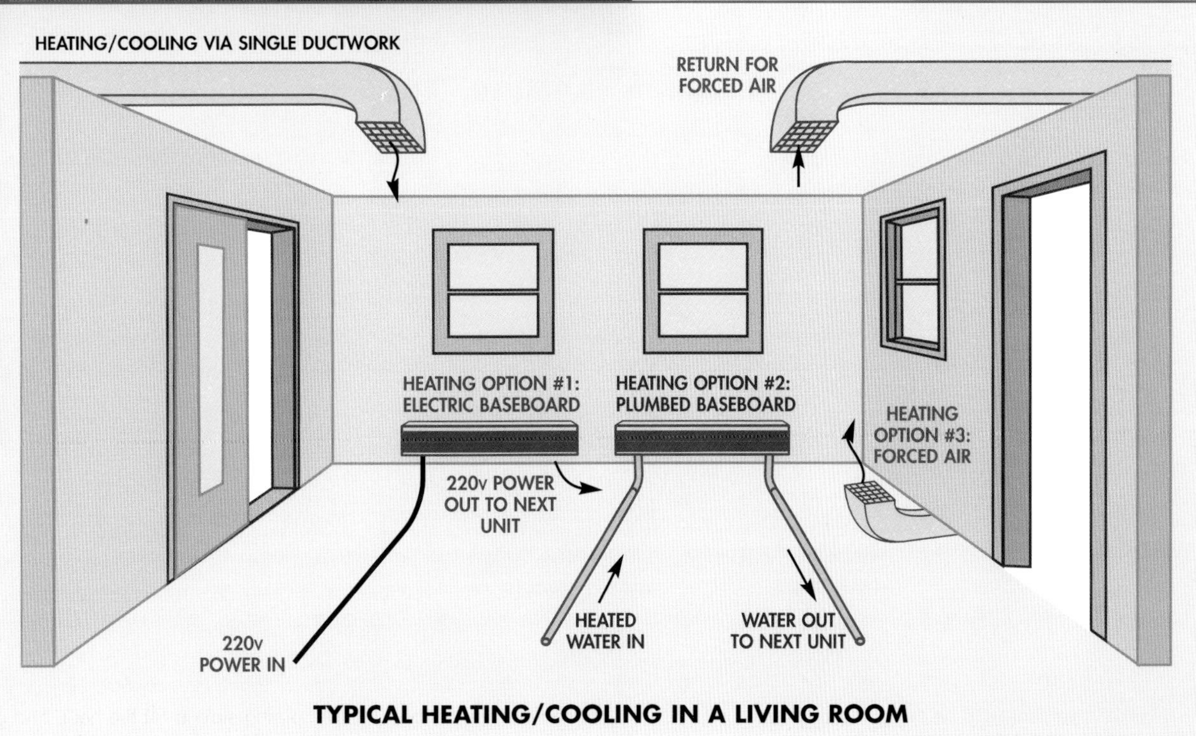

TYPICAL HEATING/COOLING IN A LIVING ROOM

FRAMING

If your makeover plans call for moving or modifying a wall, you need to have a solid understanding of basic wall framing; see the chart below for common framing terms.

Wall studs are spaced 16" on center and tied to a single sole plate attached to the subfloor and one or two top plates; see the drawing on the opposite page. In the past, all of these framing members were often 2×4 stock. This helped standardize many of the wall framing practices. But today, with greater emphasis being placed on energy efficiency, more and more homes are being built with 2×6 framing. This has a couple of advantages. First, the deeper wall cavity allows for thicker, more energy-efficient insulation to be installed. Second, since the studs are beefier, they can be spaced at 24" intervals instead of every 16".

Exterior walls are heavily insulated and have a vapor barrier installed on the warm side of the wall (typically a thin sheet of continuous plastic) to prevent moisture from entering the house. The cold side of the wall can be further insulated with rigid foam board,

COMMON FRAMING TERMS

Term	Definition
Blocking	horizontal blocks that are inserted between studs every 10 vertical feet to prevent the spread of fire in a home
Cripple studs	short vertical studs installed between a header and a top plate or between the bottom of a rough sill and the sole plate
Double top plate	a double layer of 2-by material running horizontally on top of and nailed to the wall studs
Header	a horizontal framing member that runs above rough openings to take on the load that would have been carried by the wall studs; may be solid wood, built up from 2-by material, or an engineered beam such as MicroLam or GlueLam
Jack stud	a stud that runs between the sole plate and the bottom of the header; also referred to as a trimmer stud
King stud	the wall stud to which the jack stud is attached to create a rough opening for a window or door
Rough sill	a horizontal framing member that defines the bottom of a window's rough opening
Sheathing	panel material, typically plywood, that's applied to the exterior of a wall prior to the installation of siding
Sole plate	a horizontal 2-by framing member that is attached directly to the masonry foundation or flooring; also referred to as a sill plate or mudsill
Stud	a vertical 2-by framing member that extends from the bottom plate to the top plate in a stud wall
Top plate	a horizontal 2-by framing member that's nailed to the tops of the wall studs

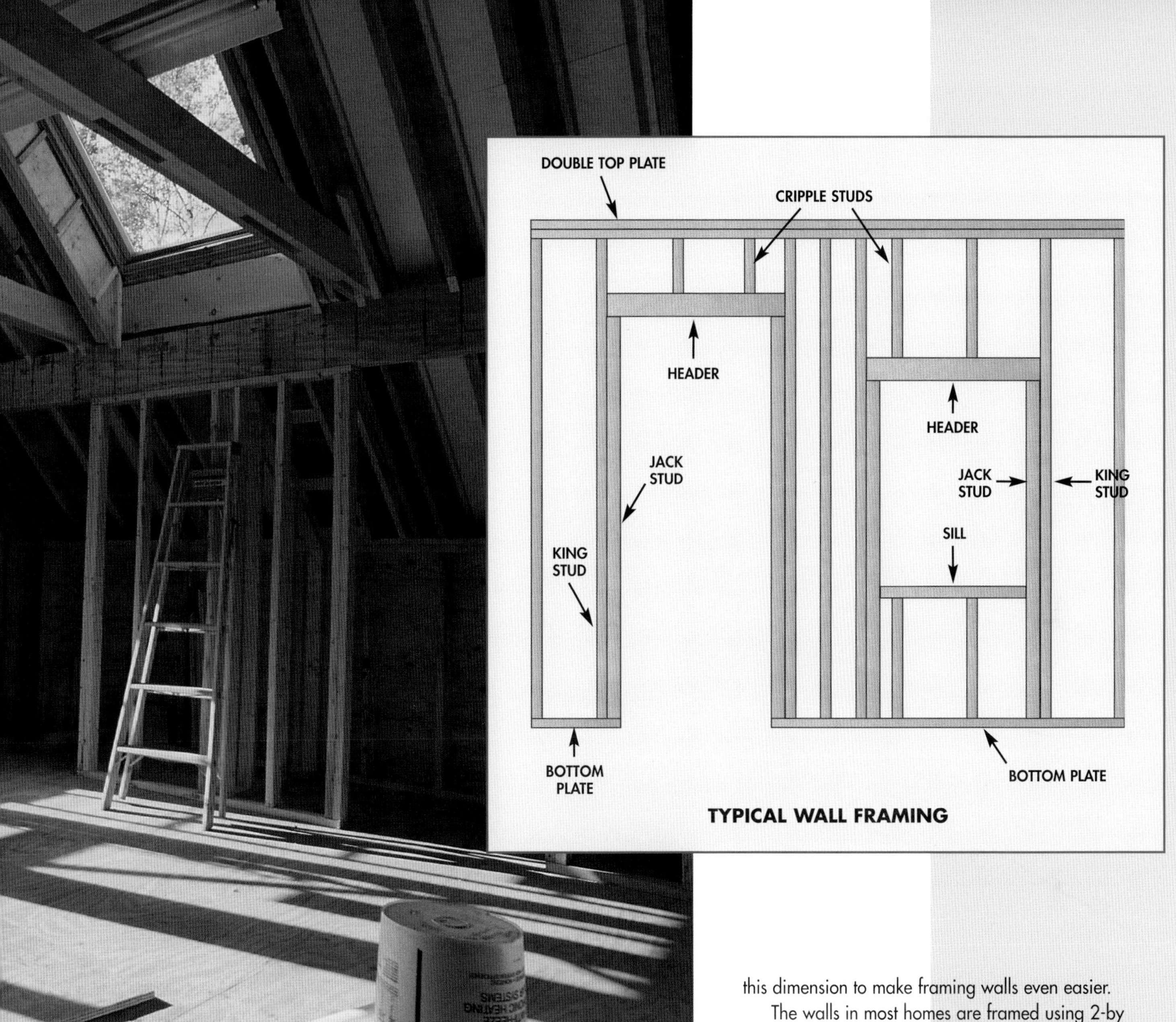

which siding is then installed over. Interior walls are often left uninsulated and are covered directly with either drywall or another wall covering.

The standard height for ceilings is 8 feet. Since the ceiling covering cuts into this height, you can't install a full 4×8 sheet of drywall to the walls without trimming it. The accepted solution to this is to frame the walls slightly higher (typically 8 feet, $\frac{3}{4}$"). If you were to subtract the thickness of a double top plate and a single sole plate, you'd end up with 7 feet, $8\frac{1}{4}$" ($92\frac{1}{4}$") for the length of the wall studs. Most lumberyards offer studs precut to this dimension to make framing walls even easier.

The walls in most homes are framed using 2-by stock. The standard is the 2×4, but the walls in homes in colder areas of the country occasionally are framed using 2×6's. A basic wall usually consists of vertical wall studs that run between the sole or bottom plate attached to the subfloor, and the top plate or double top plate, as shown in the drawing above.

Anywhere that a window or door requires an opening in the wall, a horizontal framing member called a header is installed to assume the load of the wall studs that were removed. The header is supported by jack studs (also called trimmer studs) that are attached to full-length wall studs known as king studs. Cripple studs are the shorter studs that run between the header and the double top plate or from the underside of the rough sill of a window to the sole plate.

Every wall in your home falls into one of two categories: A wall is either load-bearing or non-load-bearing.

Load-bearing wall. A load-bearing wall helps support the weight of a house; a non-load-bearing wall doesn't. All of the exterior walls that run perpendicular to the floor and ceiling joists in a structure are load-bearing walls because they support joists and rafters, either at their ends or at their mid-spans, as shown in the drawing below.

Also, any interior wall that's located directly above a girder or interior foundation wall is load-bearing (the center wall in the drawing that sits directly below the center truss of the roof framing is an example of an interior load-bearing wall).

Non-load-bearing wall. Also frequently referred to as partition walls, non-load-bearing walls have less rigid design rules and code requirements, such as wider stud spacing (24" vs. 16" on center) and smaller headers. This is because they don't support any of the structure's weight; see the drawing below.

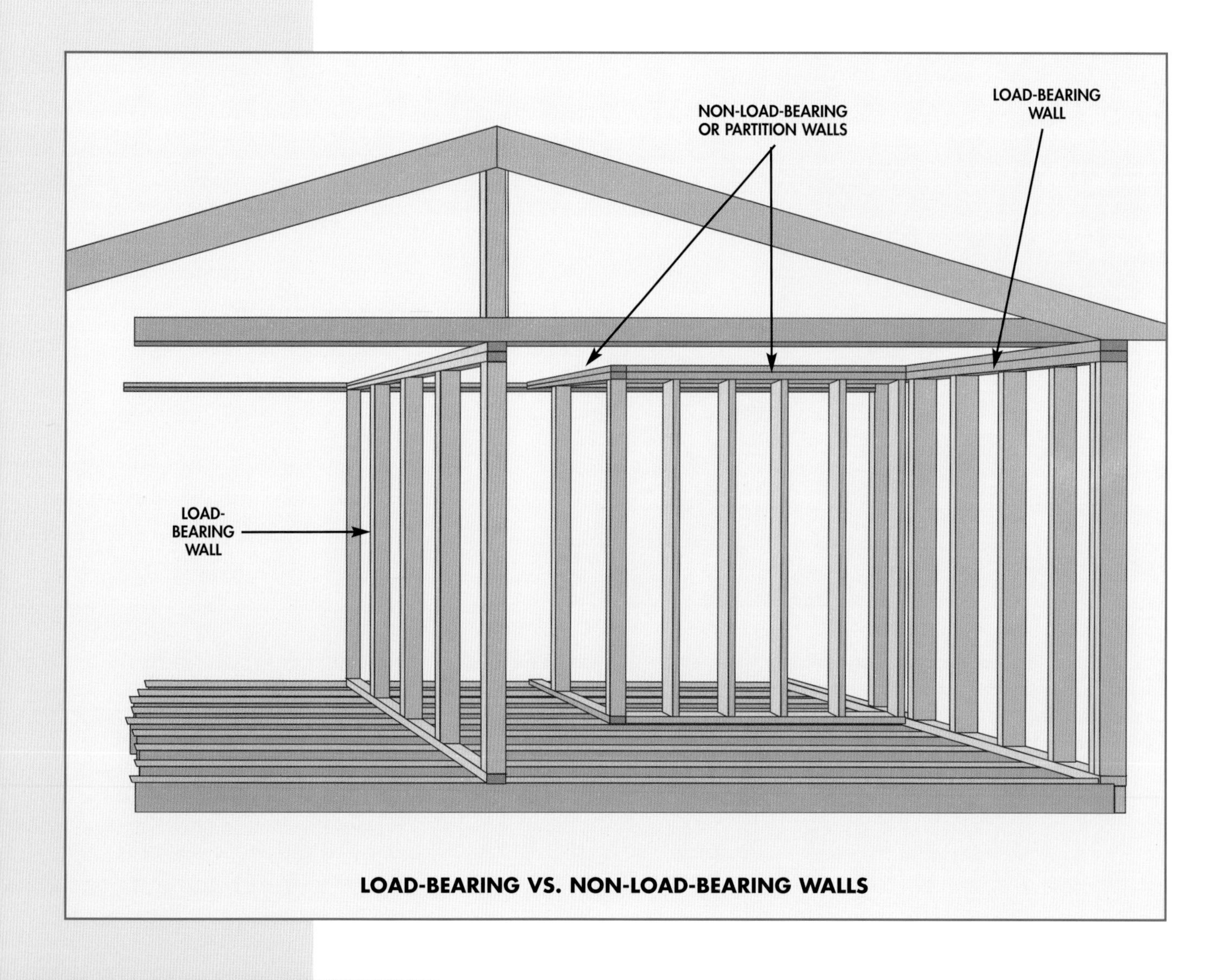

LOAD-BEARING VS. NON-LOAD-BEARING WALLS

PART 2

Real Makeover Examples

ORIGINAL DINING ROOM

HIGH-END MAKEOVER

Is your makeover budget small, medium, or large? Is your taste classic, country, or contemporary? Since only you know the answers to these questions, we show upgrades that may fit into all these plans. This section features three different makeovers in each of three different rooms: a living room, dining room, and bedroom. In each space, we show what kind of moneysmart looks you can achieve at three spending levels: budget, mid-range, and high-end. That totals nine different makeovers, to give you ideas for your own home improvements.

Each of the makeovers includes photos of the subject rooms "before" and "after," and a list of projects we did for the makeover, along with approximate costs.

These nine makeovers are intended as suggestions and examples of what you might do, with lots of room for your own tastes and preferences. We give you an idea of what the various projects cost and the results you can achieve. So, you can select the jobs, materials, styles, and patterns that will produce the customized looks you want in your home. Once you "shop" these pages for ideas and real-world inspiration, move on to Part 3: Creating Your New Look.

ORIGINAL LIVING ROOM

Here it is: the basic, boring box that comes standard issue with so many homes. The best that could be said about this 1980s living room was that it offered a bare canvas, a blank slate, for a trio of dramatically different transformations. The usual, plain ceiling fixture was attached to a popcorn ceiling; it illuminated featureless white walls and an off-white, sheet-vinyl floor. Taken separately, none of the elements was awful, but all together they presented a look that would have to get juiced up to be described as "bland."

When the homeowner said "Help!", we happily jumped in. Since there were no mechanical problems to speak of (like water-stained walls, uneven floor, or electrical nightmares), this makeover subject was mostly in need of cosmetics. As you'll see in the three makeovers, at each of the three spending levels (economy, mid-range, and high-end), we were able to create a distinctive, final look, at relatively modest costs.

Economy Living Room

WHAT WE DID

Painted walls ($50)
Wallpaper border ($50)
Track lighting ($75)
Sisal rug ($150)
Total cost: $300 – $500, depending on materials selected

At the low end of the makeover spending range, we couldn't resist punching up the living room with bright colors and casual furnishings, a decorating duo that is often available at lower costs. Caribbean blue paint on the walls is topped by a whimsical wallpaper border, while new beach-bright cushions and rattan end tables anchor an inexpensive wicker settee that was already in the home.

Funky track lighting enlivens the ceiling (while offering more diffuse light), and a sisal rug keeps the casual theme going while muting the vinyl floor. Add an indoor tree and jewel-bright wall accents, and you have a bold new look for a very timid price.

MID-RANGE LIVING ROOM

A little more money brings a more "grown-up" look to the room: an Arts & Crafts, or Mission-style, theme that continues to be a favorite. Versatile, prefinished hardwood becomes the handsome new foundation for the room, setting a more formal tone. Painted walls of a soft clay hue gently lead the eye up to an arresting border stencil of brick red and gold.

A collection of handsome furniture in white oak (the table is cherry) coordinates with the wall clock, while a mica-shaded library lamp casts a warm glow overall. To add more visual interest, we chose a floor rug in a timeless pattern of olive, rust, and cream.

WHAT WE DID

Painted walls ($50)
Stenciled walls ($75)
Prefinished wood flooring ($1,200)
Wool-blend rug ($250)
Total cost: $1,300 – $2,000, depending on materials selected

High-End Living Room

WHAT WE DID

New carpeting ($1,000)
Wallpapered walls ($300)
Ceiling fan ($300)
Ceiling paneling ($1,500)
Built-in entertainment center ($2,500)
Total cost: $4,500 – $6,500, depending on materials selected

For the high end, we went with a style best called "Transitional"—not completely traditional, certainly not contemporary, but a blend of both. The biggest change: installing a corner built-in entertainment center in beautiful light maple with distressed-glass cabinet doors (looks custom, but we crafted it from stock cabinets). It anchors a room now papered in a slub-textured, pale sage tone, complementing the soft green in the oversized armchair.

More big changes grace the ceiling, where light maple ceiling planks surround a low-profile fan with coordinating blades. Underneath it all? Go-with-everything ivory-hued carpeting—perfectly usable if the owner wants to tackle yet another look later.

Original Dining Room

Spacious, yes; inviting, no. That was the verdict on this 1970s dining room that had lots of elbow room, but precious little style. The newest thing in the room was the sheet-vinyl floor, but its swampy brown hue didn't do much for anything—or anyone. The most interesting element—the wall of built-in shelving at the far end—was poorly constructed and lacked both detail and visual interest.

With no wall treatment to add texture or tone, a plain-vanilla ceiling, and a ho-hum ceiling fixture, the overall feeling was uninspiring. The homeowners wisely opted to retain some kind of built-in storage (in a room this size, you want dining accessories close at hand), but otherwise were open to all possible changes. "Just give us a room people will want to spend time in," they implored, and we think we did just that in three different ways.

Economy Dining Room

Inexpensive aqua accents really punch up the cool, pale gray paint of the built-in shelving, while white trim makes the whole unit stand out. A glass-and-wrought-iron dining set continues the contemporary theme, sparked by vivid artwork on the wall.

Shining down on the new look is a swoopy, playful, three-bulb ceiling fixture of silver-toned metal. Underfoot: new sheet-vinyl flooring in a soft green with blue undertones, complementing the freshly white-painted walls. Very little money went into making this a room with much more personality, a personality that's modern, open, and ready to greet guests.

WHAT WE DID

Painted walls ($75)
Painted cabinets ($75)
New lighting ($125)
Sheet-vinyl flooring ($600)
Total cost: $600 – $800, depending on materials selected

Mid-Range Dining Room

Country French is a perennial crowd-pleaser, so we employed the popular yellow-and-blue motif to produce this comfortable space that invites you to sit, eat, chat, and relax. Refacing the cabinetry in red oak immediately warmed up the room (plants and knickknacks help), and we extended the look of wood further with laminate flooring in a beech finish.

A new chair rail defined the areas of mottled blue wallpaper (below the rail) and a yellow/blue floral with fuchsia accents (above it). The antique table (ash over milk-paint blue) was a local find; ditto the wall-hung flower bracket of painted tin. Atop it all: a simple country-white chandelier, suspended from a light-weight foam medallion.

WHAT WE DID

Wallpapered walls ($300)
Chair rail ($75)
Refaced cabinets ($1,500)
Laminate flooring ($800)
New lighting ($150)
Ceiling medallion ($45)
Total cost: $2,500 – $3,000, depending on materials selected

High-End Dining Room

Proving again that you get what you pay for, the high-end version cost the most and got the most raves from the homeowners. This time, we replaced the built-in shelving with new honey-toned maple cabinets, featuring glass doors, glass shelving, under-cabinet lighting, and a tiled countertop. Now the unit complements the owners' substantial dining table, building an Arts & Crafts theme echoed in the mica-and-bronze ceiling fixture.

The warmth of hardwood flooring could have made the room a bit too "woody"—if we hadn't added the welcome light of a new acrylic block window in the previously solid wall. Sponge-painting the wall in a pale coral shade, and draping the chairs in ivory covers, added a bit of softness to the overall linear, solid look. Sure, you get what you pay for—but you don't have to pay a fortune to create a room this impressive.

WHAT WE DID

Wood flooring ($1,200)
Removed old built-in ($0)
Installed new cabinets ($3,500)
Under-cabinet lighting ($50)
Tiled countertop ($300)
New lighting ($250)
Acrylic block window ($400)
Ceiling molding ($300)
Total cost: $5,000 – $7,000, depending on materials selected

Original Bedroom

"Bleak" best describes the appearance of this bedroom in its "before" state. The white, semigloss-painted walls, joined with the chilly tone of the bluish gray, worn carpet, gave an overall cold feel to the room. On the plus side, at least the two windows give a glimpse of green, and the louvered closet doors help break up the sea of white—well, at least a little.

The good news about such a plain space is that it invites unlimited creativity, limited only by our budgets for economy, mid-range, and high-end looks. In a space like this, textiles (as in bed and window coverings), wallpaper, paint, and flooring are all you need to completely redo the whole room. Textiles alone can have such impact that we could have left the walls white and still gotten a range of different looks by changing out just the bedding and draperies. But with all the choices today for covering walls and floors, we wanted to explore these options, too.

Economy Bedroom

Frilly and feminine? You bet—and it's all a matter of fabric and pattern in this lace-and-flowers Victoriana retreat. Against new wallpaper in a classic cabbage-rose pattern, we placed delicate, eyelet-trimmed curtains. They filter light onto the ivory, crochet-edged bedding, plumped with pillows that extend the crochet treatment.

A graceful headboard in a bronzed finish, wall candle sconces, and a lacy bedside table cover all help stitch together the look of comfy, old-time elegance. Underscoring the feel of the room: a wool area rug in a Victorian pattern that picks up the room's color scheme with shades of dark rose, cream, and olive green.

WHAT WE DID

Wallpapered walls ($250)
New window treatments ($200)
Room-sized rug ($300)
Total cost: $600 – $900, depending on materials selected

Mid-Range Bedroom

Jewel tones and luxurious fabrics mark this makeover that's deservedly dubbed "exotic." From the royal-purple bedspread to the sequined throw pillows, from the gilt-and-paisley wallpaper border to the deep-ruby curtains, this is a look that suggests a sultan's lair (on a budget, of course).

Laminate flooring in a rich oak tone helps set off the deep colors and must-touch fabrics. It's the biggest change in the room, and worth the investment—what look wouldn't look good with this floor? Pale lavender walls keep the room from becoming too dark. Add a beaded hanging lamp, a rattan bedside table, and themed accents, and the stage is set.

WHAT WE DID

Painted walls ($75)
Wallpaper border ($75)
Removed old flooring ($0)
Laminate flooring ($750)
New window treatments ($250)
Total cost: $800 – $1,200, depending on materials selected

High-End Bedroom

Timeless elegance that transcends trends: That's what we had in mind for this makeover, summed up as Transitional style. For the walls, we used a sponge-paint technique that gives a soft yellow texture to lighten and brighten. Topping it off is new crown molding with distinctive corner treatments. Textiles, again, really drive this entire look: Jacquard striped bedding in sage, cream, and pale coral is accented by the deep green of the chenille drapes and the bed throw.

Underscoring the trendless appeal of this room is quality wall-to-wall carpeting in a light biscuit shade, with flecks of light and dark brown. Retaining the light look with maple headboard and end tables, we created a room that will look fresh next year, and the year after, and for years to come.

WHAT WE DID

Faux-painted walls ($125)
Crown molding ($400)
New carpeting ($1,400)
New window treatments ($600)
Total cost: $2,200 – $2,800, depending on materials selected

Makeover Details

Any makeover is the sum of all its details, and adding just one more can raise a room to a whole new level. In each of our three living spaces, these are some of the details (small, medium, and large) that took the rooms from "nice" to "knockout."

PART 3

Creating Your New Look

Now that you've looked at styles, designs, products, and prices, it's time for the really fun part: rolling up your sleeves to begin your own living space makeover.

Step by step, we'll show you how to do the projects detailed so far in these major categories: flooring, walls, lighting, windows/doors, ceilings, electrical, cabinets, and overall systems. Of course, your makeover plans are uniquely yours, and maybe you'll want to try just one, two—or even all—of the projects covered.

At the beginning of each category there's an "after" photo to show the results of the tasks involved. And each project features several in-process photos, plus a list of the tools you'll need, to help you every step of the way.

MAURICE RAVEL

FLOORING

They take the dirt we track in, the heavy objects we drop, the daily pounding of feet—about the only thing that today's floors *don't* take is high maintenance. Thanks to advances in technology and materials, most of the preferred types of flooring are built to stand up to years of use. But, whether you're refinishing wood or installing new laminate, take care to do the job right so your floor can give its best service. Take care, too, to match the flooring to its room: You wouldn't, for example, carpet a kitchen, or install a hardwood floor in a bathroom; neither covering mixes well with water. That said, if you haven't shopped for flooring lately, prepare to be, well, floored by the choices in patterns, colors, and styles. No matter what look you want to complement or what style note you want to strike, your floor can play a leading role.

Refinishing a Hardwood Floor

TOOLS

- Orbital floor sander (rental)
- Random-orbit sander
- Shop vacuum
- Screwdriver
- Lamb's-wool applicator

Are your hardwood floors looking tired and worn out? Give them a facelift with a rented floor sander. There's nothing complicated about refinishing a wood floor. Actually, the biggest hassle is dealing with the clouds of dust that the sander will generate. One way to reduce this is to use an orbital floor sander instead of a drum-style floor sander. The more aggressive drum sander will do the job quicker, but at a price: Drum sanders generate copious amounts of dust, and it's easy to accidentally sand a groove or dip into your floor.

That's why an orbital sander is better—it's slow, not as aggressive, and virtually foolproof. Even if you use an orbital sander, you're still going to generate a lot of dust. Don't underestimate the insidious nature of dust—it'll seek out and pass through even the smallest cracks and create a mess wherever it goes. Hold this to a minimum with proper room preparation; see the sidebar on the opposite page.

Sand the floor. Instead of using sandpaper for refinishing floors, consider using sanding screen. Even coarse sandpaper will quickly clog up with old finish. But sanding screen, with its open weave, will go a lot longer without clogging. Place a piece of screen beneath the pad of the rented orbital sander and drape the electrical cord over your shoulder to keep it out of harm's way. Slip on a dust mask and turn on the sander (left). Start in one corner and work a 3-foot-square section at a time, keeping the sander in constant motion. Don't let the sander come in contact with the wall or baseboards, where it can cause damage—stay about 3" to 4" away (you'll sand this area next with a portable sander).

Sand the perimeter. Although most rental stores will try to rent you an edging sander to sand the perimeter of the room, we don't recommend them. Most edging sanders are just large disk sanders. Disk sanders, by their very rotating nature, will leave swirl marks on a wood floor. A better swirl-free alternative is to use a random-orbit sander (below). These sanders are surprisingly aggressive with a coarse sanding disk or screen, but are designed not to leave swirl marks. If your sander accepts hook-and-loop sandpaper, you can use sanding screen by sandwiching a piece of abrasive pad between the sanding pad and the screen. The Velcro-like hooks of the sanding pad will grab the abrasive pad and hold it firmly in place. If the sander uses pressure-sensitive adhesive paper (PSA), start with a coarse grit (60 to 80) and work up to 120-grit paper.

Vacuum thoroughly. Once you've completely removed the old finish with the power sanders and you're satisfied with the smoothness of the floor, it's time to vacuum, vacuum, and then vacuum (above). Leftover sanding dust is the number one cause of a poor finish. Use a shop vacuum to go over the entire floor. Then empty the vacuum, clean the filter (this is important, as a dirty filter will blow a lot of dust back into the room), and repeat. Allow the dust to settle for a couple of hours and then go back and vacuum again.

Apply the first coat. When the floor is as clean as you can get it, it's time to apply a finish. Contact your flooring supplier for a finish recommendation. It most cases, they'll suggest applying a polyurethane designed specifically for floors, with a lamb's-wool applicator (top right photo). This type of applicator holds a lot of finish and makes it easy to obtain a smooth, even coat. Start in one corner and work your way across the room, taking care to overlap strokes. Tip: Keep your lamb's-wool applicator pliable between coats by wrapping it tightly with a plastic bag and taping it shut so air can't get inside.

Apply additional coats as needed. Allow the first coat to dry according to the manufacturer's instructions (usually overnight), then apply a second coat (bottom right photo). Depending on the finish you're using and the amount of gloss you're after, you may have to put on additional coats. At the very minimum, you should apply at least two coats. Let the final coat cure for at least two days before moving any furniture into the room. To prevent scratches, apply felt pads to furniture feet, especially on heavy items such as sofas and chests.

DEALING WITH DUST

Take the time to prepare the room being refinished to prevent sanding dust from covering everything in your home. Begin by removing the furniture, window treatments, and anything on the walls. If there's an overhead light, remove the diffuser. Cover electrical outlets and switches with tape to block out dust. Then attach a plastic drop cloth from ceiling to floor with masking tape. Overlap two drop cloths or cut a slit in the plastic to serve as a door. Attach a furnace filter to the intake of a square fan, and place it in an open window to pull dust out of the room. Place the filter on the inside so it'll trap dust on the way out the window.

Installing a Hardwood Strip Floor

TOOLS

- Handsaw
- Circular saw
- Staple gun (optional)
- Stud finder
- Chalk line
- Hammer
- Nail set
- Flooring nailer (rental)

There's nothing like the natural beauty of a solid-wood strip floor. When you also consider that hardwood floors are extremely durable and can be refinished multiple times, it's easy to see why many homeowners invest in this hardy flooring. Although the basic technique for installing hardwood strip flooring isn't difficult, it does require some familiarity with wood and basic carpentry skills. Plus it's plain hard work: There's a lot of cutting, trimming, and nailing. It's the nailing that gets especially tiresome. Even with a rented flooring nailer, it's hard on the lower back. But most will agree that the natural beauty of a hardwood strip floor is worth the effort.

There are a number of things you'll need to do to prepare a room for hardwood strip flooring. Since this is the thickest of all flooring types, you'll need to deal with the added thickness it adds to your existing floor. This means thinking through the transitions to other types of flooring and dealing with any doors and door casings. You'll also need to lay down felt paper as a moisture retardant. And it's important to get the actual flooring into the room where it'll be installed at least three weeks prior to installation so that it can acclimatize. Skipping this simple step is a leading cause of gaps and buckling. The wood strips need to adjust to the room's humidity before they're nailed to the subfloor. If you install them and then they shrink or swell, gaps will open and the floor may buckle.

Trim casing and doors if necessary. Instead of trying to sculpt the wood strips to fit around the intricate edges of doorstop and door casings, it's a lot easier to undercut casings and slip the flooring underneath. To do this, place a scrap of flooring next to the casing to be trimmed. Then, with a handsaw lying flat on the scrap, cut into the casing (below). If any doors open into the room in which you're installing new flooring, remove and shorten them. Add 1/4" for clearance to the thickness of the flooring and cut this off the bottom of the door. For wide doors, use a straightedge as a guide for a circular saw (inset).

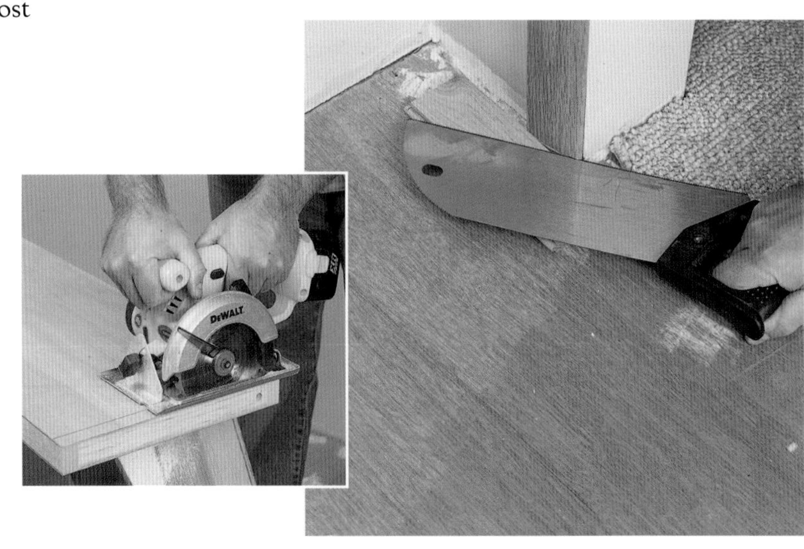

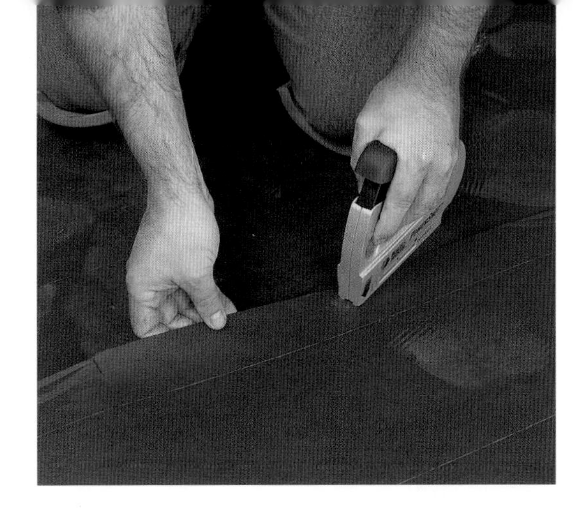

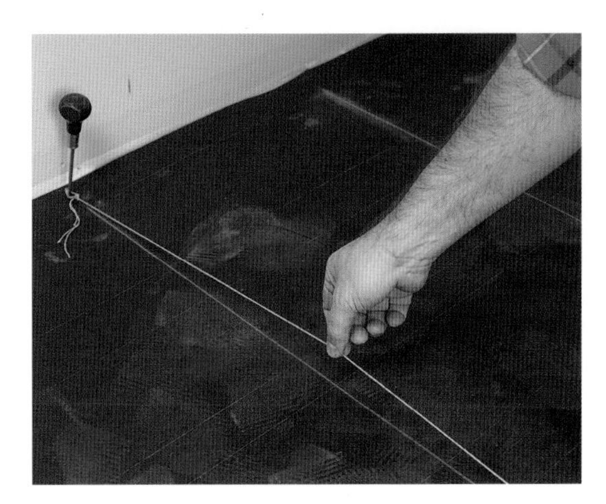

Install felt paper. Wood constantly reacts to changes in humidity: It swells and shrinks as moisture comes and goes in a room. So the more you can do to reduce this, the better. Since moisture frequently comes up through the subfloor, lay down a layer of felt or building paper as a moisture barrier. Start by laying felt paper along the longest wall, and work your way across the room, overlapping the strips 3" as you go (top photo). A couple of staples will prevent the ends from curling and keep the paper in place until the flooring is installed.

Locate and mark floor joists. Strip flooring is best secured directly to the floor joists. To locate them, use a stud finder and mark their locations on the felt paper. Then snap a chalk line at every joist location to serve as a nailing guide (middle photo). Next, find the midpoint of the room and snap a line to mark the center. Now measure equal distances from the ends of the centerlines to roughly 1/2" from the starting wall and snap a line there; this is where you'll start laying strips. Doing this ensures that the highly visible strips in the middle of the room will look straight even if the room is out of square.

Face-nail the starter strip. The first rows of flooring that you lay down have to be face-nailed in place because a flooring nailer needs about a foot of wall clearance to operate. With the groove facing the wall, align a long strip with the starter line you snapped earlier. Some rental centers supply a special face-nailer that's designed to work close to the wall along with the flooring nailer (photo below). Following the manufacturer's instructions, nail the starter strip in place. You can also face-nail manually by predrilling a slightly smaller hole than the nail and driving the nail in place with a hammer. Use 2 1/2"-long nails, and nail into the joists where possible.

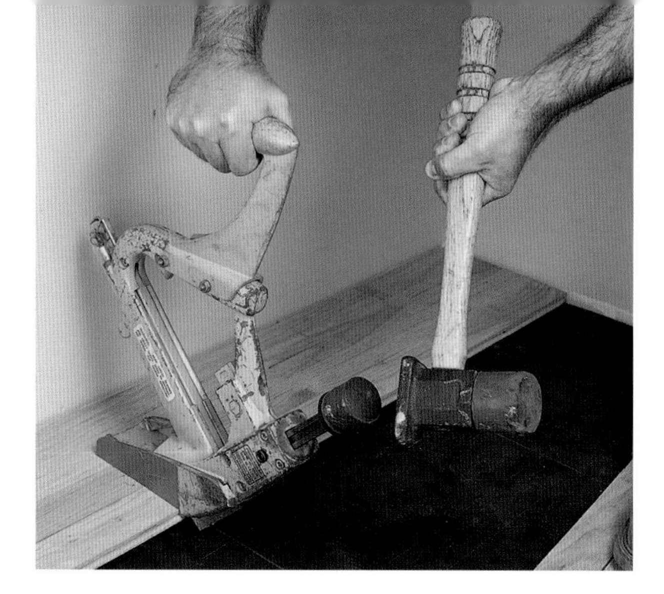

Arrange the fields. After you've face-nailed the first course, lay down at least two more courses—but blind-nail these to the joists by hand, as you did with the starter strip. Make sure to leave a 1/2" gap wherever the flooring meets a wall. Next, lay out or "rack" seven or eight rows or "fields" of flooring, staggering end joints in adjoining rows by at least 6" (above). The basic idea here is to arrange the wood strips into an attractive pattern before nailing them in place. If you select strips as you nail, you can end up with mismatched grain and a floor that's not pleasing to the eye.

Nail down the strips. After the third course is down, you can use the flooring nailer. Start by tapping the strip with the rubber end of the mallet supplied with the nailer to close any gaps. Then hook the lip of the nailer over the top edge of the strip and strike the plunger with the metal end of the mallet to drive in a fastener (top right photo). Drive fasteners at the joists and halfway between them. Make sure the nailer drives the fastener at least 1/8" below the surface. Keep a nail set on hand to countersink any that protrude.

Drive strips together as needed. Chances are that many of the wood strips you'll be using won't be absolutely straight. This means you'll probably need to nudge most strips in place to close up any gaps. If you've rented a flooring nailer, the mallet that comes with the nailer may have a rubber face on one end that can be used for this. Warning: Don't be tempted to strike the edge of a strip with a hammer—it'll dent the edge and leave an unsightly gap. Instead, use a short scrap of flooring and a hammer or mallet to drive the strips together, as shown in the bottom photo.

Cut strips to fit as needed. When you reach the opposite wall, you'll likely need to trim the final strip to fit the remaining gap (top left photo). If the wall is uneven, it's best to "scribe" the piece to fit against the wall. Start by aligning an edge with the edge of the nearest strip to the wall. Then measure the largest gap between the wall and the strip and add 1/8" to this. Poke a hole in a piece of cardboard large enough to span the gap this distance away from the wall. Now all you have to do is butt the cardboard against the wall and run it slowly against the wall as you press down on the pencil (inset). The pencil will scribe the unevenness of the wall onto the strip so you can cut it to match.

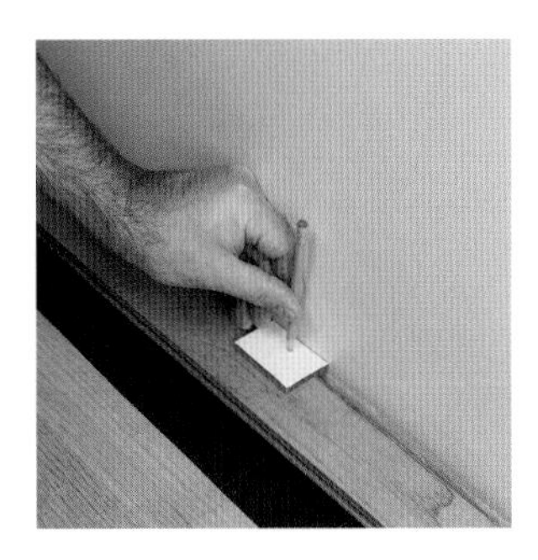

Finishing up. The flooring is down and the room looks great. Just about done, right? Well, not exactly. To finish the job, you'll need to first sand the floor to smooth it out, leveling any high points in the strips and removing any imperfections, and then apply a couple of coats of clear finish. As an optional step, you can also apply a stain to the floor to match existing furniture or flooring. Both of these jobs are messy, but are easy to do with the right tools. Use the same technique as described on pages 66–67 to sand and finish the floor, but use sandpaper instead of sanding screen when sanding.

TRANSITIONS

Reducer strip. At a threshold you'll need to transition from the strip flooring to the flooring in the adjoining room. Reducer strips are usually used for this; these have a notch in the bottom to fit over most flooring.

Expansion strips. If strip flooring meets ceramic tiles, metal doors, or a laid stone floor, install a strip of cork between the flooring and the nonwood material. The cork fills the gap but still allows the strip flooring to expand and contract with seasonal changes in humidity.

Reversing direction. If you're planning on extending flooring out of the room and into a hallway or closet, you'll need to reverse the direction of the tongue-and-grooves. This is necessary so the flooring nailer will be able to get in close to the wall in the closet or hallway. Most flooring dealers sell a slip tongue for this.

PREFINISHED WOOD FLOORING

TOOLS

- Hammer and nail set
- Air nailer (optional)
- Miter and circular saw
- Rubber mallet

Two of the biggest chores of installing strip wood flooring—sanding and finishing—are eliminated with prefinished flooring. Basically, you just nail it in place and you're done. Prefinished strip flooring is available in a variety of stains and finishes, with oak being the most common wood. Finishes can vary from satin to high gloss. It's important to realize that these are still solid-wood strips and they will move with changes in humidity. Be aware that since you're not sanding out any highs and lows once the strips are nailed in place, a prefinished floor will commonly not be as level as a floor that was sanded in place.

Install starter strip. As with unfinished strip flooring, the first or starter strip needs to be face-nailed in place (right photo). Also, if the wall is uneven, you'll need to scribe it and cut it to fit. See page 71 for directions on how to scribe a strip to fit a wall. We used a finish nailer fitted with 2½" nails to install this flooring. A finish nailer will drive and set a nail with a pull of the finger. The only disadvantage to using an air nailer versus a flooring nailer? The air nailer doesn't drive the strips together as the nail is driven in place like a flooring nailer does. But as long as you tap the strips together with a scrap block (as described on page 70), this shouldn't be an issue.

Stagger as you go. Once the starter strip is in place, you can begin laying strips. As with unfinished strips, it's important to lay out fields to ensure a pleasing pattern of wood grain. Once you're satisfied, nail the strips in place. Here again, we used the finish nailer. Its angled head allows the tip to fit nicely in the side of the strips for easy nailing.

Continue laying strips. Continue staggering and laying strips out in fields before nailing them in place. When you reach the opposite wall, you'll probably need to scribe and cut the final piece to fit. Remember to leave a 1/2" gap between the last piece and the wall so the strips can expand and contract as they react to changes in humidity.

Installing Vinyl Tiles

TOOLS

- Chalk line and tape measure
- Utility knife or scissors
- Hammer or air nailer (optional)
- Circular saw
- Framing square and straightedge
- Seam and flooring roller (rental)

Self-adhesive vinyl tiles, frequently called "peel-and-stick" tiles, are the simplest of all flooring you can install. You just peel off the protective paper backing and press the tile in place. It really is that easy. Besides a rented flooring roller that you'll use to ensure a good bond between the tiles and the subfloor, you won't need any specialized tools. Vinyl tiles are one of the easiest flooring materials to cut—all it takes is a utility knife or scissors. One important requirement for this type of flooring is that the subfloor must be flat, level, and free from dirt. Cleanliness is extremely important with these tiles: Even the tiniest bit of dirt can contaminate the bond, resulting in a weakly attached tile.

New underlayment. The most reliable way to create a flat reference surface for vinyl tiles is to install a fresh layer of 1/4" plywood over your existing floor (bottom left). It's fairly quick work and there are only a couple of things to be aware of. First, make sure the existing floor is level and there are no dips. Second, to prevent cracks in the new flooring, it's important that the seams of the new plywood don't match up with any seams in the existing floor. Cut the plywood as necessary to prevent this, and nail or screw it in place—just make sure the nails or screws are below the plywood surface to keep from interfering with the vinyl tiles.

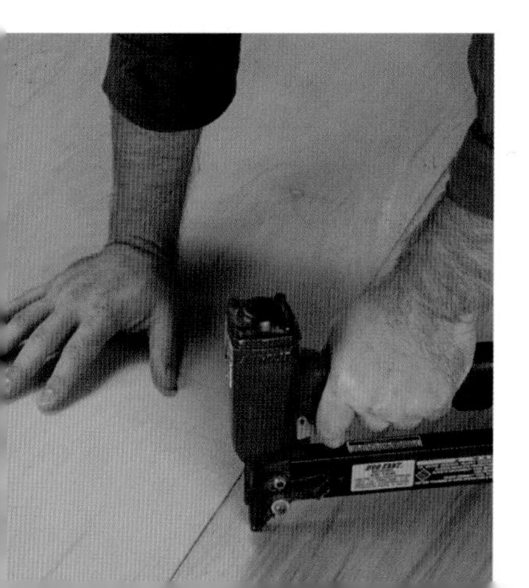

Reference lines. Accurate reference lines are the foundation of a successful tile install. To do this, start by measuring and marking the center of the room. Next, use a framing square to lay out a line perpendicular to the first line. Use the 3-4-5 triangle to check that the lines you just marked are perpendicular: Mark a point 3 feet from the intersection of the lines; then mark 4 feet from the adjacent side; now measure from the 3-foot to the 4-foot mark. If the lines are perpendicular, it will be exactly 5 feet. If the distance isn't, adjust one of the lines until it is.

Test the pattern. To keep from ending up with narrow tiles at the perimeter of the room, temporarily set out a row of tiles, starting at the centerlines you just marked and working toward the walls (left photo). If you find a narrow gap between the last full tile and the wall on either end, shift the appropriate centerline to eliminate it. Repeat this process for the opposite direction so you won't have any narrow tiles on the remaining walls.

Start at center and peel-and-stick. To install self-adhesive tile, start by peeling off the protective paper backing (inset). Then position the first tiles carefully along your reference lines (middle photo). Position tiles and press down firmly with the palms of both hands. Place adjacent tiles so they butt firmly against one another. Work on one quadrant of the floor at a time. Note: Most tiles have an arrow printed on the back to indicate the direction they should be laid. Make sure all arrows are facing the same direction as you install them so the patterns of the individual tiles will blend together correctly.

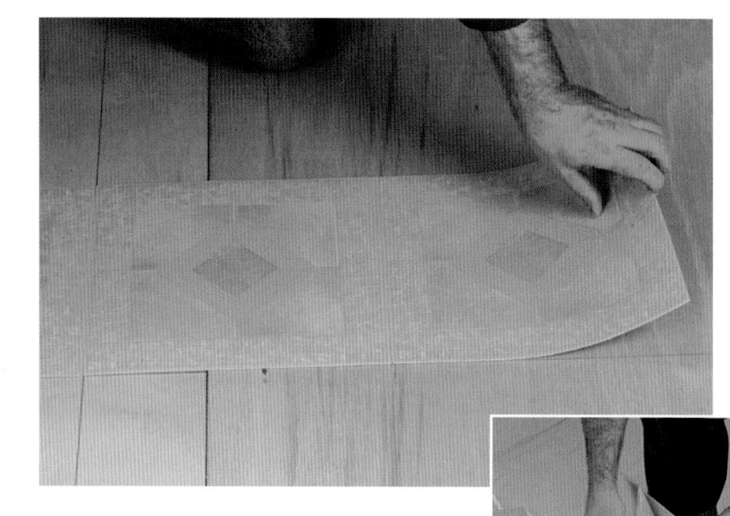

Add remaining full tiles. Once you have one quadrant laid and the tiles are pressed into place, move on to the next quadrant (bottom photo). Since you'll be generating a lot of waste with the backing, it's a good idea to have a helper handy to collect and dispose of the backing. After all the full tiles are pressed in place, go around the perimeter and measure, cut, and install the border tiles; see page 75.

Cut and install partials. If you need to cut a tile, you'll find that most self-adhesive tiles are thin enough to be cut with a pair of heavy-duty scissors. Don't remove the paper backing and then cut the tile. Instead, leave it in place and make your cut. This way the tile won't stick to the scissors. If you're looking to cut a straight line, however, you'll be better off cutting the tile with a utility knife and a straightedge (left). Be sure to slip a scrap of wood under the tile before you cut.

Flooring roller. To create the best bond between the subfloor and the tile, the tiles need to be firmly and evenly pressed into the subfloor. Without a doubt, the best tool for this job is a flooring roller rented from a nearby rental center (top right photo). Thin tile can be pressed with a 75-pound roller; thicker tiles (such as rubber) are best pressed in place with a 100-pound roller. If you're doing only a small area, you can get by in a pinch with a rolling pin; keep your weight over the pin as you roll for maximum pressure.

REMOVING VINYL TILE

If you need to remove an old vinyl tile floor, use one of the methods described below.

With floor scraper. Use a flooring scraper to pry under and lift up the tiles. Keep the angle of the scraper low to the floor to prevent the sharp blade from digging into the underlayment. Wear gloves and goggles to protect your hands and eyes. This work is tough on the lower back, so take frequent breaks or, better yet, get a helper. While one scrapes, the other can pick up the tile residue in an area that's already completed.

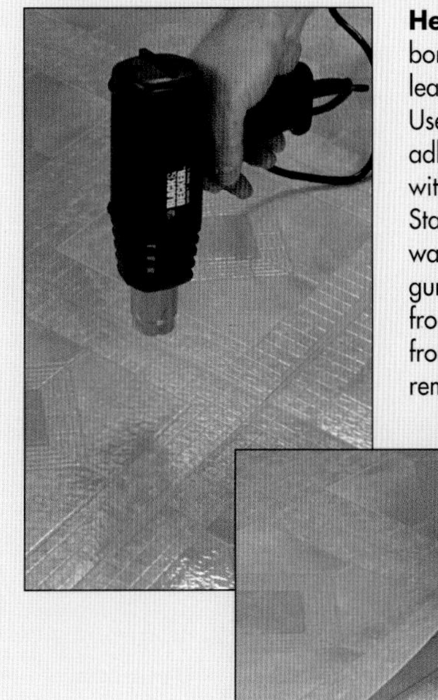

Heat and strip. Really stubborn tiles can be persuaded to leave by applying a little heat. Use a heat gun to soften the adhesive so you can pry it up with a wide-blade putty knife. Start at a seam and work your way across the tile. Hold the heat gun approximately 6" away from the tile, keeping it moving from side to side. When you've removed the tile completely, go back while the adhesive is still soft and scrape it off with the putty knife. Wipe this residue off the blade immediately with a clean rag.

Installing Sheet Vinyl

TOOLS

- Compass
- Utility knife
- Level and tape measure
- Trowel
- Framing square and straightedge
- Staple gun (optional)
- Seam and flooring roller

Sheet-vinyl flooring is an excellent choice for high-traffic areas like entryways—especially where water is involved. Unlike its easier-to-install cousin, individual tiles, sheet vinyl is tougher to install but doesn't have any seams. Plus, it's virtually impervious to water and dirt. Sheet vinyl is attached to the underlying flooring in one of two ways: with adhesive or with staples. When attached with adhesive, it's referred to as a full-adhesive installation. A full-adhesive installation has a couple of advantages. Since the entire floor covering is firmly glued in place, it's very durable. This is especially true if the sheet flooring is a single piece; without seams, water, dirt, and dust can't sneak under it to weaken the glue bond. Being firmly attached to the subfloor also helps prevent tears and rips that are common with stapled flooring.

When sheet vinyl is attached to the underlying floor with staples, it's referred to as a perimeter installation. The only thing holding the flooring in place is staples around its perimeter. The rest of the flooring rests or "floats" on the subfloor. A perimeter install is easier and not as messy as a full-adhesive installation. A perimeter install works best with non-backed solid vinyl flooring; it's very flexible and can be stretched tight as it's stapled down. This makes it much more forgiving than paper-backed vinyl. Unfortunately, perimeter-installed sheet vinyl is prone to rips and tears since the bulk of the vinyl is not attached to the subfloor.

Make it level. Floor levelers are mortar-like, cement-based coatings that go down smoothly and set up quickly—some as fast as 10 minutes. Most are ready for the next step in the installation process (such as applying flooring adhesive) in less than an hour. In addition to leveling out low spots in a subfloor, levelers are a great way to prevent old embossed flooring from telegraphing its pattern over time onto a new flooring such as resilient sheet vinyl. A thin coat of leveler will fill in all the indentations in the old tile to prevent this.

Make a template. The best way to avoid mistakes when installing a single sheet of vinyl is to make a template of the floor and use it to cut the flooring. To make a template, start by butting the edge of a roll of heavy paper (builder's paper or red rosin paper works great for this) into one corner of the room. Fasten the paper to the floor by first cutting small triangles with a utility knife in the paper (top photo), near the edges at regular intervals; then remove the paper triangles and press a strip of masking tape over each hole. Next, continue rolling paper out along the perimeter of the room. Overlap the pieces 2", and fasten them together with strips of masking tape at the seams. Cut triangular holes in the paper as you did for the first strip, and fasten each piece to the floor as you work.

Scribing the pattern to fit. If there's more than a 1/4" space between the paper and the wall, use a compass to "scribe" the wall's unevenness onto the paper. To do this, set the compass about 1/2" wider than the largest gap between the paper and the wall. Then place the point of the compass against the wall and the pencil on the paper; slide the compass point along the wall, keeping constant contact (inset). The pencil will scribe the profile of the wall on the paper so you can trim it to butt perfectly up against the wall. This same technique works for almost any profile or obstacle.

Transfer pattern to sheet vinyl. When you're done making the template, remove all of the tape covering the triangle cutouts and carefully lift it off the floor and roll it up. Transport it to the room where you've laid out the sheet flooring and place the template on the flooring. Position the template carefully so that you'll end up with the pattern you want. Use the same triangle cutouts to fasten the template to the flooring.

Cut to size. Once you're sure the template is fastened to the flooring correctly, you can cut it to match the template. Start by making the straight perimeter cuts with a utility knife and using a metal straightedge as a guide. Slide a scrap of plywood under the area you're cutting to protect the existing floor. Use firm, steady pressure as you cut. Most sheet vinyl will cut cleanly in a single pass with a sharp blade. Slight tapers can also be cut using the straightedge by angling it slightly to match the taper.

Trowel on adhesive. Position the flooring on the subfloor, taking care to slip it around obstacles. If you're working with one piece, pull one side back toward the center and apply flooring adhesive with the recommended-sized notched trowel—usually 1/8" (top photo). Then carefully fold it back into position. Repeat this process for the other half.

Press with flooring roller. Before you begin pressing the flooring into the adhesive with a rented flooring roller, go around the room to make sure the flooring is positioned properly. Once you start pressing it in place, it's a lot more difficult to lift and reposition. Begin rolling in the center of the room, working your way toward the wall (middle left photo). This pushes out air bubbles so they can escape, and moves any excess adhesive to the edges, where it can be removed.

Clean up excess. Have a soft cloth dampened with solvent on hand to clean up the inevitable mess (above). If you're working with multiple pieces that will need to be seamed (see page 79), it's best to roll and press one piece in place at a time. This gives the other piece a solid edge to butt up against—there's just a lot less slipping and sliding this way.

PERIMETER INSTALL

For a perimeter install, start by cutting and positioning the sheet in the room. Then start in one corner and pull the flooring tight against the wall and staple it to the subfloor. Use a lot of staples—one about every 2". Continue working around the room, pulling and stapling. You'll be surprised how much non-backed vinyl will stretch. Keep the staples as near to the wall as possible. They'll be covered later when you install cove base molding other trim, or thresholds. If a staple doesn't go all the way in, give it a tap with a hammer.

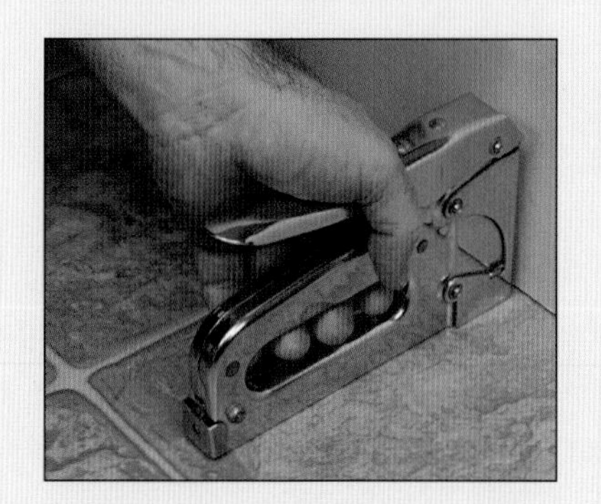

SEAMING SHEET VINYL

If the subject room for sheet vinyl is large or odd-shaped, you may need to use multiple pieces and seam them together. How you do this will depend on whether it's a full-adhesive or a perimeter install.

In either case, cutting the flooring to create a perfect seam is the toughest part. Here's how. When you go to cut the flooring using your templates, leave about 6" extra at the edges to be seamed. Then position and install one piece. If you're doing a full-adhesive install, do not apply adhesive around the seam area—stay about 8" away from the seam. Then position and install the second piece so the excess overlaps at the seam. Next, slip a scrap of plywood under the seam to protect the flooring and use a sharp utility knife guided by a metal straightedge to cut through both layers of flooring at the same time. If your flooring has imitation grout lines, try to split the line in half as you cut.

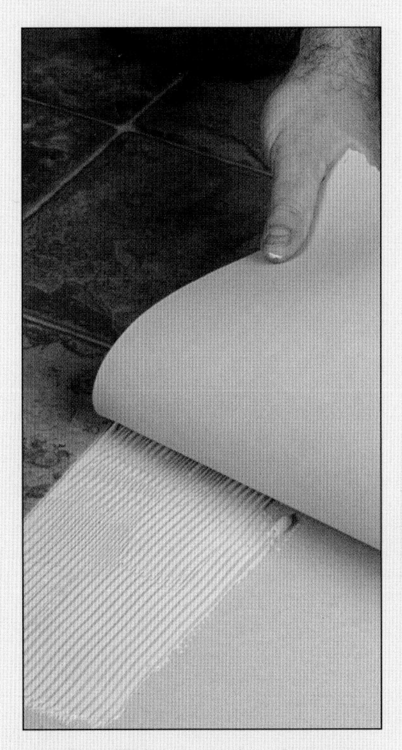

Apply adhesive under the seam area. With the pieces in place on the floor, fold back one piece at a time near the seam and apply adhesive to the subfloor with the appropriate-sized trowel. Make sure to use the adhesive recommended by the manufacturer. Repeat for the other half of the seam. After the adhesive is applied, fold back each section of flooring and press the edges together to form a tight seam.

Press the seam together. Now, using a small hand roller, rolling pin, or laminate roller, press the flooring firmly into the adhesive. Wipe up any squeeze-out with a soft cloth dampened in solvent. Strips of duct tape applied across the seam every 4" to 6" will help hold it together until it has set up.

Seal the seam. Following the manufacturer's instructions, allow the adhesive to dry and then apply a sealer to the seam. There are a couple of different types of applicators; most have a T-shaped metal tip that slips under both edges of the seam and lets you apply sealer to both the edges and to the underside of the vinyl. Most sealers actually fuse the edges of the vinyl together to create a tight seam. Make sure to follow the directions regarding how long you should wait before walking on the seam.

Installing Carpeting

TOOLS

- Hammer and metal snips
- Utility or carpet knife
- Stapler and putty knife
- Tape measure and chalk line
- Knee kicker
- Seaming iron (optional)

Soft underfoot and an effective noise reducer, carpeting is a top choice for many living spaces—bedrooms, living rooms, etc. With the variety of materials, colors, and patterns on the market, it can be a challenge to choose the right carpet—and to install it properly.

It's important to recognize up front that installing carpet is not easy. Special tools are required and, for the most part, carpet is a relatively uncooperative material to work with. For your first carpeting project, consider doing a fairly small square or rectangular room. Leave the larger rooms to a pro. Cutting and seaming carpet has a fairly well-deserved reputation for being nerve-wracking, for several reasons. First, quality carpet is expensive, so a mis-cut can be a costly mistake. Second, proper seaming technique requires a hot-glue seaming iron. Since the iron melts the glue just long enough for you to join the pieces together, you must work quickly and without hesitation.

INSTALLING TACKLESS STRIPS

Carpet is stretched and held in place by hooking its underside onto tackless strips secured to the subfloor around the perimeter of the room.

Start in one corner. Tackless strips come in a standard width of 3/4" and can be used to install carpet on most subfloors. Wider strips are available for installations on concrete. Put on gloves (the pins on these strips are very sharp) and, with the angled pins of the strip pointing toward the wall, begin by nailing a strip to the floor in one corner of the room. Maintain a consistent gap between the wall and strip with scrap-wood spacers—check the installation instructions or contact a flooring contractor for the correct gap.

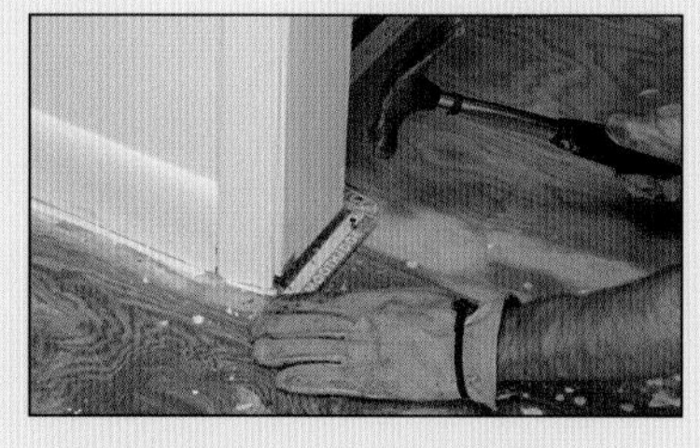

Working around obstacles. Continue nailing tackless strips to the floor around the perimeter of the room. When you encounter an obstacle, such as a radiator, threshold, built-in, or door molding, cut the strips as needed into short lengths so you can work around the obstacle. Take care to maintain the same gap that you used for the previous strips, and nail the cut strips to the floor.

Cutting strips. Tackless strips have angled pins protruding from one face and nails for securing the strips to the floor from the other. This makes them a challenge to cut. You can't lay them flat on a surface to cut with a handsaw (if you do, they'll scratch the surface), and they're too thick to cut with a utility knife. The best tool is metal snips. Again, be sure to wear leather gloves whenever handling tackless strips.

INSTALLING PADDING

Once the tackless strips are in place, the next step is to cut and install the padding.

Roll out the pad. Carpet padding often has a slick side and a rougher side; always install it with the slick side up to make it easier to slide the carpet around during installation. If your padding is wide enough to cover the entire room, roll out enough to cover the floor. To install narrow padding, start by rolling out a strip to span the length of the room. Cut it to rough length and roll out the next strip. Work slowly and try not to pull the padding excessively. If it catches on something, stop and lift it off—don't pull: Carpet padding has very little resistance to tearing.

Staple and tape. When working with a single piece of padding, work around the perimeter of the room, stapling the padding to the floor every 8" to 10" and at 1-foot intervals throughout the interior of the padding. For narrow pieces, staple the seams to the floor and then run a strip of duct tape to join the pieces together at the seam; then staple the padding in place as you would for a one-piece padding. Don't go overboard with the staples—the carpet will hold the padding in place for the most part. Staples only help to prevent the pad from shifting or bunching up over time.

Cut and trim. Position the padding into one corner and check to make sure it butts up against or overlaps the tackless strips along the length of the padding. Use a sharp utility knife to cut away any excess padding at the corner and along the edges. In most cases, you can cut this freehand; if you're looking for extra precision, use a metal straightedge to guide the knife. The padding should butt solidly up against the tackless strips, but not overlap them.

Position carpet. With the padding in place, you can install the carpet. In most cases, a roll of carpet is both heavy and cumbersome. Enlist the aid of a helper to bring in into the room and help you unroll it. Start by positioning the roll along one wall, leaving about 6" of excess to run up the wall (top photo). Then carefully roll the carpet out until you hit the opposite wall.

Leave excess and cut. Where the roll butts up against the opposite wall, mark the back of the carpet at each edge. Then measure up about 3" and make another mark. Pull the carpet away from the wall and snap a chalk line to connect the marks. Cut along this line, using a sharp utility knife or a carpet knife. Make sure to insert a scrap of plywood or other protective material under the folded-back carpet before cutting. Alternatively, if you've got a good eye, you can slice though the front of the carpet with a carpet knife as shown in the middle photo.

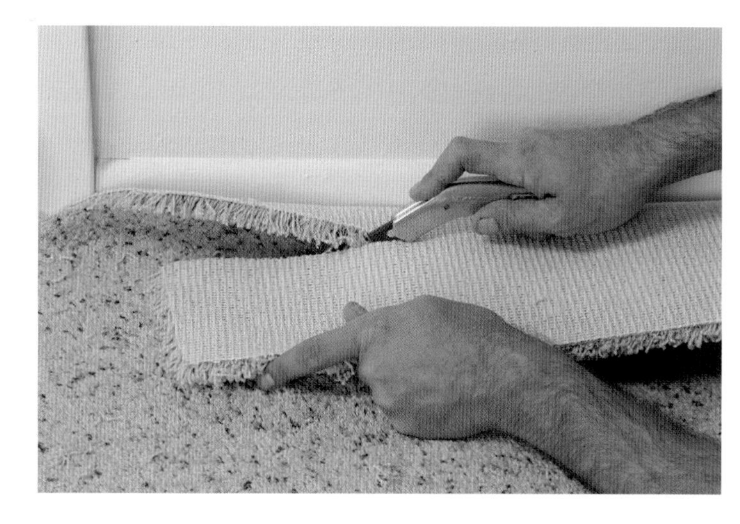

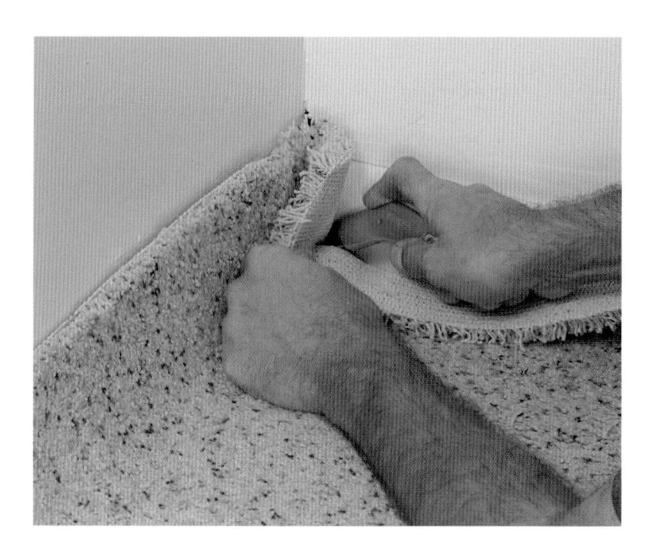

Relieve buckling in corners. With the carpet cut to rough length, the next step is to slide it over so the long edge extends up the wall. To do this, straddle the carpet and pull it until it runs up the wall about 3". You'll notice immediately that the carpet doesn't want to cooperate at the corners. Use a carpet knife or utility knife to relieve the buckling by slitting the carpet in the corners (bottom photo). Cut just the couple of inches necessary to get the carpet to nestle into the corner—don't cut too far—you'll fit these corners later after stretching the carpet.

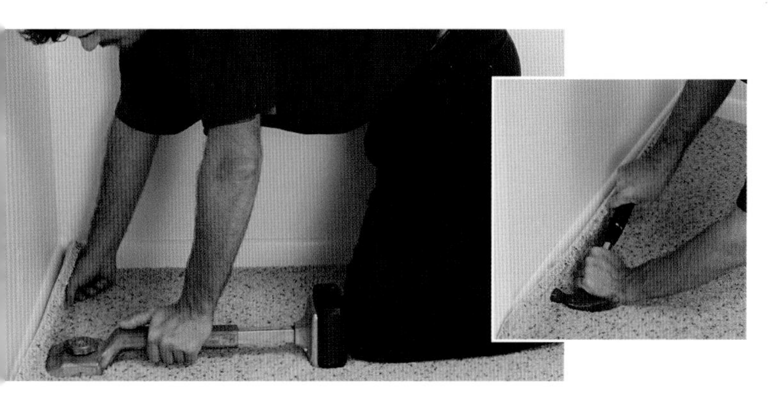

Stretch with knee kicker. Carpet is stretched with a knee kicker—and these devices take some getting used to. It's a good idea to practice a bit first before doing the actual installation. Start by positioning the knee kicker about 3" to 5" away from the wall. This way you won't accidentally break one of the tackless strips loose. Holding the knee kicker securely with one hand, strike the pad on the end sharply with your knee to stretch the carpet toward the wall. You may find that it'll take a couple of whacks to fully stretch the carpet (photo above). Once in place, press the carpet firmly onto the pins of the tackless strips with the head of a hammer (inset).

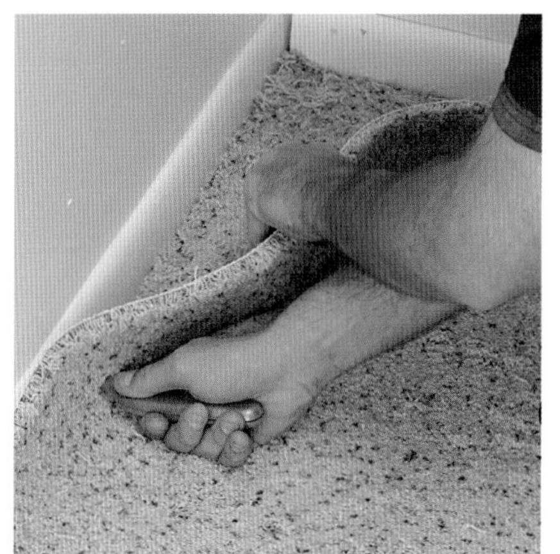

Trim to fit. In a pinch, you can use a carpet knife or sharp utility knife as shown to trim surplus carpet from the edges of the walls. The best tool for the job, however, is a carpet edge trimmer. You can rent one of these from your local rental store, or purchase one from some home centers and most flooring suppliers. To use a carpet edge trimmer, hold it flat on the carpet and press it firmly into the wall as you move it slowly along the wall. Since it can't make it into corners, you'll need to complete the cut with a utility knife.

Tuck the edges. Once the edges have been cut, work your way around the room, tucking the edges of the carpet into the gap between the tackless strips and the wall. You can do this with a wide-blade putty knife or a special kind of chisel called a stair tool (below right). Depending on the stiffness of the carpet, you may or may not need to use a hammer on the knife or chisel to persuade the carpet edge to cooperate.

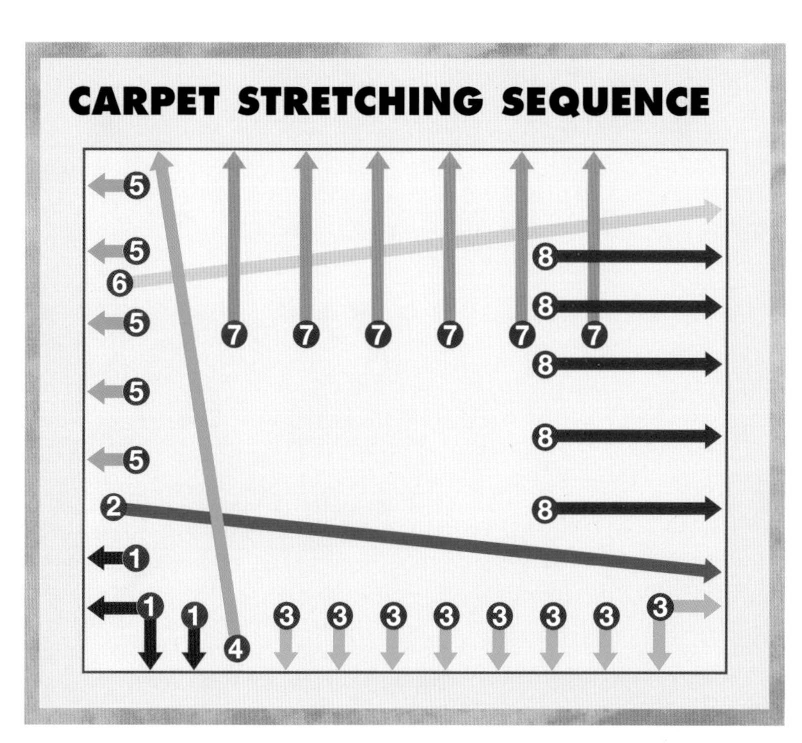

Cut carpet at the seam. If you need to join pieces of carpet, start by positioning each piece as you did earlier. Be sure to include an extra 3" at each wall plus an extra 3" for the seam. Position the cut pieces, making sure that the pile all runs in the same direction. Roll back each side of the carpet one piece at a time, and snap a chalk line about 2" back from the factory edge. Then use a straightedge and a utility knife or carpet knife to cut along the line with a scrap of plywood underneath (top photo).

Position seam tape. Now you're ready to join the two pieces of carpet together. Although you can try gluing the carpet to the floor at the seams, a better method is to use hot-glue seam tape. You can find this wherever carpet is sold. The glue on the tape is melted with a special seaming iron available at most rental stores. These irons take a while to heat up, so plug it in and turn it on as you cut the seam tape. Measure and cut a piece of tape to length for each seam, and position the tape under the seam with the adhesive facing up (middle photo).

Use sealing iron. Next, slide a protective scrap piece of plywood under the seam tape. Place the iron under the seam directly onto the tape and plywood (inset). In about 20 to 30 seconds, the glue will melt and you can slowly slide the iron along the tape. As you move the iron, let the carpet pieces fall onto the hot glue (bottom right photo). Work slowly in roughly 12" sections. Don't get nervous here—the iron won't burn the carpet or the glue. Every foot or so, stop sliding the seaming iron and press the edges of the carpet pieces down into the seam tape with your hands while squeezing the cut edges together. Hold the edge together for 10 to 15 seconds and move down the seam a couple of inches. Continue until you're close to the seaming iron.

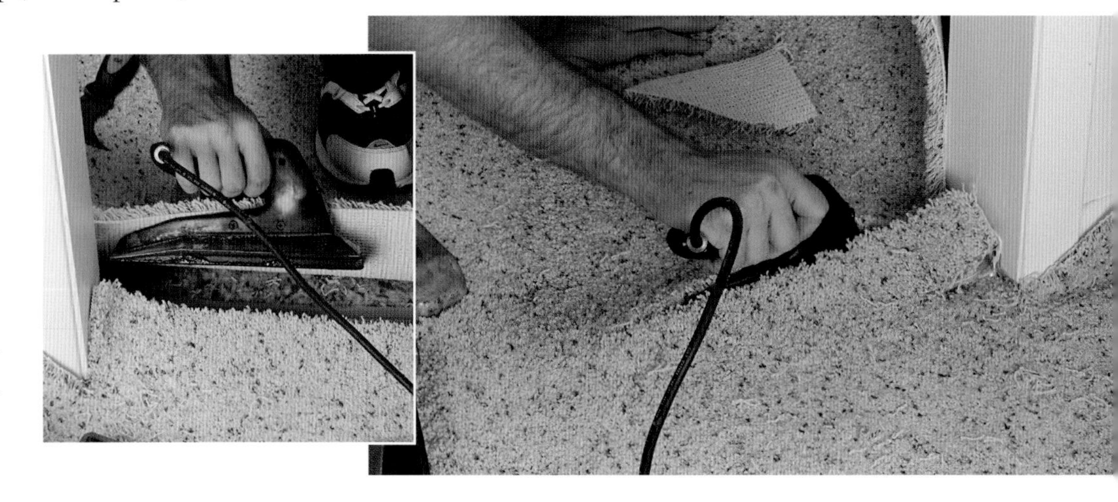

REMOVING CARPET

If you're replacing old worn-out carpeting with new carpet, you'll first need to remove the old carpeting. Here's how:

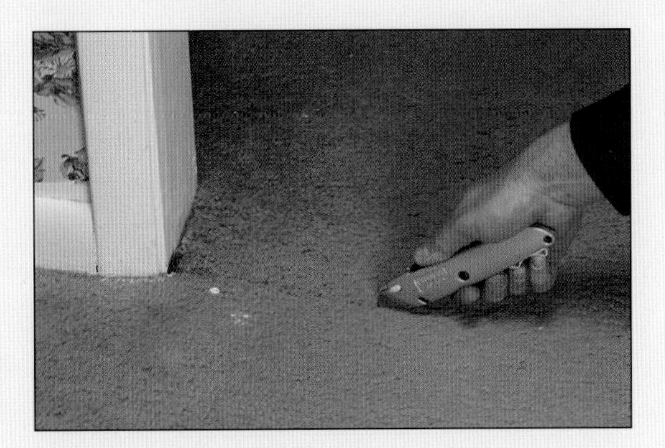

Cut around thresholds. Start by cutting through the carpet near the door thresholds where the carpet is attached. Depending on the thickness of the carpet and the sharpness of your utility knife, you may be able to cut through both the carpet and the pad at one time. If not, you can always go back after the carpet has been removed and cut and roll the pad. This is also the time to remove any old metal thresholds with a pry bar.

Cut and roll carpet and pad. Next, cut the carpet into strips that will be easy to roll up; 3-foot strips work well. After cutting the carpet into strips, roll them up and set them aside for disposal. If you cut through both carpet and pad, you may be able to roll them up together. If not, pull up the pad and roll it separately. Most carpet padding is stapled down—just give it a good yank and it'll pull right up.

Remove tack strips. If you're planning on laying new carpet, inspect the tackless strips to see whether they can be reused—the points need to be sharp and angled toward the wall. Replace any worn-out sections with fresh strips. If the tackless strips are in bad shape or you're not reinstalling carpet, work around the perimeter of the room, removing the strips with a pry bar.

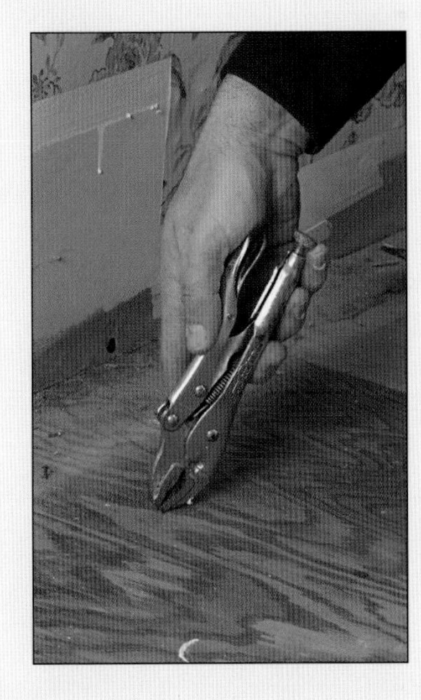

Remove staples. Finally, use a putty knife, needle-nose pliers, or locking-jaw pliers to pry up and lift out any staples remaining from the carpet padding.

Laminate Flooring

TOOLS

- Utility knife or scissors
- Installation kit (optional)
- Hammer and handsaw
- Framing sqaure, compass, and straightedge
- Miter, saber, or circular saw

One of the biggest benefits laminate flooring has to offer is that it can be laid down over most existing flooring. Not having to first remove the old flooring will save you both time and money. There are a couple of exceptions to this: Laminate flooring can't be laid over carpeting; and if you're planning on installing laminate directly over concrete, you'll need to do a moisture test. To do this, cut a couple of 2-foot squares of plastic and duct-tape them to various areas on the floor. Wait 72 hours and check for moisture. If you find beads of moisture on the underside of the plastic, you've got a moisture problem—call in a flooring contractor for advice. If the plastic is dry, you can install laminate flooring. Just make sure to first lay down a vapor retarder before installing underlayment.

Since laminate flooring is made of materials similar to those used to make kitchen countertops (like fiberboard, cellulose paper, and hard melamine resins), it can stand up to a lot of abuse over time. As with hardwood flooring, it's important to purchase your laminate flooring in advance of the intended installation date so the planks can acclimatize to the room. Unlike hardwood strips, which take weeks for this, cartons of laminate flooring need to be placed in the room where they'll be installed 72 hours in advance.

Install foam underlayment. All floors require some type of underlayment to be installed before laying down the flooring. Laminate manufacturers offer a variety of types. You'll find rolls of foam are the most common. The subfloor should be level and free from dips and high spots. To install foam underlayment, place the cut end of the roll against the wall in one corner of the room and unroll it (inset). Cut it to length with a utility knife or scissors. To prevent tearing the underlayment as you work, most manufacturers suggest laying one strip of foam at a time and then covering it with flooring.

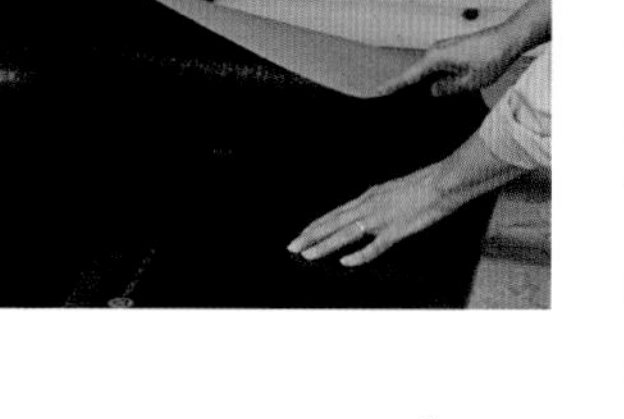

Tape seams and undercut moldings. Butt the edges of the foam together and tape the seams (bottom photo). Make sure that the foam doesn't overlap. The final thing to do before installing flooring is to undercut any moldings (door casings, etc.). Place a scrap of flooring on the floor and lay a saw flat on the flooring. Then cut just through the molding; this way the flooring can slip underneath the molding and won't have to be cut to fit around it.

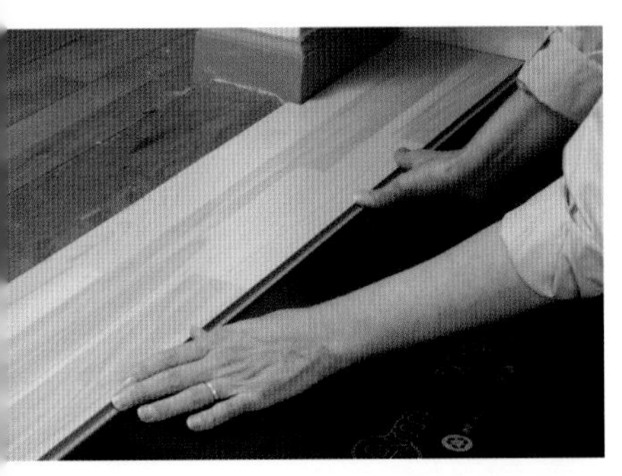

First course. The first rows of laminate flooring you lay down will have an impact on the overall success of the installation. It's important that these planks go down flat and straight so that the rest of the planks will be easy to install. Start by choosing the longest, straight wall as your starting point. Starting in one corner, lay down a plank, inserting spacers between the plank and the wall to create the appropriate expansion gap. Most laminate manufacturers specify a 1/4" gap. You can use scraps of 1/4"-thick plywood or a combination of plastic spacers that come in an installation kit (which can be purchased or rented from most home centers). Push the plank and spacers firmly against the adjacent walls as tightly as possible.

End to end. Since the ends of snap-together laminate flooring use the same snap-together profiles as the long edges, you'll need to connect all the planks in a row end-to-end before you can snap two rows together. Take care with these end joints, as their narrow width, combined with the heft of the long plank, makes it easy to break the fragile, profiled edges. Snap together all the planks in a row end-to-end, cutting the final plank to length as needed. Note that it's important to stagger the end-to-end joints in progressive rows. Most manufacturers suggest staggering the joints by at least one-third the length of a plank. Typically, if you use the cutoff from the first row to start the second, the joints will be staggered correctly.

Push and snap next course. Now you can snap the hooked-together row onto the previous row. For long rooms, a helper is useful in getting the row to snap in place. As you slide each piece to mate with the previous row, use a tapping block and mallet to force the planks together. Slip the profiled edge of the tapping block over the tongue of the plank. Then tap it with a hammer; slide the block along the plank, tapping as you go until any gaps close.

SNAP-TOGETHER LAMINATE FLOORING

In the past, all laminate flooring needed glue to hold the planks together; modern flooring uses "snap-together" technology to make glue obsolete. The edges of snap-together flooring are molded to create a unique profile: It uses ridges and valleys that, when mated, pull the planks together for a perfect joint. In most cases, this "mating" does require some persuasion in the form of a tapping block and a mallet or hammer.

Working around obstacles. As you work your way around the room, you'll most likely need to trim a few planks to fit around obstacles. Whenever possible, use a framing square or straightedge and mark directly onto the plank so you can cut it to fit (as shown in the top left photo). Alternatively, you can use a compass or piece of cardboard to scribe an odd shape onto the plank; see page 77 for more on scribing.

Cutting and drilling planks. Laminate flooring is easy to trim with a circular or saber saw. Circular saws will cut best when fitted with a carbide-tipped bit. A simple way to safely cut flooring is to place it on a scrap of 1"-thick foam insulation board as shown in the top right photo. Set your blade to cut just through the laminate, and make your cut. The foam board provides a stable platform for cutting and can be used over and over again.

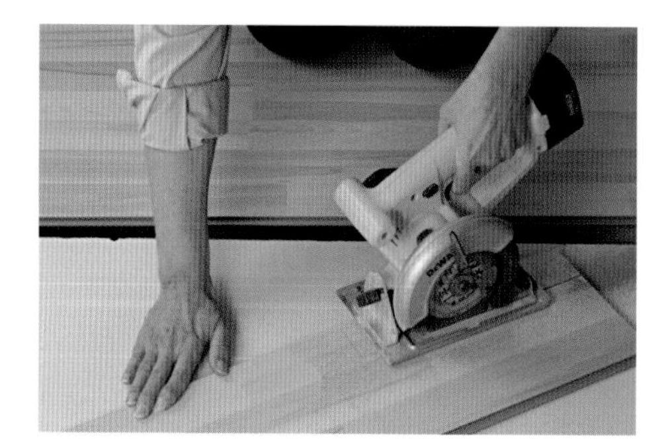

Trim. Once you've installed all the flooring, work around the perimeter of the room, installing molding to conceal the expansion gap between the flooring and the walls (bottom right photo).

LAMINATE FLOORING TRANSITIONS

Most manufacturers of laminate flooring sell transition strips and molding to match their product. T-molding joins two areas of laminate flooring or other similar-height flooring. Reducer strips handle transitions between floors that are different heights.

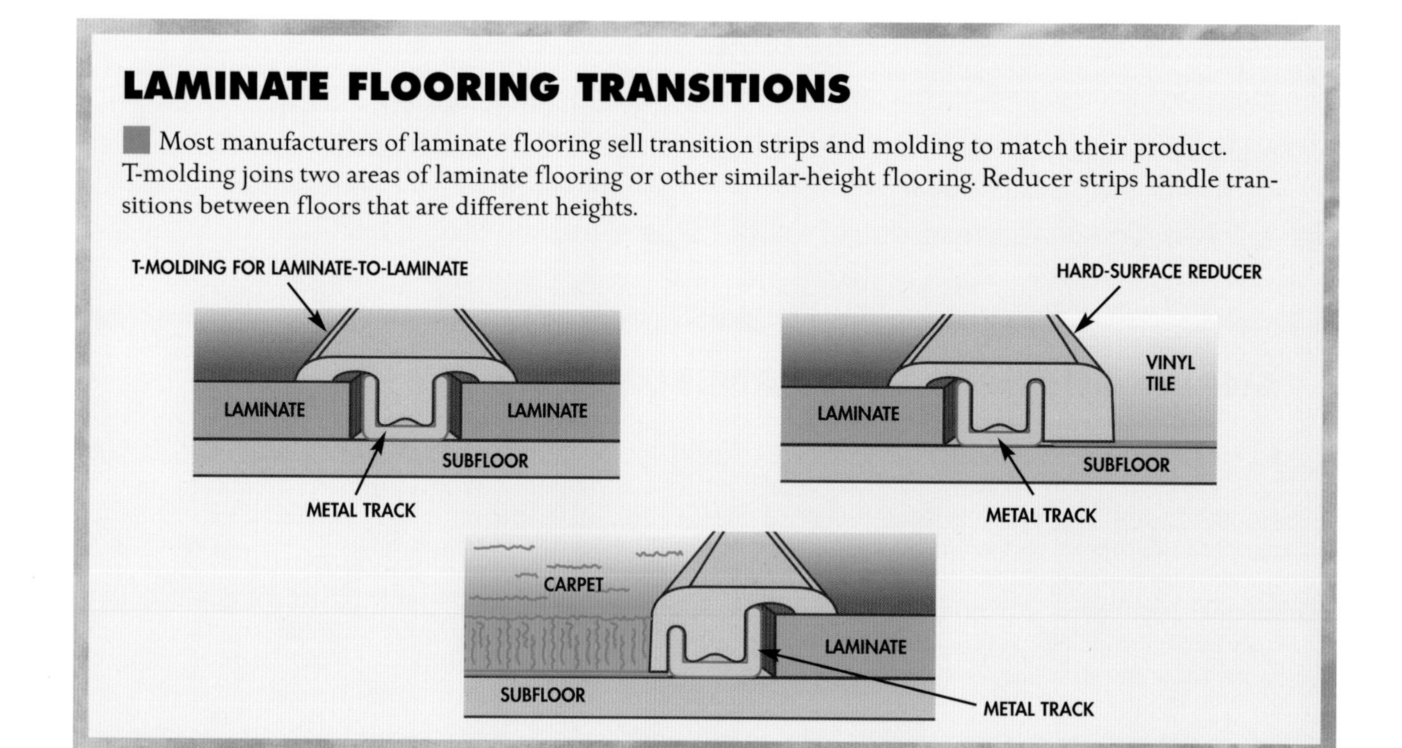

GLUELESS LAMINATE FLOORING

Pergo recently introduced a variation of laminate flooring under the brand name Paradigm. What makes this flooring special is that although it still uses snap-together technology for easy installation, it also has a pre-applied glue on the tongue of the planks. This glue is activated with water applied with a special applicator. This way, you can glue the planks together without the mess of dealing with glue. Why glue the planks together when they snap together? It has to do with moisture. Flooring that's joined by snapping together planks is still prone to water damage. Gluing the planks together seals the joints and keeps water out. So, this type of flooring is perfect for entryways and other areas where moisture is a concern.

Applying water. To activate the glue, place the sponge activator on top of the tongue on the long side. Then press down and hold to recharge the water supply to the tip and move it along the length of the tongue; moisten only the preglued side of the tongue. As you apply water to the tongue, you'll see a change in the color of the glue that indicates you've applied sufficient water to activate the glue. The plank tongue should turn yellow. Do not install a plank if this color change is not evident.

Snapping planks together. Once the glue has been activated, install the planks as you would standard laminate flooring. As usual, you'll likely need to give the planks a tap or two with a mallet and a tapping block to drive the planks tightly together and close any gaps. If a plank needs to be removed after it has been installed, you'll have roughly 5 to 7 minutes before the glue sets up to the point where you won't be able to pull them apart without damage.

SAN ANDREAS
MARCO POLO, IF YOU CAN
The Tommyknockers

CABINETS & STORAGE

For a project that elevates an ordinary room into a living space with something special, cabinetry—the built-in kind—installs the perfect combination of function and form. Your moneysmart makeover might be to simply give a fresh coat of paint to an existing built-in...or maybe you're more ambitious, and want to create your own new, showpiece storage unit. Whatever your plans, your time will be well spent, since storage space is something few of us have too much of. Tired of the electric cord tangle dangling behind your television, DVD/VCR, cable receiver, and sound system? Or maybe you need to give new life to a built-in that holds all your "stuff" but looks somewhat the worse for wear. There are lots of options for revamping, upgrading, and creating new storage in your home. At the same time, you'll increase the usability of the space you have, and maybe get rid of some visual clutter in the bargain.

Painting Cabinets

TOOLS

- Screwdriver and awl
- Stiff-bristle brush
- Sanding block
- Putty knife
- Paint tray
- Paint roller and brushes

It's fast, it's low-cost, it makes a big impact, and you can do it in a weekend. But there's one caution about painting cabinets: Before you break out the brushes and rollers, you need to know that your cabinets will actually take paint; only certain kinds of cabinets will. Wood and metal cabinets accept paint well; cabinets where the doors, drawers, and face frames are covered with any kind of plastic laminate (such as melamine) cannot be painted. The same thing that keeps these cabinets from staining also prevents them from accepting paint. If you're not sure, you can check by brushing on a bit of paint in an inconspicuous spot (like the back of a door). When it's dry, try to scrape off the paint with your fingernail. If the door is covered with plastic laminate, the paint will flake right off.

Remove doors and drawers. The first step to painting cabinets is to remove all the doors and drawers (bottom photo). To make it easy to re-install them when done painting, start by making a rough sketch of the cabinets and label all parts. Then mark each of the doors and drawers. Drawers can be labeled under the drawer bottoms, as these won't be painted. The doors are trickier because usually both sides are painted and you'd paint over your label. One way to get around this is to label the door where the hinges mount. If the hinges fit in mortises (like those shown in the inset photo below), you can mark in the bottom of the mortise. Alternatively, consider using an awl to scratch a label where the hinge mounts. This way, even if it gets painted, you'll still be able to read your label.

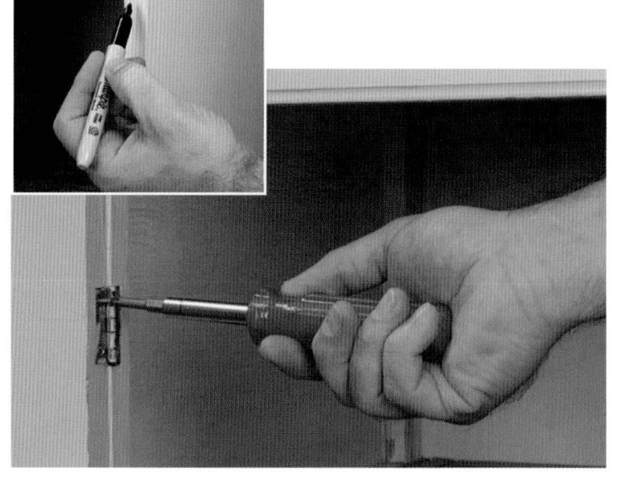

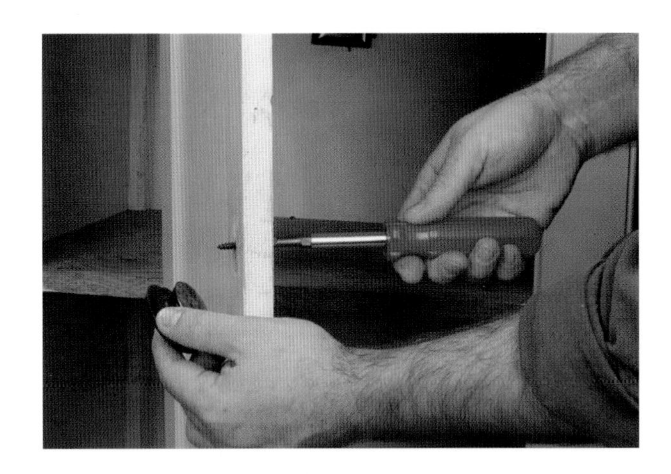

Remove hardware. After the doors and drawers are off, remove any hardware (above). Remove the door and drawer knobs and pulls and all of the door hinges.

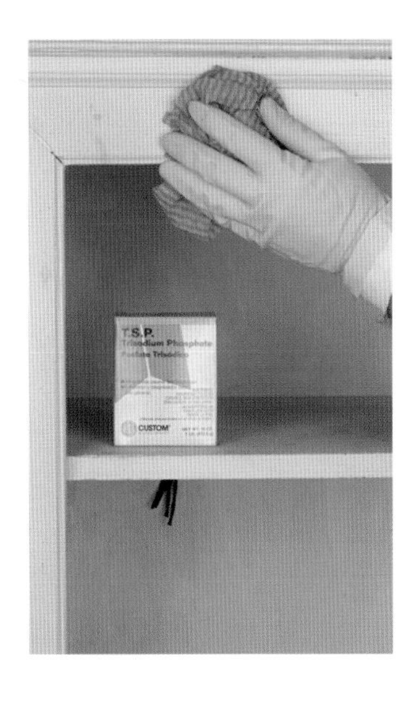

Clean with TSP. For paint to adhere well to a surface, it must be clean and dry. Even if your cabinets appear to be clean, don't skip this important step. Clean the doors, drawer fronts, face frames, and cabinet interiors with a solution of TSP (trisodium phosphate) and water (middle photo). A stiff-bristle brush will do a good job of lifting off any dirt and grime. TSP can be found wherever paint supplies are sold. After you've scrubbed all the cabinet parts, allow them to dry overnight before proceeding.

Sand if glossy. If your cabinet parts have a glossy finish, it's best to scuff-sand the surfaces with a sanding block wrapped with sandpaper (right). Scuff-sanding roughens up the surface and gives the paint something to "bite" into. Open-coat aluminum-oxide sandpaper is your best bet for this job, as it doesn't clog up as fast as other types of sandpaper. The idea here is to just roughen the surface, not sand it down to bare wood. If you're working on a large cabinet, consider using a power sander to speed things up.

Fill old hardware holes. If you're planning on using new hardware that doesn't fit the existing holes in the doors, drawers, and cabinet face frames, fill the old holes with putty as shown in the bottom photo. Make sure to use putty that dries hard and can be painted. Wax-type putty sticks do not dry and will not accept paint. After the putty dries, go back and sand the surfaces smooth with a sanding block wrapped in sandpaper.

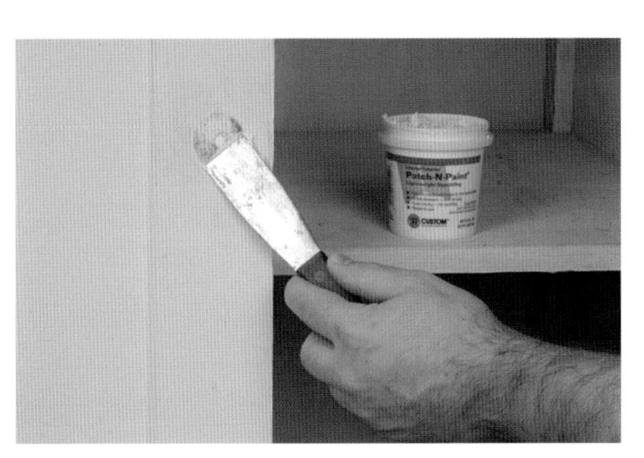

Paint the insides if desired. Depending on the type of cabinet and condition of the interior, you may or may not want to paint the insides of the cabinets. For the open shelf cabinets shown here, painting the insides was essential. A small foam roller, like the one shown in the top photo, will make quick work of this job. Paint the top first, then the sides, followed by the back and then the bottom. Also, if you're painting a dark surface a lighter color, it's a good idea to first prime all surfaces with a primer that's tinted to match the final paint color.

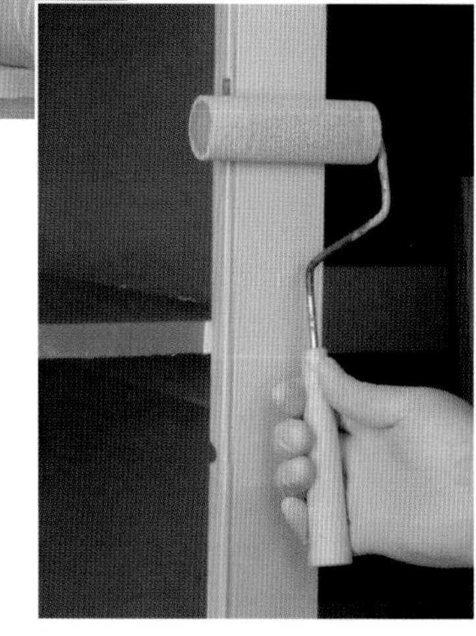

Paint face frames. Next, you can paint the face frames. Start by painting the inside edges of the frames with a small foam brush. Then, using a foam roller, paint the fronts of the face frames (middle photo). You may need two or more coats of paint; if so, wait the recommended period between coats and then apply a second coat.

STRENGTHENING SHELVES

Since many cabinets in living spaces sport open shelves, you'll likely find shelves that have sagged over time. There are a couple of simple ways you can strengthen these shelves before painting. All of the strengthening methods shown here use a cleat to shore up the sagging shelf. If you've got access to a woodshop, or have a friend with one, the simplest way to strengthen a shelf is to cut a groove the length of the cleat to fit over the shelf (photo at right). If you don't have access to a woodshop, you can slip the cleat under the shelf and secure it with screws. Finally, you can attach the cleat to the front of the shelf with biscuits, dowels, or a spline.

METHOD 1
DADOED CLEAT

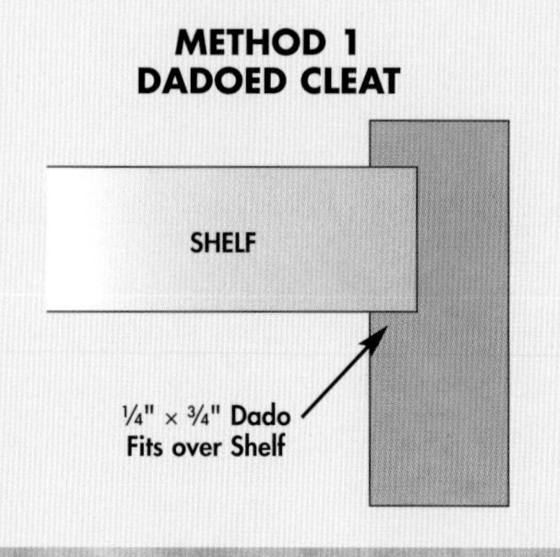

METHOD 2
ATTACH CLEAT UNDER SHELF

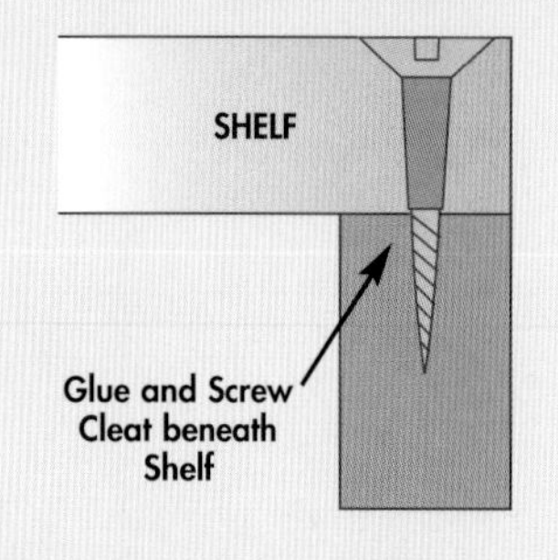

METHOD 3
ATTACH CLEAT TO FRONT OF SHELF

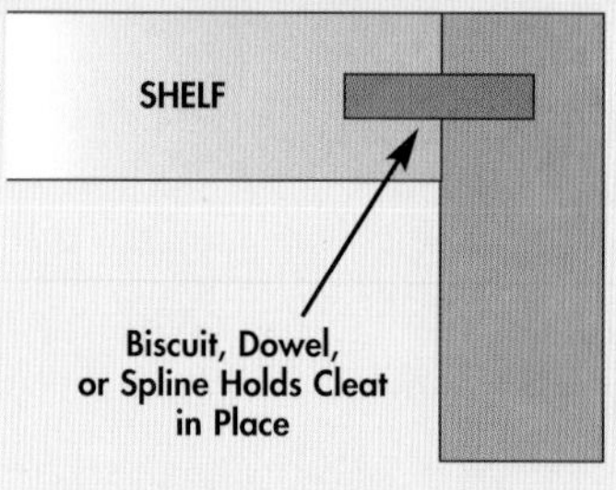

Paint the doors and drawer fronts. While the face frames are drying, you can get started on painting the doors and drawers. Here again, a small foam roller will speed things along (top photo). Set up a workstation by placing plywood on a pair of sawhorses. Paint the backs of the cabinets first and set them on newspapers or scraps of cardboard to dry. When dry, flip them over and paint the fronts. Finally, paint any drawer fronts. Allow the paint to dry overnight before remounting the doors and drawers to the cabinet.

Re-install the doors and drawers. When the paint is dry, remount the drawers and doors. Start by attaching the hinges to the doors, then attach the doors to the cabinets (left); slide any drawers back in place. (For more on installing hardware, see page 101.)

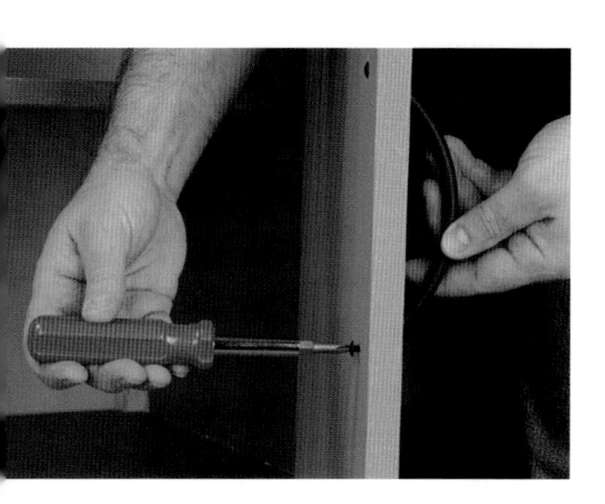

Add hardware. All that's left is to add the door and drawer pulls or knobs (bottom photo). If you are using the old holes, this is just a matter of threading the mounting screws through the existing holes and tightening them with a screwdriver. If you need to drill new holes, use the drilling jig described on page 101 to accurately position the new holes.

DEALING WITH STRIPPED SCREWS

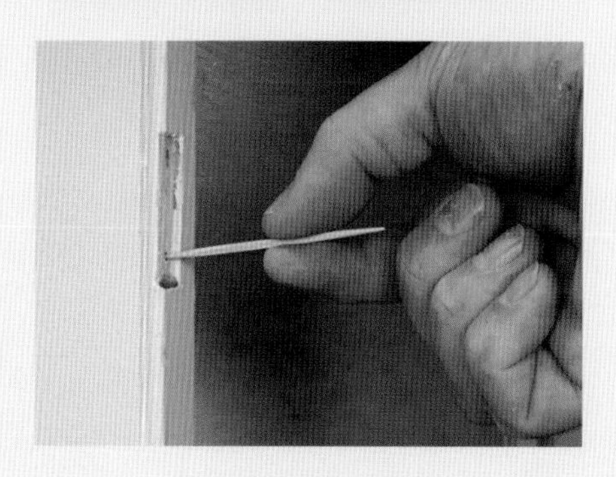

If you do decide to use the existing hardware holes for your new hardware, you may encounter a hole that has been stripped. Here's an easy way to fix this.

Just dip the end of one or two wooden toothpicks into glue and insert them into the stripped hole. Snap the end off so it's flush with the face frame, and then drive in the screw. The toothpick will give the threads of the hinge screw something to bite into as it's driven home.

Refacing Cabinets

TOOLS

- Tape measure and hammer
- Scissors and utility knife
- Screwdriver and putty knife
- Try square or combination square
- Veneer applicator
- Saber saw
- Sanding block
- Straightedge
- Handsaw or laminate trimmer

Refacing is an excellent choice for a number of reasons. It's a whole lot cheaper than replacing—by a factor of 5 or more. And outside of the weekend it takes you to do the actual refacing, it won't disrupt your life the way installing new cabinets does. Add to this the fact that it's easy to do—almost fun—and you'll be looking around at the other cabinets in your home, wondering what they'd look like in oak...or maybe maple....

Refacing cabinets consists of replacing the old doors and drawer fronts with new parts and applying wood veneer or plastic laminate over the face frames. Refacing supplies (doors, drawer fronts, matching end panels, peel-and-stick veneer—even crown molding) can be ordered from most home centers; material choices typically include oak and maple in a variety of finishes, plus white melamine. We used materials supplied by Quality Doors and were impressed with both the product and the ease of installation.

It's important to note that your old cabinets must be in good structural condition to be refaced. They can look awful, but must be sound: Surface veneers if used must be firmly attached; joints where face frame parts connect together must be flush and secure. That's because any surface imperfections will telegraph through the new veneer.

Measure and order parts. The first step to refacing cabinets is to measure them so that you can order parts. Follow the manufacturer's instructions; typically this involves measuring the drawer and door openings with a tape measure and making a list (bottom photo). Then you add a set width for overhang. You'll also need to specify how much veneer you'll need and any specialty items such as molding and end panels. Double-check each measurement, fill out the form, and place the order. Be prepared to wait 3 to 5 weeks for your order to arrive.

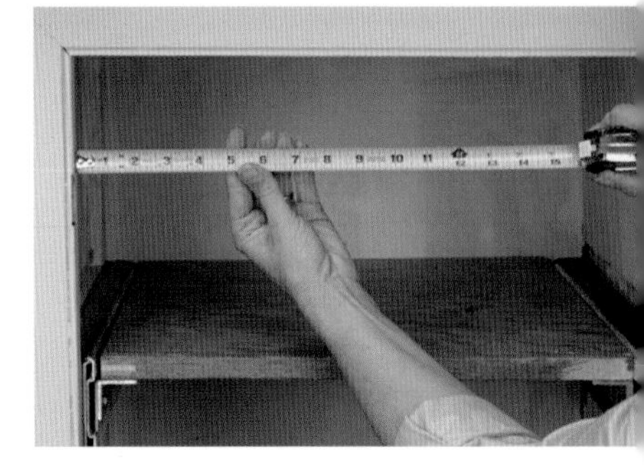

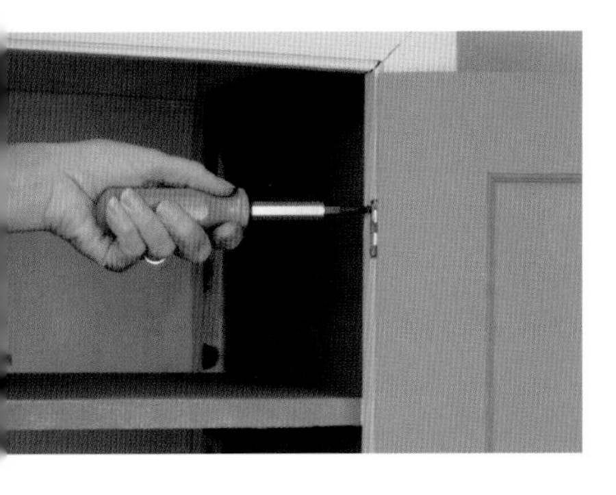

Remove the doors and drawers. When your order shows up, carefully unpack everything and double-check it against the packing list. Then hold up each door and drawer front to the existing cabinets to make sure they'll fit. Contact the manufacturer about any discrepancies. When all looks good, start refacing by removing the old doors and drawers (top left photo). Label the drawers so you know where they go back. If the drawers have false fronts, remove these as well. Remove hardware, including pulls, knobs, hinges, and catches. Set aside those you'll be reusing.

Wash face frames. For the new veneer or laminate to bond well with the existing face frames, the face frames must be free from grease and dirt. Clean face frames with mild dishwashing detergent and water (top right photo). Use a damp rag only; do not soak the wood. Rinse with clean water and allow to dry completely.

Fill holes and sand. When the face frames are completely dry, fill any screw holes and imperfections with wood filler or spackling compound. Since the face frames of the cabinets we were refacing had a decorative bead routed in the frames, we filled these recesses as well (right photo). Once the filler is dry, sand it flush with the surface. Also, if the existing surfaces are glossy, scuff-sand them with a sanding block wrapped in sandpaper (inset); sand just enough to roughen the surface slightly.

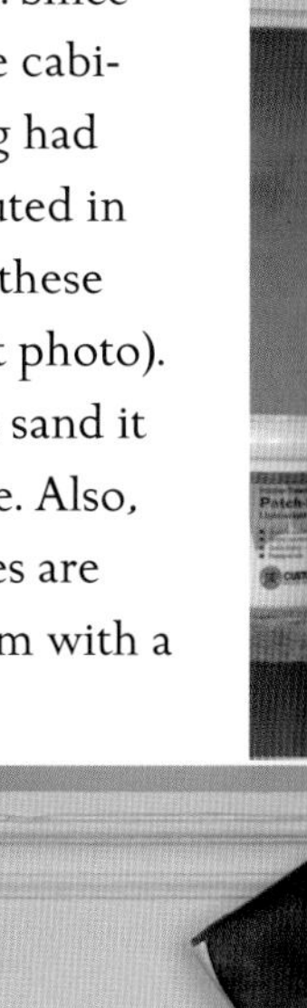

PAINTING INSIDE CABINETS

If the cabinets you're working on have open shelves, as ours did, you'll want to do something to the interiors to match the rest of the cabinets. Although you could order matching prefinished plywood and cut it to fit, this would be both time-consuming and expensive. A less expensive and quicker alternative is to paint the insides of the open shelves. The trick is to get the paint to match the refacing materials. To do this, just take a piece of veneer or wood to your local paint center and ask them to color-match it. This way you can paint the interiors so they'll blend perfectly with the refacing materials.

Cut veneer to size. Now that all your surfaces are prepped, you're ready for the fun part—applying the veneer. The vertical parts of a cabinet frame are the stiles; the horizontal pieces are rails. It's best to cut veneer strips for one opening at a time. Measure the length and width of one section of the face frame and cut strips 1/2" wider and 2" longer. Peel-and-stick veneer is easy to cut with sharp scissors or a utility knife and a straightedge (top photo).

Apply veneer to stiles. Start by applying veneer to the stiles of the base cabinets. Peel off the backing and position the strip with the top up against the countertop. Make sure the veneer extends out equally on each side of the stile (top left photo on opposite page). Then press the veneer firmly into the stile. Most refacing suppliers sell a special applicator for this. Alternatively, a plastic scraper for removing ice and snow from your car's windows in the winter is

END PANELS

If one or more sides of the cabinets you're working on are exposed, you'll need to treat these before you apply veneer to the face frames. Sides are covered with pieces of 1/4" matching plywood. If the face frames of your old cabinets are flush with the exposed sides of the cabinets, installation is just a matter of cutting a plywood end panel to match and attaching it with glue and nails. If, however, the face frames extend past the ends (typically 1/4" or so), you'll need to trim these flush with the ends. This will allow you to attach the plywood end panels flush with the face frame. Then when the veneer strips are applied to the face frame, these will cover the exposed edge of the plywood.

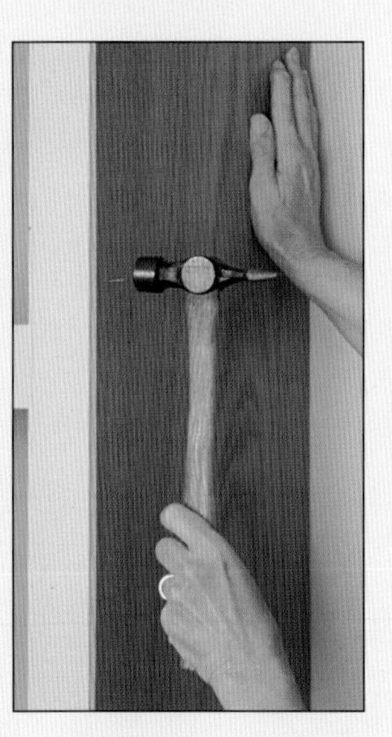

Attach the end panels. Measure and cut plywood end panels to match the side of the cabinet. Attach the panel to the side with glue or a bead of construction adhesive and 3/4"-long brads.

Sand the panel edges flush. Next, use a sanding block fitted with 120-grit sandpaper to sand the plywood panel flush with the face frame.

Seal the edges. Finally, spray the exposed edges of the plywood with spray-on adhesive. This will both seal the edge and help the veneer stick onto the edge of the plywood.

an inexpensive way to press the veneer in place, as shown in the inset photo below.

Apply veneer to rails. With the stile veneer in place, you can veneer the rails. Peel off a couple of inches of the backing from a strip and position one end so it overlaps the stile about 1". Align the strip on the face frame so there's an even overlap on the top and bottom of the rail. Then press and smooth out the strip, working toward the other end, peeling the backing off as you go (below). Use the applicator to press the veneer firmly in place.

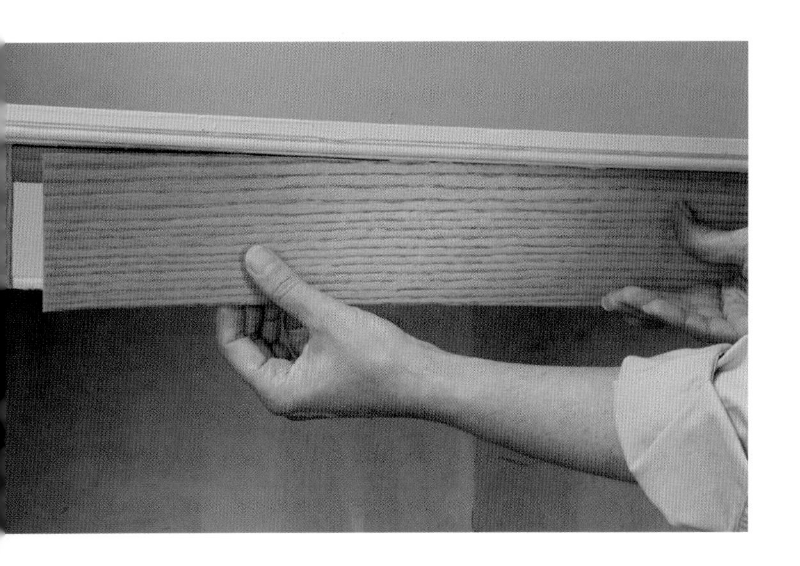

Trim away excess veneer. With both the stile and rail veneers in place, go back and trim away any excess veneer. Use the inside of the frame as a guide. Slice through any overhanging veneer with a utility knife; take several light passes to cut completely through the veneer (right photo).

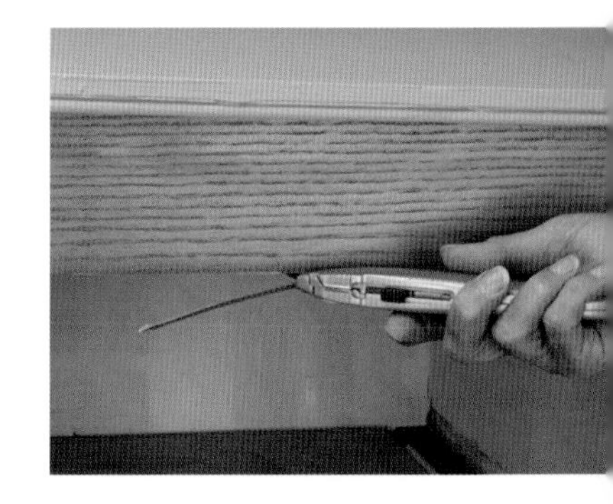

Cut the veneer joint. Creating a perfect seam between the rail and the stile veneers is easy. Here's how. Position a try square or combination square so the edge is directly over where the rail joins the stile. Now cut through both layers at once with a utility knife (bottom right photo). Then use the tip of the knife to lift up the cut end of the veneer and pry out the waste piece underneath (inset below). Press the rail veneer back in place for a perfect seam.

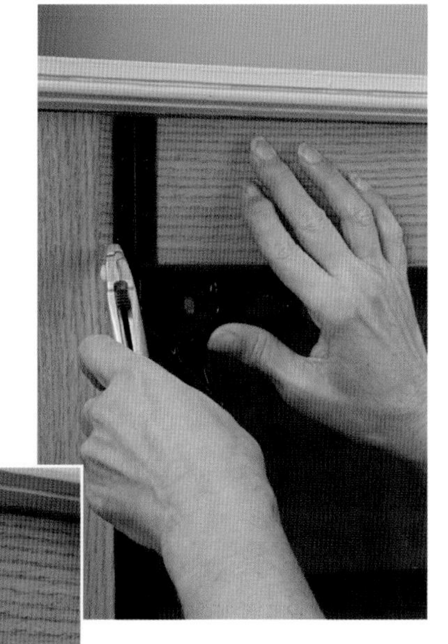

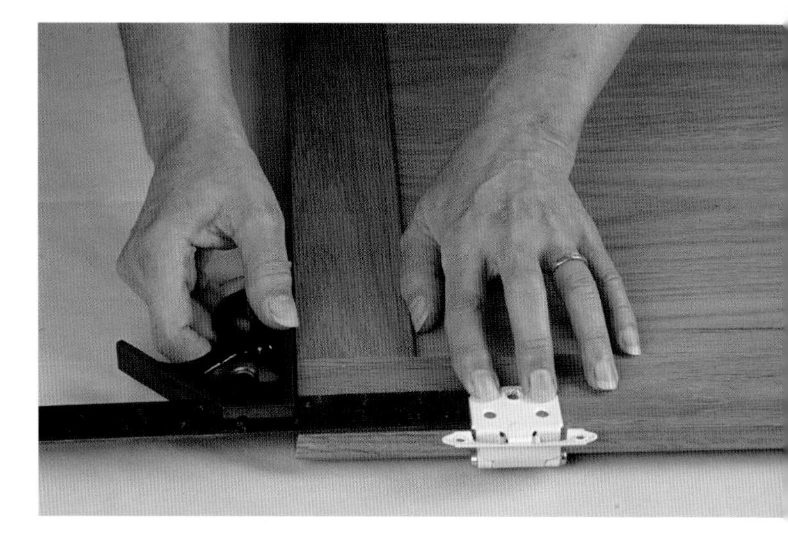

Sand edges smooth. Once you've cut all the veneer joints, go back and sand the edges of the veneer flush with the faces of the cabinet with a sanding block (top left photo). Sand toward the inside of the cabinet only, to prevent the sanding block from pulling the veneer away from the face frame. Repeat for the remaining openings.

Attach new hinges. With the face frames veneered, you can add the doors. Start by attaching the hinges. A quick way to do this is with a combination square. Set the blade of the square so that it extends out the distance you want the bottom of the hinges in from the cabinet edge. By using this to position each hinge as shown in the photo above, all hinges will be in alignment. Drill pilot holes and secure the hinges with screws (see page 101 for more on installing hinges).

Attach new doors and add hardware. You're finally ready to mount the doors to the face frames. To make sure all the doors align, consider using a cleat to support the doors so you can secure them to the cabinet as shown in the bottom left photo. Position the guide under the doors, set the doors on the guides, and center them in the opening. Then drill hinge holes and secure the doors to the face frames. Attach any drawer fronts to drawers and slide them into place. The final step is to add the new hardware. See page 101 for more on drilling accurate mounting holes and installing hardware.

New Hardware

TOOLS

- Electric drill
- Screwdriver
- Shop-made drilling jig
- Self-centering drill bit
- Clamps

Cabinet hardware will look good and work well only if it's installed properly. This means that each piece must be carefully positioned and precisely installed.

Self-centering bits. Hinges are often the toughest piece of hardware to install. That's because so many things can go wrong: The hinge itself can twist out of alignment as it's screwed in place, the door can twist out of alignment as it's being secured to the face frame, and the door can be improperly centered on the opening. Fortunately, each of these can be prevented. Use the guide shown in the bottom photo on page 100 to center and align the door or doors on the opening and to prevent it from twisting out of alignment.

Then use a self-centering bit (often referred to as a Vix bit) to keep the hinges from twisting as they're screwed in place. A self-centering bit is a totally reliable way to install a hinge without the usual skewing and misalignment. The "magic" of this bit is an inner and outer sleeve that spins around a twist bit (inset drawing). When the tip of the self-centering bit is inserted in a hinge hole and depressed, an inner sleeve retracts up into the outer sleeve. This positions the twist bit so that it can drill a perfectly centered hole for the hinge screw.

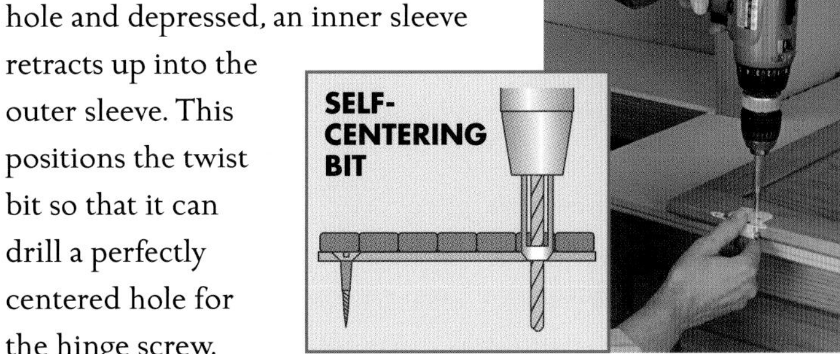

DRILLING JIG

To accurately install cabinet pulls and knobs, it's worth the time and effort to make a drilling jig. This is just a piece of scrap wood with cleats on both faces to serve as lips to automatically position the guide for drilling. Once you've decided on hardware placement, measure the distance up from the bottom and offset from the adjacent edge; transfer these to the jig. Then drill the desired-size mounting hole in the guide at this location. To use the guide, position it on the corner of a door or drawer so the cleats butt up against the edges of the part (left photo). Then simply drill through the hole in the guide. It's a good idea to clamp a scrap to the back of the door to prevent tear-out as the drill bit exits the back of the door (right photo).

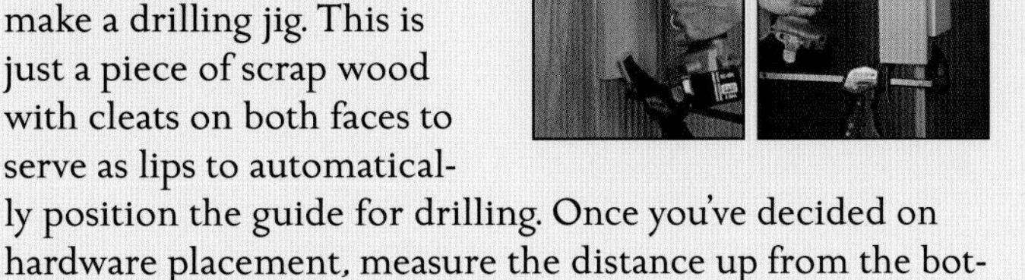

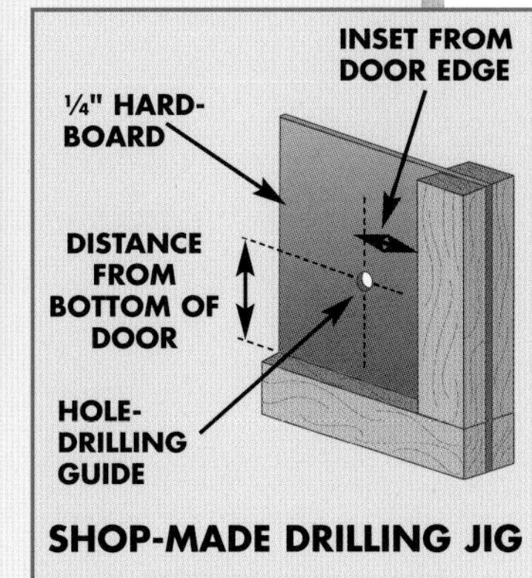

SHOP-MADE DRILLING JIG

Crown Molding

TOOLS

- Tape measure
- Level
- Spring clamps
- Miter saw
- Finish nailer or hammer

Crown molding adds elegance to any cabinet. It's especially useful for concealing gaps between ceiling-height cabinet tops and the ceiling, which are commonly caused by an uneven ceiling. You can attach crown molding manufactured from matching wood, as shown here. Another popular look is to use paint-grade molding (sold at most home centers) and paint the molding to match the accent colors used in the room, to create a striking contrast. As a general rule, you should choose crown molding that's around 3" to 4" wide for a standard 8-foot ceiling. Anything wider would appear out of scale. Although attaching crown molding to cabinets is fairly straightforward, cutting the complex molding to wrap around the cabinets—especially in places that aren't 90-degree corners, such as around a corner cabinet—can be tricky. Fortunately, with the aid of a power miter saw, this can be done without too much head-scratching.

Mark reference lines. To install crown, start by using a level to mark reference lines on top of cabinets (photo above). To provide a nailing surface for the molding, locate the line about 1/4" up from the tops of the cabinet doors.

ADDING A BASE MOLDING

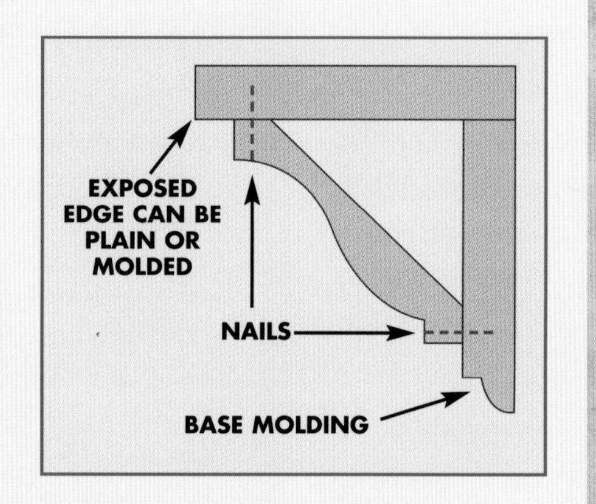

Since crown molding will always butt up against a wall or cabinet at an angle, it has only two small flat sections that make contact. This makes it difficult to attach, especially on walls and ceilings, since you need to hit a stud or joist for the nail to hold. One way to get around this is to first attach a base molding. The base molding is easy to attach to the wall, ceiling, or cabinet and provides a continuous nailing surface for the crown molding. In addition to providing a nailing surface, these moldings also provide a more complex and pleasing profile.

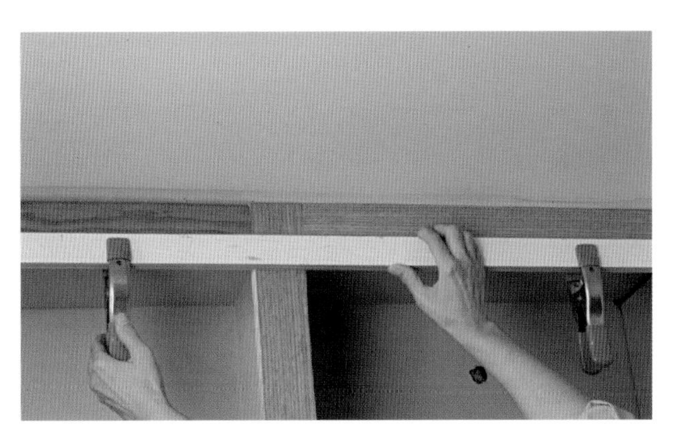

Add support cleats. Installing a long piece of crown molding by yourself can be a real hassle. To make it easy to position and hold the molding in place, clamp a strip or two of scrap wood to the top of the face frame to support the molding (above).

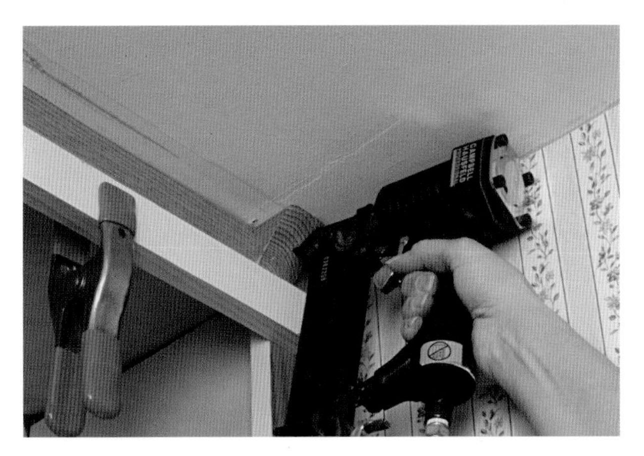

Attach support blocks and cut molding. Besides using a base molding as described on page 102, the next most secure way to attach crown molding to a cabinet top is to cut and attach support blocks. The blocks are just scraps of 2×4 that are mitered to match the flat portion on the back of the molding. Mark along the top of the cabinets every 16" or so, and attach a block at each mark with glue and nails or screws (above). With the support blocks in place, you can cut your molding. Cutting crown is tricky. It's a good idea to practice your first few cuts on scrap until you get the hang of it. In general you want to place the molding upside down and backwards on your miter saw when cutting.

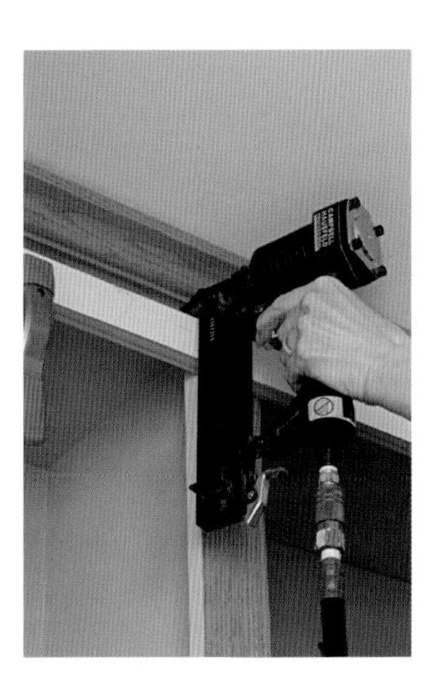

Attach crown molding. The best tool for attaching crown molding is an air-powered nailer like the one shown in the top right photo (you can find these at most rental centers). An air nailer will drive and set the nail exactly where you want it with the pull of a trigger. Sure, you can attach crown with a hammer and nails, but the chances of dinging the molding are extremely high. Also, since the finish nailer is used one-handed, your other hand is free to hold the molding in place—not so with a hammer and nails. Start by attaching the crown to the support blocks you installed earlier. Then nail the top edge into any ceiling joists if applicable.

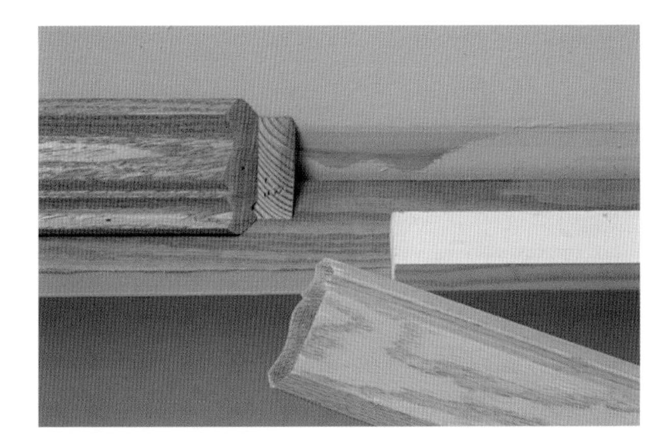

Scarf together when necessary. Finally, if you need to join together two lengths of crown molding, cut the ends at opposing 45-degree miters to create an almost invisible "scarf" joint (bottom right photo). When possible, cut miters first and then trim the molding to length, always erring on the long side.

Removing Old Cabinets

TOOLS

- Prybar
- Putty knife
- Screwdriver
- Shop-made cabinet brace

Although tearing out an old set of cabinets may seem like a simple job, it rarely is. To properly remove cabinets, you have to reverse-engineer the installation process; that is, you need to know how they were installed. Some older cabinets were actually built on site; others were assembled from stock cabinets. In either case, go slow and keep an eye out for hidden screws that hold the parts of the cabinet unit together.

Remove any trim around cabinets. To start, remove any trim around the perimeter of the cabinet (photo below). This includes baseboard, side trim, and crown molding. If you won't be reusing the trim or old cabinet, just pry off the molding with a prybar. If you do plan on reusing any parts, sandwich the prybar between a pair of wide-blade putty knives to keep the prybar from damaging either surface.

Remove doors and drawers. Then to make it easier to remove and carry the cabinets, take the time to remove all the doors and drawers to lighten the load, as shown in the top photo. If you'll be reusing the cabinets for storage somewhere else (they make great shop cabinets), label the parts with masking tape before you remove them so you can easily reassemble them later.

Remove face frame if site-built. If your cabinets are site-built (like the one shown here), the next step is to remove the face frame from the cabinets. A couple of taps of a hammer will usually free most frames, and then you can remove them by hand. Take care to protect your hands with leather gloves and your eyes with safety goggles.

Remove the countertop (if any). If the cabinets you're removing had an integral countertop, it's time to remove it. Look under the countertop to see whether it is secured from below. If so, remove the screws. On site-built cabinets, the countertop is typically attached to the base cabinets with nails driven through the top of the countertop. In this situation, free the countertop from the base cabinets with a prybar as shown in the top right photo. Lift it off and set it aside for disposal.

Check for base cabinet screws. Many older base cabinets are secured to the floor with screws or nails. Carefully inspect the bottom edges of the base cabinets to locate any screws or nails, and then remove them (middle photo).

Remove base cabinets. The base cabinets may also be secured to the wall studs through their backs. Locate any screws or nails and remove them if possible. For nails, you can usually just pry the cabinet off the wall (inset). Now you should be able to pull the cabinets away from the wall. If you encounter resistance, you've probably missed a screw. Locate and remove the screw and try again—in old cabinets, these may be hard to find, as installers often covered screw heads with putty to make them less visible.

SUPPORTING WALL CABINETS

The wall units can now be removed. Before you remove your first screw, make a simple brace from scraps of 2×4 and plywood to support the cabinets temporarily. Wedge the brace under the cabinet and start by removing the screws in the face frame securing the cabinets together. Then locate and remove the screws in the back of the cabinet that secure it to the wall. Lift the cabinet off the brace and set it aside. Repeat for the remaining wall units.

Installing Base Cabinets

TOOLS

- Stud finder
- Level
- Driver/drill and bits
- Circular saw
- Screwdriver
- Clamps
- Air nailer (optional)

Unlike kitchen cabinets that typically have to be shoehorned into an exact space, cabinets that are installed in other rooms in the home often have a more forgiving space. That is, they are often installed only along one wall and may or may not need to fit into an exact space. This makes installing cabinets much more do-able for the average homeowner. To tackle an install like this, you'll need a basic understanding of cabinet construction, and modest woodworking skills that include scribing, cutting, planing and fitting parts together, and mitering and coping molding. If this doesn't sound like you, consider hiring a professional cabinet installer.

Cabinets are usually shipped directly to your home from the manufacturer. When the shipment arrives, check each package carefully for signs of damage before accepting shipment. If you find damage, open the package with the delivery person present. Note any broken items on the bill of lading and contact the distributor or manufacturer for a replacement. Do not uncrate the rest of the cabinets at this time, as the packaging often has the part numbers you'll need to identify which cabinet goes where.

Find highest point on floor. The secret to a successful cabinet installation is identifying the highest point on the floor. This is the starting point for all layout and measurement. To do this, place a 4-foot level on the floor at various points and mark the high point on the walls, as shown in the bottom photo. Then draw a level line along the wall at this point. Now measure up the height of the base cabinets and draw a level line around the perimeter of the room wherever the cabinets will be installed.

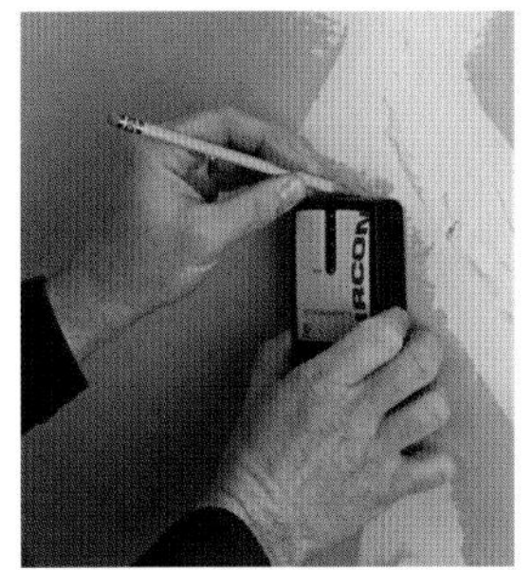

Locate the wall studs. Next, you'll want to locate and mark the locations of all the wall studs (left photo) behind the cabinets, as these are what you'll be securing the base cabinets to (as well as the wall cabinets).

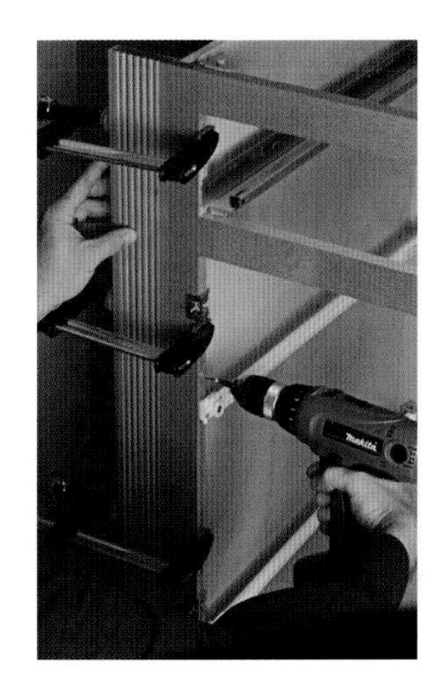

Add filler strips if necessary. Whenever a cabinet butts up against a wall, a filler strip is typically added to the wall side of the cabinet so that it can be scribed and planed or cut to match the wall profile; see the sidebar at right. Once you've scribed the face frame to fit (see page 77 for more on scribing), temporarily clamp it to the side of the cabinet and drill pilot holes for screws. Then secure it to the cabinet by driving screws through the face frame and into the strips (above).

Level base cabinet and shim. Depending on your cabinets, you'll likely begin installing cabinets in a corner and then work your way out in one or two directions. Since this first cabinet will serve as the foundation for the rest of the installation, you should spend considerable time shimming the cabinet bottom until it's both level and plumb (left photo). Each cabinet is shimmed as necessary to level the top of the cabinet from side to side and from front to back; also, check to make sure the cabinet front is plumb.

Secure to wall at studs. Once you've got your corner cabinet level and plumb, drive screws through the back of the cabinet and into wall studs located during the layout process as shown in the top right photo. All of the standard base cabinets are added in turn.

FILLER STRIPS

Since there are no standards for room sizes and layouts, and cabinets come in standard sizes, there will inevitably be gaps between cabinets and walls—sometimes even between cabinets, because of the configuration. Here's where filler strips come in. Filler strips are just planks of wood finished to match your cabinets. The strip is attached to the closest cabinet to the wall with screws. When done right, the cabinets will look like they were custom-built on site to fit from wall to wall.

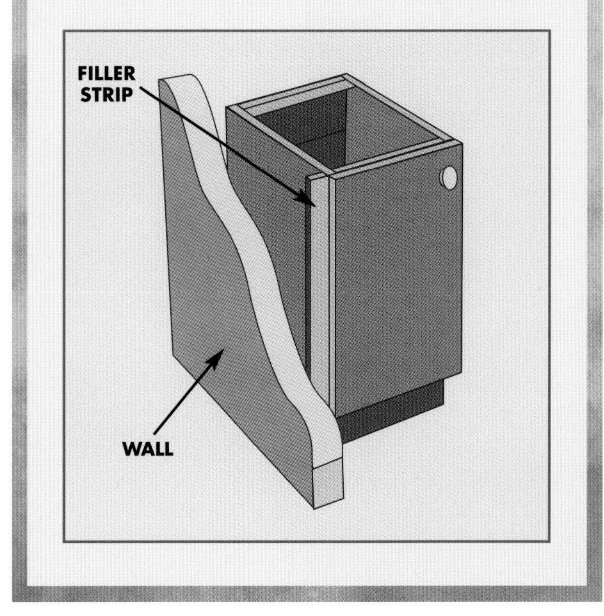

Add blocking to offset center cabinet. A common way to give stock cabinets a custom look is to offset or stagger one or more of the cabinets. That's what we did for the center base and wall cabinets. When you offset a cabinet like this, it can't be screwed to the wall, so you need to add a support structure that's commonly referred to as blocking. This is often made from scrap 2×4 lumber, as shown in the top photo. Once you've constructed the blocking, secure it to the walls at the studs. Now you can secure the offset base cabinet to the blocking.

Install second cabinet and level. Slide the offset cabinet into place and then shim it as needed so the top is level, as shown in the bottom left photo. Then insert shims as necessary between the blocking and the back of the cabinet so the front of the cabinet is plumb (inset).

Screw cabinets together. Before you secure the offset cabinet to the blocking, it's best to secure the side of the offset cabinet to its adjoining cabinet (photo above). If possible, apply temporary clamps to keep the cabinets from shifting, and then drill pilot holes through the side of the cabinet and into the face frame of the adjoining cabinet. Secure the cabinets together with screws. Continue adding base cabinets until all of them are installed.

Add door panel to end cap. In cases where the sides of the cabinets are exposed, you'll need to apply matching plywood or end panels, or both, to the sides of the cabinet. That's because the sides of cabinets are not finished with matching wood. For the installation shown here, we added end panels (basically matching doors) to a plywood end cap that attaches to the end cabinet via a fluted filler strip (top left photo).

Cut and install toekick strip. Like the sides of most cabinets, the toekick area under the base front is also not finished. You can either cut matching plywood to cover this and attach it with glue and brads (as shown in the photo above), or you can cover it with standard vinyl cove base molding that's held in place with cove base adhesive.

Attach end cap to end cabinet. Once the end panels were attached to the end cap, this was attached to the side of the end cabinet as shown in the bottom left photo. Clamps were used to hold the assembly in place until pilot holes were drilled and screws installed.

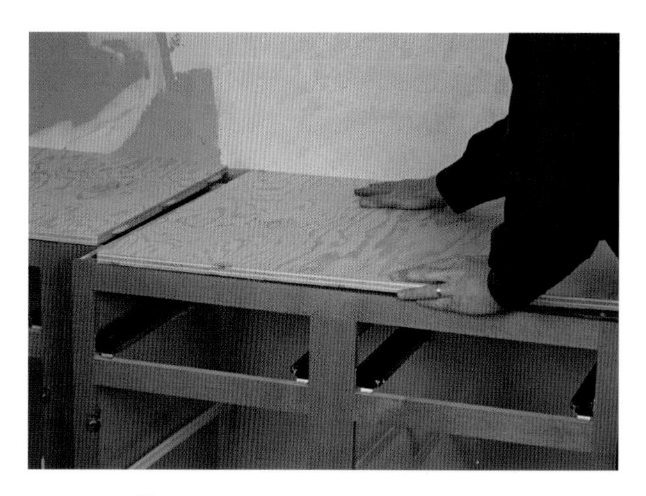

Install countertop. To complete the base unit, add a countertop if applicable. For the cabinets shown here, we installed a tile countertop with matching wood edging. For step-by-step directions on how to tile a countertop, see pages 113–117.

Installing Wall Cabinets

TOOLS

- Stud finder
- Level
- Driver/drill and bits
- Circular saw
- Screwdriver
- Clamps
- Air nailer (optional)

Once all the base cabinets are in and the countertop (if applicable) has been installed, the next step is to tackle the wall cabinets. Note that in some installations, it may be easier to install the wall cabinet first, as you may have better access to the wall cabinets this way. But this isn't possible with the cabinets shown here, as the wall cabinets rest directly on top of the countertop. Before you begin work on the wall cabinets, take a moment to temporarily remove doors to lighten the load.

Attach blocking for molding. If your cabinets call for crown molding to be installed, it's easiest to add blocking to the tops of the cabinets now. This blocking is just scraps of 2-by or 1-by material that's cut to length and secured to the top face frames with glue and screws (left photo).

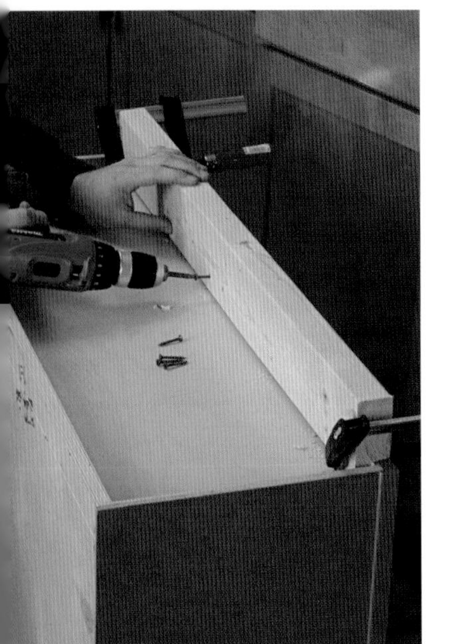

Prepare corner cabinets. Instead of installing cabinets one at a time, you may find it easier to level and plumb sections of cabinets in groups and fasten them together. For the install shown here, we attached the top two wall cabinets together with screws (inset) and then attached a single long filler strip to the side of the assembled cabinets (far right photo). The only disadvantage to this is the combined weight of the cabinets will require a helper to lift them into place.

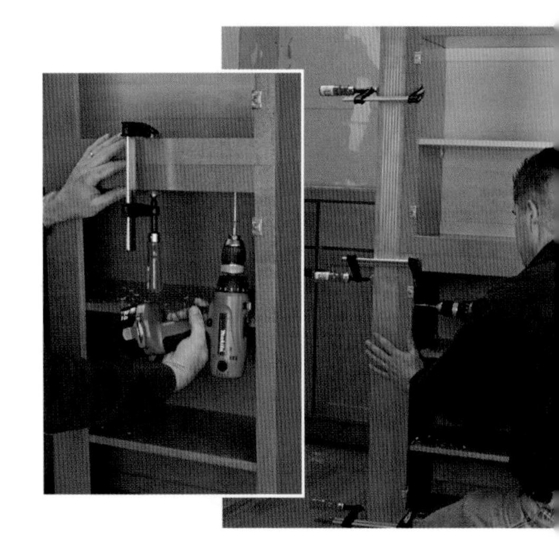

Install corner cabinets. Once the wall cabinet assemblies are complete, they can be positioned and secured to the wall. Before securing them, though, take the time to double-check them for level and plumb. If the base cabinets were installed level, the wall cabinets should be, too. But since most walls aren't plumb, it's important to check the cabinets for plumb and shim as necessary before securing the cabinets to the wall studs (above).

Install blocking to offset center wall cabinet. As we did for the base cabinets, we offset the center wall cabinet to give the wall unit more character. Not only did we offset the unit out from the wall, we also raised it up to give it an extra dimension. Just like the base unit, you'll need to make blocking and insert this between the center wall cabinet and the wall. Just make sure to secure it to the wall studs (top right photo).

Make returns for center cabinet. Because we left the space under the top center wall cabinet open, we needed to cover the exposed sides of the adjoining cabinets. We used a similar treatment like that used for the end caps and end panels, but in this case, just went with matching plywood and no end panels. Cut plywood to fit and attach fluted filler strips to the plywood. Then secure these assemblies, commonly called returns, to the sides of the cabinets as shown in the bottom left photo.

Attach remaining wall cabinets. With the center unit in place, you can install the remaining wall cabinets (bottom photo). Here again, take the time to shim each unit level and plumb before securing it to the wall studs. Some cabinet plans call for decorative trim such as the medallions shown in the inset photo. Secure these with glue and brads.

Attach the crown molding. With all the wall cabinets in place, the crown molding can be installed. Cut the molding to fit and attach it to the blocking you added earlier to the tops of the cabinets, as shown in the photo below. An air nailer is absolutely the best tool for this job, as it will drive and set a nail in the blink of an eye. And because of air nailers' one-handed operation, you can position the molding with one hand and secure with the nailer with the other.

Add shelving. For the cabinet unit shown here, we added glass shelving under the top center cabinet. The shelving is supported by shelf pins in the sides of the cabinet. A simple but accurate way to locate these holes is to use a scrap of pegboard, as shown in the inset photo above. Just locate and mark the desired hole locations on the pegboard and place it against the cabinet side. Then just drill through the marked holes, taking care to stop the bit before it breaks through the side of the cabinet. When all the holes are drilled, insert pins and set the shelving in place (top photo). For an added touch of elegance, install an under-cabinet light as described on pages 186–187.

Re-install doors and add hardware. When all the trim is in place, you can reinstall the doors (bottom right photo) and then add the cabinet hardware (inset below). See page 101 for a simple jig for accurately drilling holes for mounting the knobs and pulls.

Tiling a Countertop

TOOLS

- Tape measure and framing square
- Circular saw
- Tile cutter and nippers
- Notched trowel and putty knife
- Grout float and sponge
- Drill and screwdriver
- Staple gun and hammer
- Dead-blow hammer or rubber mallet
- Biscuit joiner (if applying wood edging)
- Small foam brush

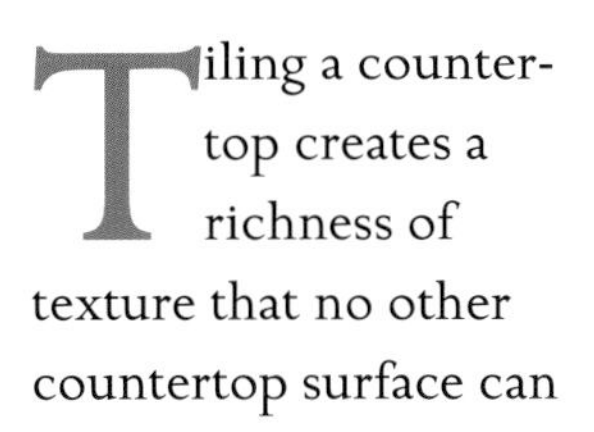

Tiling a countertop creates a richness of texture that no other countertop surface can match. Add to this the superb depth of color and the varying patterns, shapes, and sizes of tile, and it's easy to see how a tiled countertop can add distinction to any cabinet installation. There is one drawback to tile: the grout lines. Grout is a putty-like substance that fills in the spaces between the tiles. If left unsealed, the grout is easily stained. But this can be avoided by applying grout sealer (see page 117). The secret to grout longevity is to regularly reapply the sealer; see the manufacturer's instructions on how often this should be done.

Attach the plywood foundation. If the countertop you're planning on tiling is going on new base cabinets, the first thing to do is to cut and install a plywood foundation for the tile. Three-quarter-inch AC plywood is an excellent choice for this. It's strong, dimensionally stable, and inexpensive. Measure your base cabinets and cut the plywood to size. If you need to build the top from multiple pieces, take care to orient any seams so they don't end up directly over the cabinets where they join together. Secure the plywood foundation by screwing up through the base cabinet corner brackets and into the plywood, as shown in the bottom photo.

Add backer board. To create the flattest possible foundation for the tile, the next step is to cover the plywood with masonry backer board. This cement-like material is absolutely flat and accepts the thin-set mortar well that holds the tile in place. Backer board can be secured with galvanized screws, nails, or staples (as shown in the top photo), or secured to the substrate with thin-set mortar and screws. Pros will generally apply a thin layer of thin-set to the plywood foundation before installing the backer board (inset above) to ensure that the backer board lies flat—and stays flat over time.

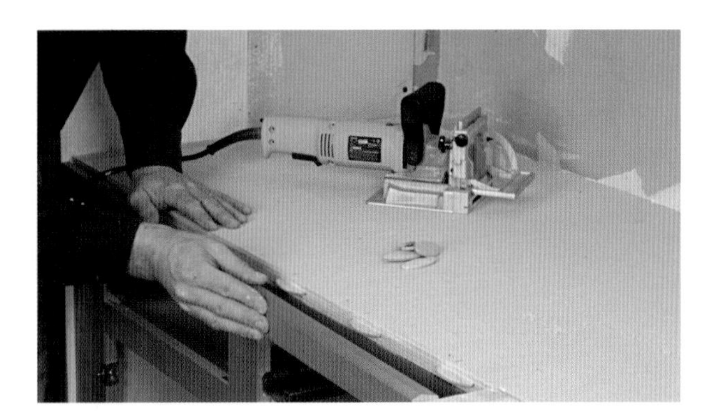

Install the edging. All tile countertops need some kind of edging to cover the foundation layers. You can purchase special trim tiles for this, but we wanted the top to blend in with the wood cabinets, so we chose to use wood edging (above). This is just strips of matching wood that are trimmed to a width of around 2" and are attached to the plywood via biscuits. If you don't have a biscuit joiner, dowels or splines will work equally well. After cutting matching slots in the edge and edging, apply glue to the biscuits and tap the edging in place.

Check the tile pattern. While the glue is drying for the edging is an excellent time to double-check your tile pattern to make sure it will lay out correctly on the top. Place the tiles along the front edge to check for partial tiles on the ends (photo below). What you're after here is partial tiles on the ends that are roughly the same width. If they're not, offset the tiles so that they are. Check the placement of any decorative tiles as well.

Trowel on thin-set mortar. When you're confident your tile pattern will work well on the top, it's time to start laying tile. Start by applying thin-set mortar to the backer board with the appropriate-sized notched trowel, working in a 2- to 3-foot-square area (bottom photo). Thin-set mortar can be bought ready-mixed or in dry form that you mix. If you're only doing a small countertop, consider the pre-mixed variety. It's a bit more expensive, but since you'll only need a small amount, the added expense will be offset by the convenience of not having to mix it.

Place full tiles. With the mortar applied, begin laying tiles by working out from the corner. Some tiles have built-in tabs for spacing the tiles; other tiles (like the ones shown in the top photo) may require rubber spacers to set the gaps between the tiles. Press a tile firmly into the mortar, wiggling it slightly as you press down to set it into the mortar. Continue filling in tiles on each side of the first tile; use spacers if necessary to create even gaps for the grout that will be applied later.

Add decorative tiles. If your countertop pattern calls for decorative tiles, lay these as needed. We used a strip of smaller mosaic tiles here as a colorful accent (middle photo). Decorative tiles tend to be expensive, so use them sparingly to add a splash of color or texture.

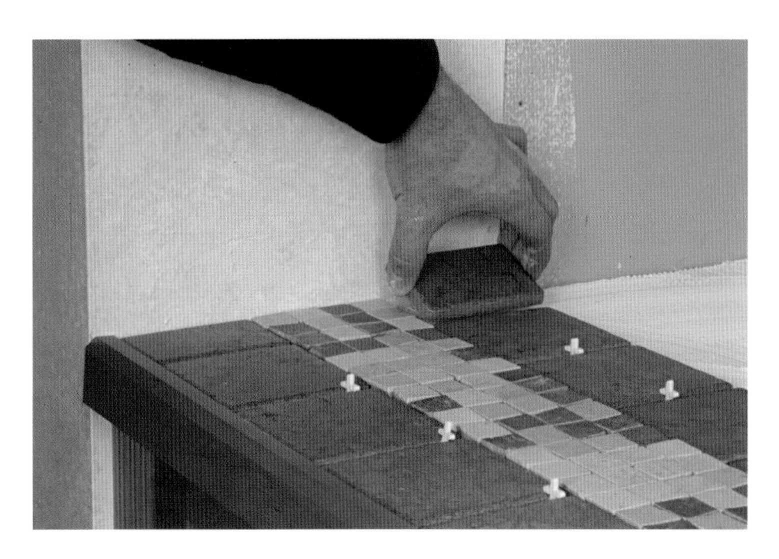

Cut and install partial tiles. When you've placed all the full tiles, you can go back and cut partial tiles as necessary to fill in any spaces, as shown in the bottom photo. Tiles can be cut with a rented wet tile saw, or scored and snapped with an inexpensive tile cutter. If you need to make an odd-shaped cut, tile nippers can be used to snip off small bits of tile until the desired shape is achieved.

Set tiles. After you've laid all the tiles, they can be set. Setting tiles presses them firmly into the mortar and also levels the surface. An easy way to do this is to place a scrap 2×4 on edge on the tile and give a few raps with a dead-blow hammer or rubber-faced mallet (top photo). Slide the 2-by along the countertop, tapping as you go until all the tiles are level.

Apply grout when dry. Allow the thin-set mortar to dry overnight, and then mix up enough grout to fill in the gaps between the tiles. Mix only enough to cover an area approximately 4-foot by 4-foot square. Apply the grout with a grout float diagonally to the surface to force the grout between the tiles, as shown in the middle photo, working in a 2- to 3-foot area at a time.

Screen off excess grout. Excess grout is removed in two steps, using the grout float first and then a sponge. Hold the grout float at about a 45-degree angle as shown in the bottom photo, and scrape the surface, taking care not to pull the grout out from between the tiles.

Sponge off remaining grout. When the grout becomes firm, wipe off any excess with a damp sponge as shown in the top photo. As with the grout float, it's important to work gently since the sponge can and will pull the damp grout right out of the joint. Work slowly and keep the sponge just barely damp, rinsing it in clean water frequently.

Wipe off haze with cloth. Once you've got the bulk of the grout off, start working on the next 2- to 3-foot area. Keep an eye on the first section; when you see that the grout has dried to a soft haze, go back and wipe off the haze with a clean, soft cloth, working in a gentle circular motion as shown in the middle photo. Stop and shake out the cloth frequently to keep it clean. Continue grouting, screening, and sponging off the excess until the entire countertop has been grouted.

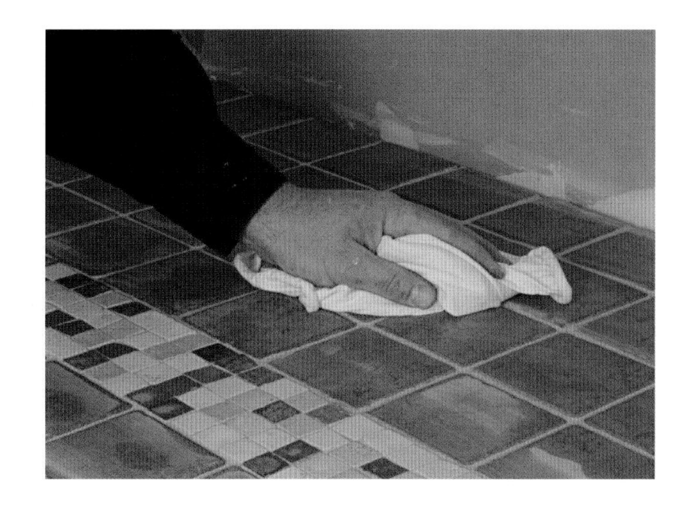

Apply sealer. Finally, you'll need to seal the grout to keep it from staining, as shown in the bottom photo. Unfortunately, you'll have to wait 2 to 4 weeks to do this. That's the length of time most sealer manufacturers recommend before applying a sealer to the grout. Check the label of your grout sealer to find out how long you should wait. This waiting time allows all the water in the grout to completely evaporate. If you apply sealer prematurely, it will trap water inside, which will eventually create mold.

Built-In Entertainment Center

TOOLS

- Driver/drill with bits
- Circular saw
- Hammer and nail set
- Air nailer (optional)
- Level and tape measure
- Stud finder
- Screwdriver
- Clamps
- Power miter saw (optional)

With the prevalence of television in our daily lives, entertainment centers are becoming increasingly popular—and not just in living rooms. Bedrooms, dining rooms, and great rooms are all places where an entertainment center will fit in nicely. The problem is that the selection of entertainment centers is slim and they're often unattractive, shoddily made, and expensive. An alternative to purchasing an entertainment center is to build one yourself from stock cabinets. The design pros at most home centers can help you create a unit to fit your media gear. The center shown here was designed by Connie Edwards, director of design for Timberlake Cabinets. It features a tall center unit that holds the TV and VCR or DVD player, and two side cabinets for displaying and storing just about anything. Only six cabinets are used; they attach to fluted columns and returns to create a unified look that's both elegant and practical.

Build the platform. The base cabinets rest on a 4"-high platform created with 2×4s on edge and covered with 1/2" plywood. This raises the shorter base cabinets up to create a viewing platform for the television. Since the platform is built to match the cabinets, assembly is fairly straightforward. We screwed the 2×4s together and then nailed the plywood on top, as shown in the bottom photo.

Build columns. The underlying support structure of the entertainment center is a pair of rectangular columns that rest on the platform and support the center top cabinet. Each is made from two pieces of matching plywood secured to blocking and capped in the front with a fluted filler. The plywood sides attach to 2-by blocking, and the fluted filler attaches to the front edges of the plywood (near right photo).

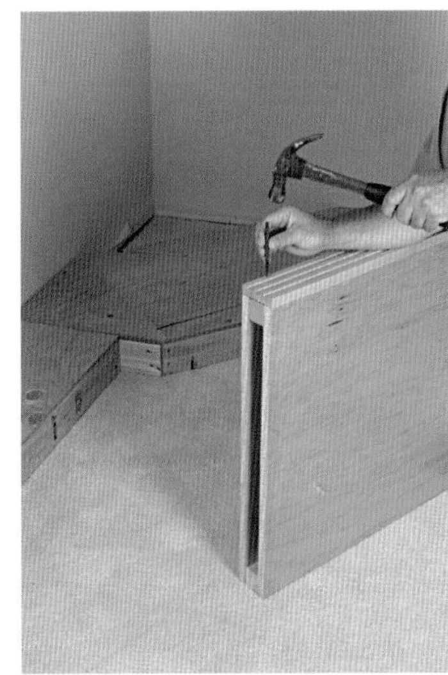

Remove doors from cabinets. Once the columns are built, the center cabinets can be attached to them. For better access and ease of lifting, start by removing the doors from both cabinets (far right top photo).

Position corner cabinet and attach to columns. Now you can set the lower cabinet onto the platform so its front edge is flush with the edge of the platform and it's centered from side to side (photo below). Set a column on each side of this cabinet and secure each column to the cabinet temporarily with clamps. Make sure the face of the fluted fillers is flush with the cabinet face frame. Drill pilot holes through the face frame of the cabinet (inset) and into the fluted filler, and secure the cabinet to the column with long screws; repeat for the other column. Typically, you'll want to use three screws on each side spaced evenly apart.

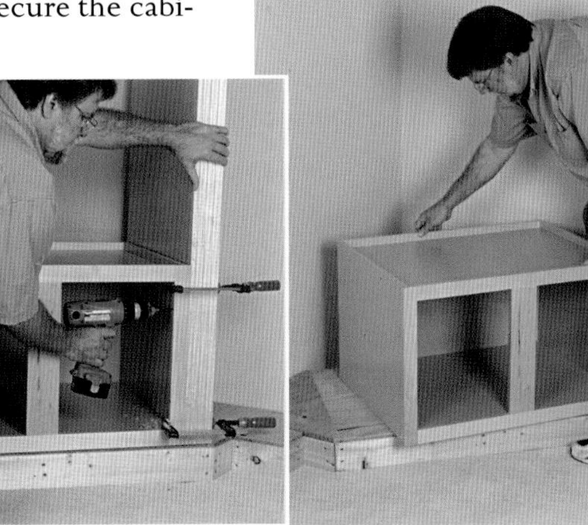

Install upper center cabinet. With the base cabinet secured to the columns, you can add the top center cabinet. The easiest way to support this cabinet in place is to cut a couple of 2×6 supports to length and position these inside the columns as shown in the photo above. This way you can rest the bottom of the top center cabinet on these while you clamp the cabinet to the columns in its final position. Make sure that the sides of the top cabinet are flush with the top edges of the columns. When everything looks good, drill pilot holes and secure the cabinet to the columns with long screws.

Add back. Gently turn the assembled center section around so you can add the plywood back that encloses the television area. Cut the plywood to size and then drill a series of vent holes to promote air circulation, to prevent any of the electronic gear from overheating. Attach the plywood to the back edges of the columns with glue and brads (right).

Install returns. Because the center cabinet is angled in the corner at 45 degrees, plywood returns need to be cut and attached to the columns so the side cabinets have something to attach to (left photo). These returns are the same height as the columns and will need blocking for support. A cleat nailed to the platform and a mitered 2×4 attached to the column top will provide the nailing surfaces you'll need. The edge of the plywood that meets the columns will need to be beveled at 45 degrees. This edge can be fastened along its length to the columns with brads.

Connect side cabinet. The side units consist of a short base cabinet topped with a taller wall cabinet with glass doors. Set the top unit on the base so the front edges are flush, and drill pilot holes through the bottom face frame (photo above). Secure the two units together with long screws.

Attach to returns. Now you can set the assembled side unit onto the platform and position it so it's flush with the front edge of the platform. When it's in place, drill pilot holes through the side frame frames and into the returns (right photo). Secure the side units to the returns with long screws.

Attach to studs. To make the entertainment center as stable as possible, secure it to the wall studs. Since you can't do this for the center cabinet as it doesn't rest against the wall, you'll have to settle for securing both side cabinet assemblies to the studs. Use an electronic stud finder to locate the wall studs, and mark their locations with a pencil. Drill a pilot hole through the top back edge of the cabinet and then drive a long screw through the cabinet back and into the stud (top photo).

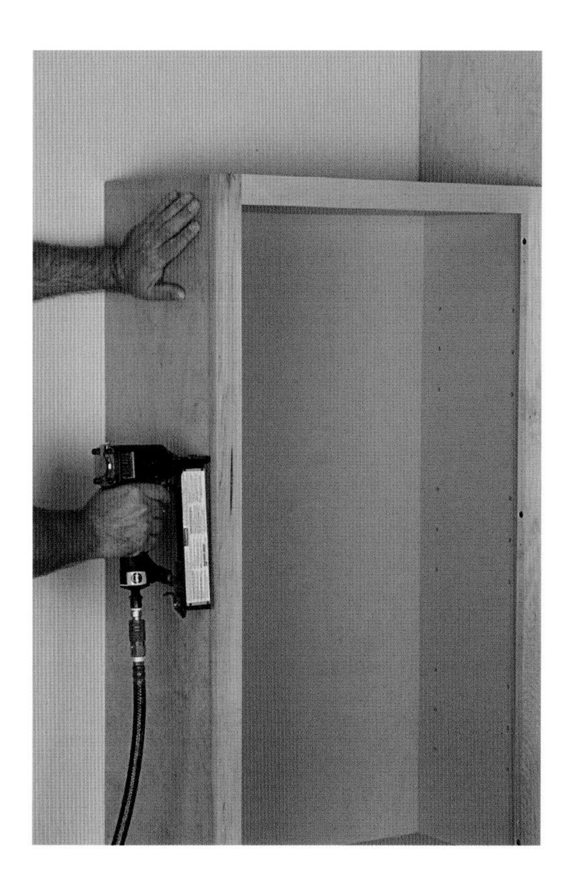

Cover sides of cabinets. Since the sides of the cabinet are unfinished, you'll need to cover them with plywood that matches your cabinets (above). Measure the sides and cut 1/4" plywood panels to match. Secure them to the cabinet sides with glue or construction adhesive and brads.

Add decorative panels. For the best appearance, consider adding decorative panels to the exposed sides of the cabinets, as shown in the bottom right photo. These are nothing more than doors that are secured to the sides by driving screws though the inside of the cabinet and into the face frames of the doors. Take care here to use short screws and some kind of stop on your drill bit to prevent the bit from drilling all the way through the panel.

Add base trim. With the cabinets in place and the ends covered, you can add trim. Start with the base. Measure a length and miter the end or ends as needed, working on one piece at a time. Attach each trim piece to the platform with 2"-long finish nails. As usual, an air nailer will make quick work of this nailing job (above); air nailers can be rented at most home centers and rental centers.

Install blocking for crown. Once all the base trim is attached, you can turn your attention to the crown molding. The most secure way to attach crown is to nail it to support blocks spaced every foot or so along the top edge of the cabinets. These blocks are nothing more than scraps of 2×4 cut to length, notched to fit over the top edge of the cabinet, and secured with glue and screws (above).

Install crown. After the blocking is in place, you can install the crown molding. Work on one piece at a time, measuring carefully and cutting it to length. Miter the end or ends as required. Then attach the crown molding to the support blocks as shown in the photo above. Additionally, you may want to drive a brad or two through the bottom edge of the crown into the top edge of the cabinet.

Add accent strips. Much of the crown molding available from cabinet manufacturers comes in two pieces: the crown molding and an accent strip that attaches to a flat on the molding. The system allows the manufacturers to offer different looks using the same base molding. Cut the accent strips to length, mitering the end or ends as needed and secure it to the flat section of the crown molding with glue and brads (right).

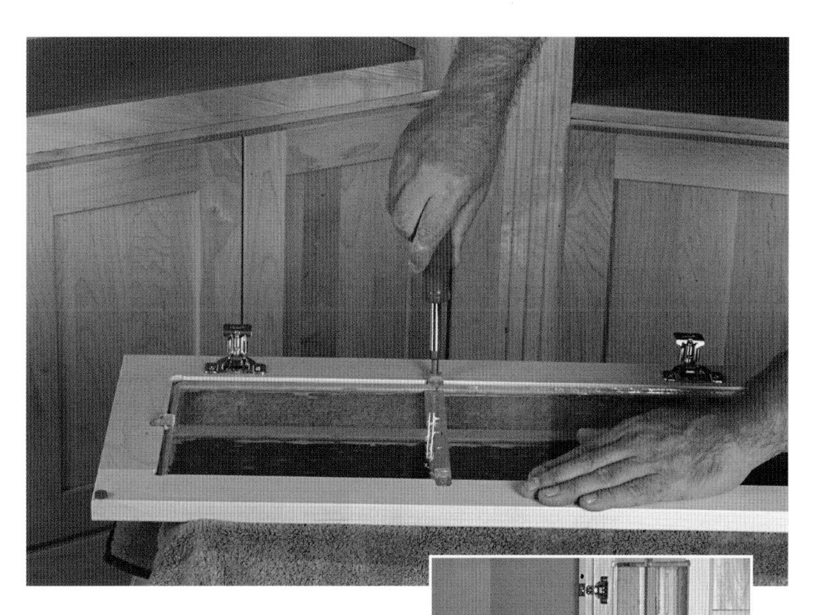

Add doors. All that's left is to add the doors and hardware. The doors shown here use decorative glass panels. These are installed right before you remount the doors. Use the hardware provided to secure a glass panel in each door as shown in the photo above. Then reattach the doors to their respective cabinets (inset).

Install hardware. Finally, mark and drill mounting holes for the door and/or drawer hardware. Secure each knob or pull with the screws provided (above). Then go around the cabinets and fill any nail holes with matching putty. Install your television, fire it up, and sit back and relax.

CEILINGS

What's the last feature you notice in a room? Probably the ceiling, and usually because there's nothing much to note. Painted white or off-white, flat or spray-textured, ceilings tend to be ignored in the makeover process, and that's unfortunate. With all that real estate overhead, a ceiling can have an enormous effect on the look of a room. So, you can create an enormous difference by not settling for the same old same old when it's time to redo a ceiling. How about a ceiling fan? You say your ceiling is too low? Then you haven't looked at the sleek, low-profile models available. And then there's paneling—not the gloomy stuff of 1950s dens, but ceiling paneling in light, fresh materials and tones that don't give a room that closed-in feeling. Finish up with crown molding, and you can turn that otherwise boring expanse overhead into a real improvement.

Installing Ceiling Paneling

TOOLS

- Driver/drill and bits
- Tape measure and chalk line
- Stud finder
- Circular saw or saber saw
- Power miter saw (optional)
- Hammer or air nailer (optional)

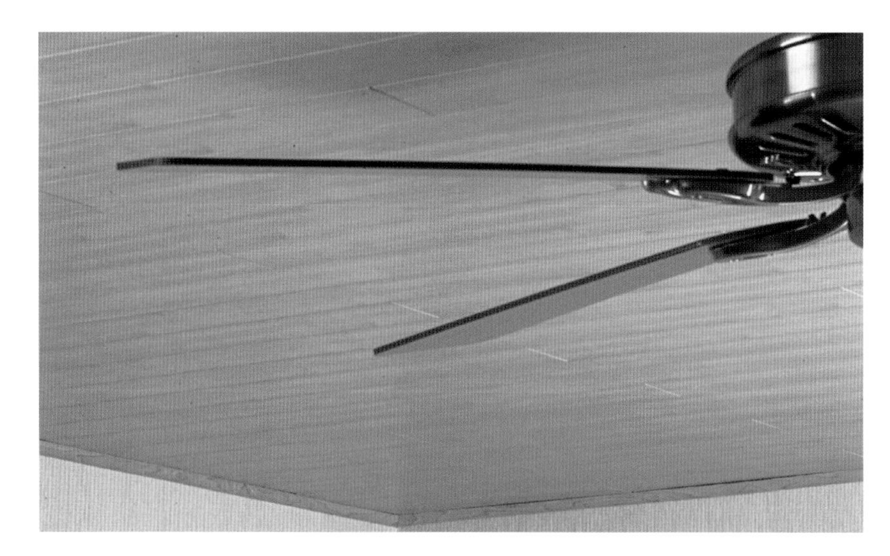

If you can use a chalk line, you can install ceiling paneling—and there are lots of reasons to do so. A bad-looking ceiling can be transformed with good-looking paneling, especially if you opt for today's wood lookalike versions that add warmth, interest, and character to a room. Installation is easier than ever thanks to new, snap-in-place systems—once you have the grid-like tracks installed, you simply pop the panels into place. And, because these panels are crafted of long-lasting laminate, they don't require any special care. (This is basically the same material used for laminate flooring, but thinner; and here, it doesn't get walked on.) These panels are a great choice for adding flair to a room, whether they're colored a warm wood tone, given a whitewashed effect, or something in between. Once installed, they may make the ceiling the first thing people notice.

SNAP-IN PANELING SYSTEM

Ceiling paneling can be installed in a number of ways. The classic method is to attach furring strips perpendicular to your ceiling joints and then attach the paneling to this via metal clips that are screwed in place, as shown in the drawing at right. A much easier way is to use a snap-in track system like the one developed by Armstrong. Their "Easy-Up" system uses metal clips as well, but instead of screwing to furring strips, the panels simply snap onto metal tracks that replace the furring strips.

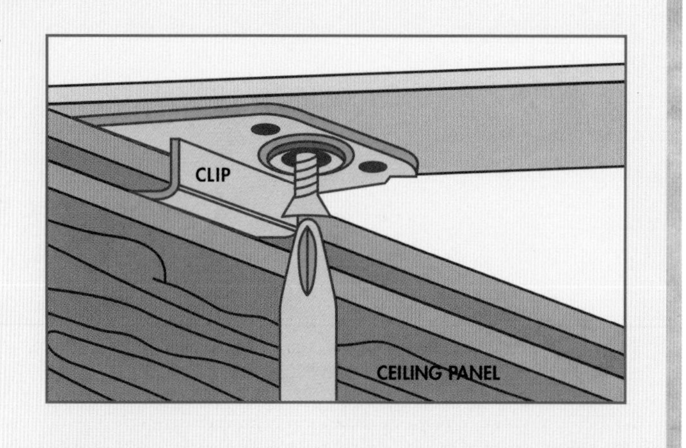

Locate ceiling joists. Since both metal tracks and furring strips need to be installed perpendicular to your ceiling joists, your first job is to locate and mark all the joists. Use a stud finder (top photo) to locate them at each end of the room and then snap a chalk line between each mark to define each joist (inset photo above).

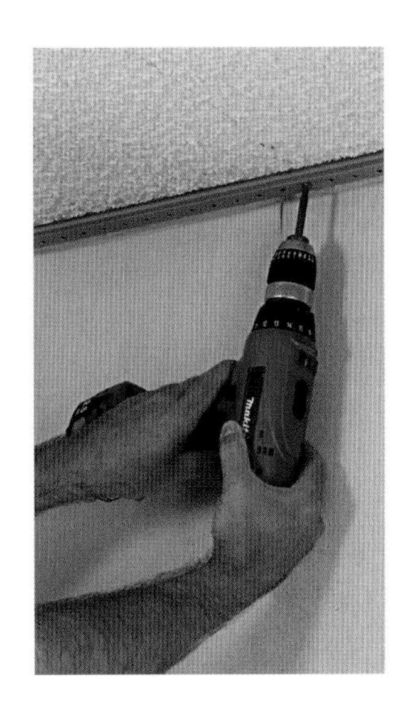

Install starter track. Now you can start mounting the tracks or furring strips. Start in one corner and fasten the track to the joist with nails or screws so the track is about 1" from the wall (near right photo). You'll find that screws are easier to work with from below and that it's easier to prevent damage to the metal track screwing it in place versus hammering it in place. Butt the next track up against the first and install it, taking care to maintain the 1" distance from the wall.

Install remaining tracks. With the starter track in place, measure out 12" and install the next track; be careful to offset the joints where two tracks butt up against each other (middle photo below). Since you can secure the tracks only to the ceiling joists, you'll find some tracks aren't quite as firmly mounted as you'd like. This isn't a problem as long as you offset the joints where the tracks meet. Continue measuring every 12" and installing tracks until you reach the other end of the room. Then install a final track 1" away from the wall.

Install starter planks. To determine the width of the first row of planks, measure the room parallel to the tracks in inches and divide this by 5 (planks are typically 5" wide). In most cases, your room dimension will not divide evenly. Take the remainder, add 5", and divide this in half—this is the width of your starter planks—and the final planks you'll install on the opposite end of the room from where you started. This will give a balanced ceiling appearance. Cut enough planks to width, and place the first plank in position. Although you can use clips to support the edge away from the wall, the edge nearest the wall is screwed to the track. Drill countersunk holes in the plank and attach it to the track with screws, as shown in the bottom right photo.

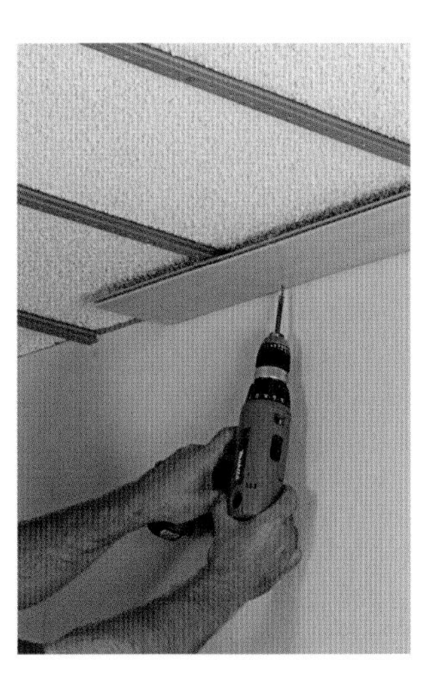

Stagger the planks. When you reach the end of the first row, you'll likely need to cut the plank to length. As you start the second row, you'll want to stagger the planks so that the end joints don't line up (top right photo). Most manufacturers recommend staggering planks in thirds. For example, use a full-length plank for the first row, a two-thirds plank for the second row, and a one-third plank for the third row.

Snap planks in place. The beauty of a snap-in paneling system will become evident right now. Just position the next plank, snap a clip on the metal track (left photo), and then slide it over until it engages the profiled edge of the plank (right middle photo). The ends of the planks are tongue-and-grooved as well to mate easily.

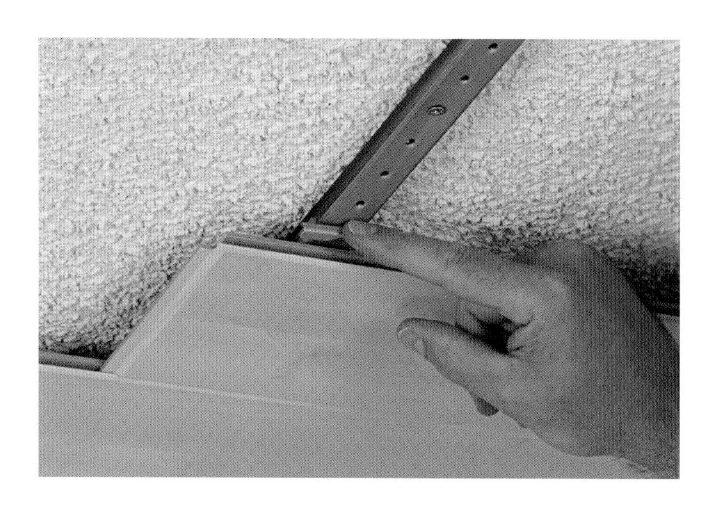

Work around fixtures. If you have any ceiling-mounted fixtures, you'll want to do any prep work to them before adding the paneling. Consult the manufacturer's directions for the recommended offset you'll need to move the electrical boxes. In many cases, this can be accomplished by simply adding a box extender. Box extenders are sold where electrical supplies are available. They can be made of plastic or metal and are designed to extend the outer edge of the box by a set increment, typically ranging from 1/4" to 3/4". The simplest way to work around a fixture is to hold the plank to be installed next to the fixture and mark the fixture location directly onto it. Then cut this out with a saber saw and snap the plank in place, as shown in the bottom left photo.

Add the final row. Continue installing planks until you reach the opposite wall. If all went well and you made your initial calculations correctly, the final plank should be the same width as your starter plank. Measure the gap between the last plank and the wall and subtract 1/4" for expansion; cut the final plank to this width. Take care to measure and cut each plank individually, since most rooms are not square and you may need to taper some of these planks slightly. Once you've cut a plank to width, check the fit (top right photo).

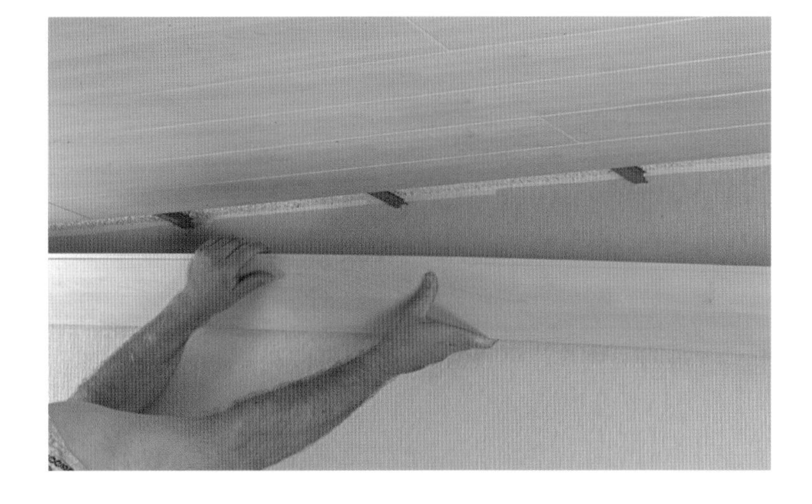

Screw final planks in place. If each of your final planks fits, start installing them by slipping the plank's edge into the second-to-last plank. As with the starter row, you'll need to fasten this last row directly to the track you installed close to the wall. Here again, drill countersunk pilot holes first and then screw each panel in place as shown in the middle photo. Make sure to drill pilot holes as close to the wall as possible so the molding you'll put up next will conceal the screws.

Install molding around perimeter. Once all the paneling is in place, you can work your way around the perimeter of the room installing molding to conceal the gap between the paneling and the wall—and to hide the screws used to install the starter and final rows of planks. Some ceiling paneling manufacturers sell matching molding; others do not. You can pick molding that matches (as shown in the bottom left photo) or molding that's different to create an accent. A common trend is to use paint-grade molding and paint it the same color as the accent color used throughout the room.

TIN-LOOK CEILINGS

Looking for that yesteryear touch to turn a foyer, dining room, or living room into a distinctive room? How about a tin ceiling? If you think it's too much work and too expensive, the market has good news. Take a look at the gorgeous tin ceilings shown here—the surprise is that they're not tin. They are tin-look ceiling tiles manufactured by Armstrong as part of their Decorator Ceilings collection. Just like an acoustical tile, this tile goes up quick and easy.

What's really nice is that the tiles all come in white, so you can paint them to match your décor, as shown in the photo at right. You can paint them any color you want or go with a metallic paint to create a true tin look: silver, gold, and copper metallic paint is commonly available wherever paint is sold—or you can have it custom-mixed to suit your needs.

Installing Simple Molding

TOOLS

- Tape measure and stud finder
- Power miter saw
- Caulk gun
- Hammer and nail set or optional air nailer

One of the most homeowner-friendly home improvement products we've come across in a long time is extruded foam molding. Most of the moldings we used throughout the makeovers featured in this book are extruded foam. They're easy to cut, very lightweight (which makes holding them in place a breeze), and quick to install. The moldings shown here are manufactured by Style Solutions (www.stylesolutions.com) and come in a dizzying array of profiles.

There are a few things to keep in mind when using a foam molding. First, foam moldings should be used for decorative purposes only; they do not provide any structural support. Second, it's important to check your local building codes to make sure the moldings meet your local specifications. Third, you can paint this molding any color you want. It takes paint well, and some manufacturers make embossed molding that looks like wood, so you can stain it to match other wood in the room.

Always use an adhesive. Foam molding should never be installed with just fasteners. It's designed to be installed with both fasteners and high-quality, urethane-based adhesive. You don't need a lot here; a 1/8" bead on both mating surfaces will do (bottom left photo).

Start in one corner. Foam molding can be cut and trimmed just like any wood molding, except it's a lot easier. Start in one corner of the room and apply adhesive to the back of the molding. Position the molding and drive fasteners through the molding and into the studs as shown in the top right photo. An air nailer works best for this, as it drives and sets the nail at the same time. (Air nailers can be rented at most home centers and rental centers.)

Scarf as needed. As you work your way around the room, odds are you'll need to fasten strips of molding together to cross long expanses, as shown in the bottom right photo. When this occurs, miter the ends of the molding in opposite directions to create a nearly invisible "scarf" joint. At corners, you can miter the molding together or cut a coped joint.

Adding a Ceiling Fan

TOOLS

- Driver/drill and bits
- Screwdriver
- Stud finder

A ceiling fan is a great addition to any room. Not only does it add a touch of style, it also offers cooling in the summer and heating in the winter. That's right—heating. No, it doesn't have a heating element, but a ceiling fan set on low in the downdraft mode can actually help drive warm air that's up near the ceiling down into the living space to create a more uniformly heated room.

Ceiling fans are rated to match the size of the room; see the chart below. There are three ways to mount most fans: flush, standard, and angled. The type you choose will depend on the height and slope of your ceiling.

The general rule of thumb is that you need at least 7 feet of clearance between the fan blades and the floor. Also, because ceiling fans are heavy, they must be installed in electrical boxes especially designed to handle this weight (see the drawing on the opposite page) or attached to heavy-duty boxes that are affixed directly to your ceiling joist.

FITTING A FAN TO A ROOM

Blade Size	Room Size	Square Footage
36"	10' × 10'	100 sq. ft.
42"	12' × 12'	144 sq. ft.
44" or 48"	15' × 15'	225 sq. ft.
52" or 54"	20' × 20'	400 sq. ft.
56"	22' × 22'	485 sq. ft.
60"	25' × 25'	625 sq. ft.

Install the plate. To install a ceiling fan, turn off power and thread the wires coming out of the box through the ceiling plate. Then, using the screws provided, secure the plate to the electrical box or joist as shown in the middle photo above.

Hang fan on plate hook. Because ceiling fans tend to be heavy, most manufacturers have added a hook on the ceiling plate to suspend the fan from so that you can connect the wires. If your ceiling plate has one of these, hook the fan onto it as shown in the top left photo. If it doesn't, enlist the aid of a helper to hold the fan while you connect the wires.

Connect wiring. Wiring for most ceiling fans is pretty straightforward. Connect black to black and white to white with wire nuts, as shown in the middle photo. Connect the ground wire to the ground wire of the fan or to the grounding lug on the ceiling plate. Most fans come with wire nuts for making these connections.

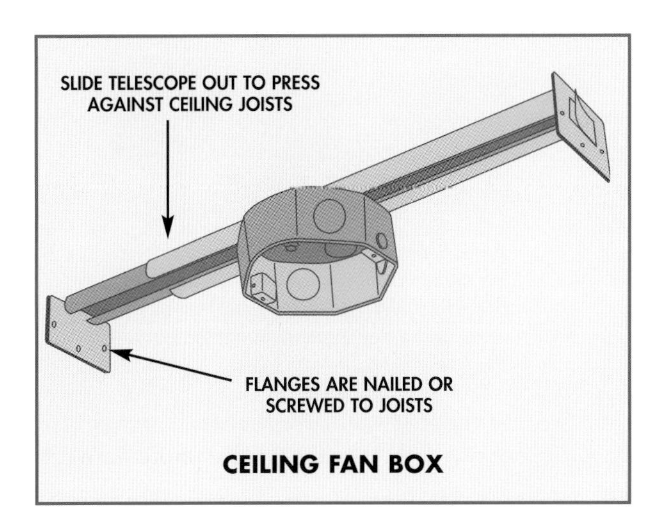

CEILING FAN BOX

Attach the fan to the ceiling plate. With the wiring complete, stuff the wires up through the opening in the ceiling plate and into the electrical box. Now you can attach the fan to the ceiling plate. Unhook it and position it on the plate so the holes in the fan align with those in the ceiling plate (top right photo). Secure it with the screws provided. Here, the weight of the fan can make this difficult. Consider getting a helper to hold and align the fan while you drive in the mounting screws.

Add the canopy. Most fans have a canopy that slips over the fan housing to conceal the inner workings and keep out dust. If your fan has a canopy like the one shown in the bottom right photo, slip it into place and secure it with the screws provided.

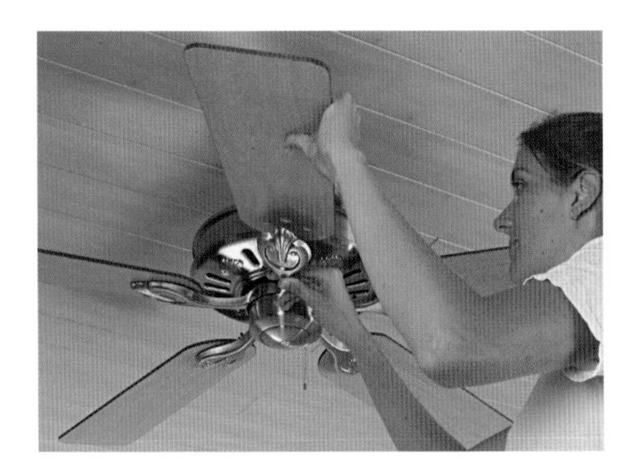

Attach blades. All that's left is to add the blades. Mounting systems differ, from screw-on to snap-in. Some fans instruct you to attach the blade brackets to the fan before mounting it to the ceiling; others don't. If you haven't attached the blade brackets to the fan, do so now as shown in the photo at left. Then attach the blades with the hardware provided. Turn power back on and test the fan. If the blade wobbles, see the sidebar below.

BALANCING BLADES

Many homeowners are disappointed the first time they turn on their new fan and it wobbles. That's because they don't realize that most new fans need to be balanced, just as you balance new tires before installing them on your car. Quality fan manufacturers include blade-balancing kits along with their fans. Alternatively, most home centers and hardware stores sell fan-balancing kits. Kits usually include a set of directions, an adjustable clip to locate the out-of-balance blade, and self-adhesive weights to correct the problem. Here's how to balance a fan.

Position the clip. Start by running the fan on high speed with the direction set to downdraft. Before you try the balancing kit, first try swapping two adjacent blades to see whether this corrects the problem. If it doesn't, turn off the fan and attach the clip to the leading edge of one blade about halfway between the outer edge of the blade and the blade bracket, as shown in the bottom left photo. Run the fan and observe the wobble. Stop the fan and move the clip to the next blade; turn it on and observe the wobble. Repeat for the remaining blades. Now move the clip back to the blade with the least wobble, except now attach the clip near the blade bracket. Turn it on and observe. Stop the fan and move the clip out toward the blade end in small increments until you find the position where the fan runs best.

Attach the weight. Finally, peel the backing off one of the self-adhesive weight strips and attach along the centerline of the blade opposite the clip. Remove the clip and run the fan. If the blade wobble is gone, stop. If not, repeat this procedure for the blade that wobbled the second least amount.

Solatubes

We all know that natural light is the best for most rooms. The problem is we don't always have the correct size, number, or placement of windows we'd like. The solution? Why not bring light in through the ceiling? That's exactly what Solatubes tubular skylights are designed to do—they capture sunlight on the roof and redirect it down through a highly reflective tube, through a diffuser, and into your room.

The only downside to one of these is that it requires cutting a hole in your roof. If you're not comfortable doing that, consider hiring a roofing contractor to install the unit. Solatubes generally consist of a dome, a top tube assembly with flashing, an extension tube, a tube bottom, and a transition box or fitting that accepts the diffuser; see the drawing at left.

Armed with modest carpentry skills, the average homeowner can install one of these units in an afternoon. The only problem will be that as soon as you're done, you're going to want to install more. Complete installation instructions can be found at Solatube's website (www.solatube.com).

LIGHT INTERCEPTING TRANSFER DEVICE
GORE
ROOF RAFTER
ADAPTER TUBE
EXPANSION JOINT SEAL
GORE
EXTENSION TUBE
CEILING JOIST

SOLATUBE CROSS SECTION

Crown Molding

TOOLS

- Stud finder and tape measure
- Caulk gun and putty knife
- Hammer and nail set or optional air nailer

Crown molding can dress up any room, adding a graceful touch with its classic profiles. The newer extruded-foam varieties are much easier to install than conventional wood crown. The molding shown here is manufactured by Style Solutions (www.stylesolutionsinc.com) and offers a unique feature that makes installing crown a snap—premade corner blocks and molding. That's right, no more upside down and backwards cuts on the miter saw. If you can cut a piece of molding so it's square on the end, you can install this type of crown molding.

Locate and mark wall studs. To install crown, start by using an electronic stud finder to locate the wall studs. Then mark these with a pencil as shown in the bottom left photo.

Add block in corner. There are two different corner treatments that Style Solutions offers: a block that fits in the corner (near left photo) and preformed corner pieces. The nice thing about using the blocks is that you simply glue them into the corners using a high-quality urethane adhesive. Additionally, since the block profile is slightly larger than the crown molding profile, it creates an additional shadow line that looks particularly nice.

Install molding. After you've installed all the corner blocks, measure the distance between them, add 1/8", and cut a piece of crown to this length. Yes, the manufacturer actually suggests cutting the molding a bit long so you end up with a nice, tight friction-fit. Unlike unforgiving wood molding, the foam molding will actually compress a bit as needed. To install the molding, start by applying a bead of urethane adhesive to the end of the molding as shown in the inset photo. Then position the molding and secure it by driving nails through the molding and into the wall studs you marked earlier (top right photo). Repeat for the remaining walls.

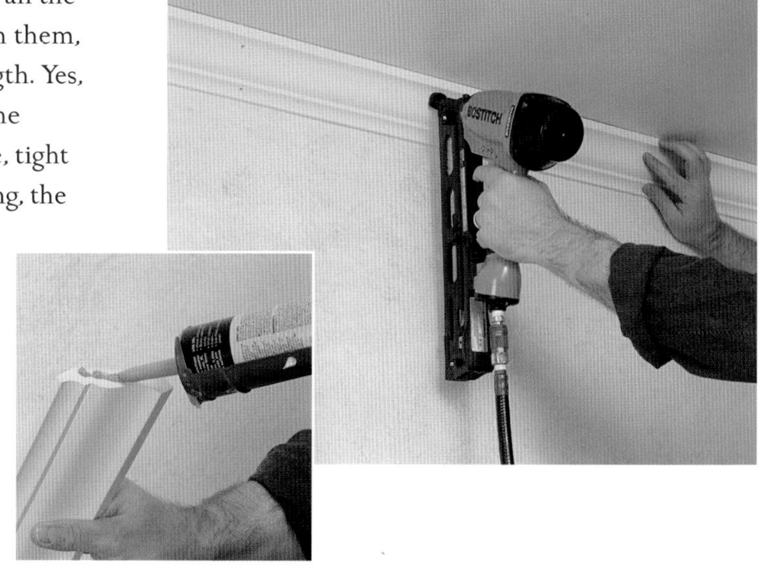

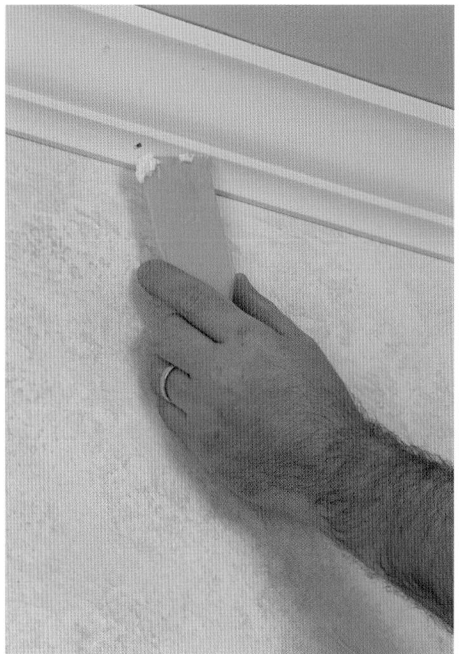

Fill all nail holes. Once all the molding is in place, go back around the room and fill all the nail holes with putty as shown in the middle left photo. Fill these just slightly proud of the surface, and then go back when dry and sand them flush with the molding surface.

Chalk if needed. Finally, fill any gaps between the molding and the ceiling or wall with a quality paintable latex caulk (bottom right photo). Wipe away any excess immediately and when dry, mask and paint the crown molding if desired.

THE CENTURY DICTIONARY AND CYCLOPEDIA
THE CENTURY DICTIONARY AND CYCLOPEDIA

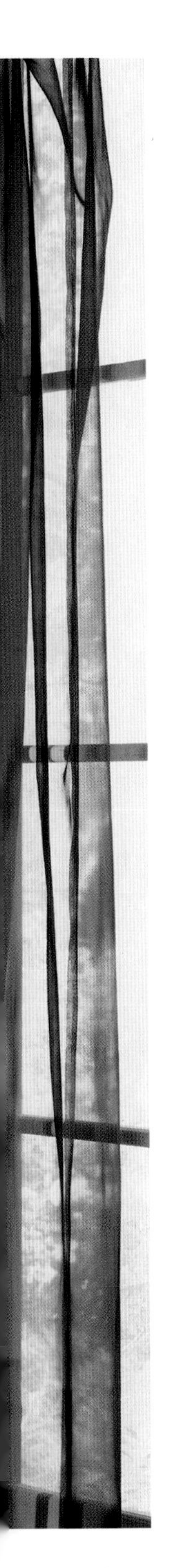

WALLS

Possibly the most fundamental makeover maneuver is to improve walls with paint or wallpaper. Within just hours, you can change the mood of a room, shrink or enlarge the visual space, hide flaws or stains, coordinate with your furnishings—and all at fairly low cost, with no more than average skills. No wonder it's the most popular home improvement around. And no wonder, too, that many homeowners mix and match surface treatments for more interesting effect. You might add wainscoting around the bottom half of a room, for example, and paper the top half—or sponge-paint the upper half and top it off with a wallpaper border. Alternatively, a chair rail can help break up a large wall surface and give you two different "canvases," above and below the rail, for your special effects. So next time, why not go beyond the fundamentals—after all, they're your walls, so make them over your way.

Painting Walls

TOOLS

- Paint tray and roller
- Trim pad
- Putty knife
- Foam brushes and rags

The fundamentals still apply: There's nothing like a fresh coat of paint to brighten up a room. You can make a drab space vivid, cool down or warm up a room with the right hues, define an accent area...the possibilities go on and on. Just stroll through the paint aisle of your local home center, and you'll be struck by the enormous color choices available. Thankfully, manufacturers make decision time a bit easier with sample color strips and design booklets (usually free), which advise what goes with what, and show how an unexpected hue could be perfect.

Just remember: Dark paint shades tend to make a room seem smaller, while light paints open a space up for a bigger "feel." As to paint formula, it's usually best to stick with latex: It goes on easily and cleans up well. And a flat finish (versus gloss or semi-gloss) is the best look for most wall surfaces.

Clean with TSP. The first step to successful painting is to clean the walls thoroughly. Scrubbing a wall lightly with a sponge or brush saturated with a cleaning solution of trisodium phosphate (TSP) will quickly strip off dirt and grime (bottom left photo). Just make sure to wear rubber gloves and rinse the wall completely with clean water when done.

Mask as needed. When the walls are dry, take the time to fill any holes or dings with putty and sand them smooth. Then go around the room and mask off any areas that will not be painted, such as window and door trim. Remove any receptacle and switch covers and tape over these as shown in the bottom right photo; do the same for electrical wall or ceiling fixtures. Also, make sure to cover the floor and any furniture with drop cloths or old sheets. Tape the cloths or sheets with masking tape or duct tape to wrap around obstacles as needed.

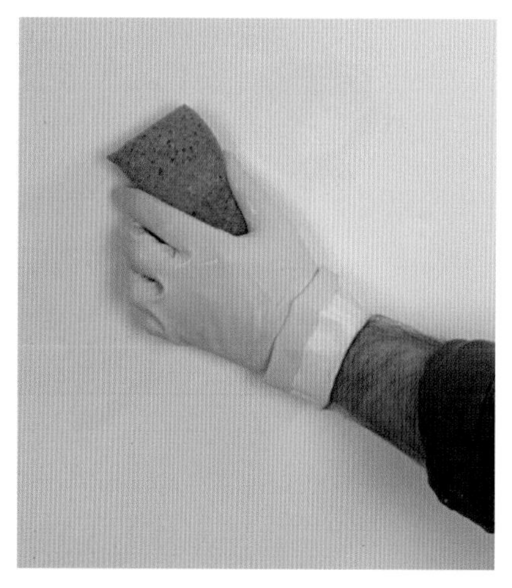

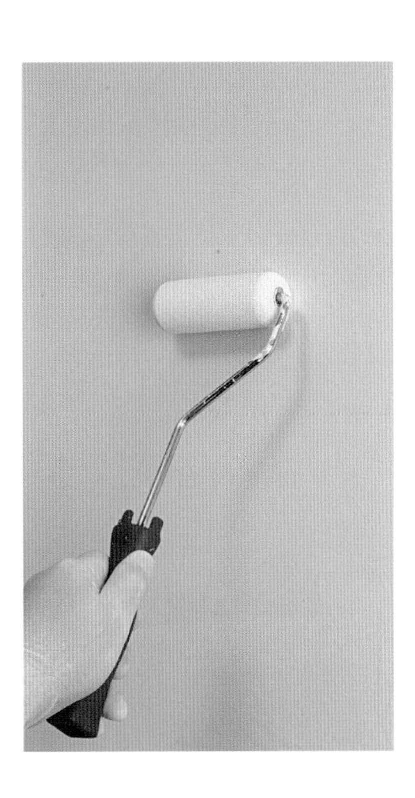

Prime the walls. Even if the walls don't look like they need to be primed, do so anyway (top left photo). Primers help ensure a good bond between the old surface and the new paint: They're formulated to make the old surface more "receptive" to the paint. Priming also seals damaged areas and hides stains. And if you have the primer tinted to match the paint, you may need only one coat of finish paint.

Paint the perimeter. When the primer has dried, you can start painting by working around the perimeter of a wall. One of the best tools for this job is a trim pad with rollers, like the one shown in the bottom left photo. These also work great for painting around the edges of windows and doors. The only trick to working with a trim pad is to keep the rollers free of paint. Check the rollers each time you load the pad, and remove any paint with a clean cloth.

Roll on the paint. As soon as you've painted the perimeter of the wall, fill in the large spaces with paint. Use a standard roller fitted with a disposable sleeve for this, as shown in the top right photo. After you've rolled paint on a wall to cover it completely, go back and do what's called "striking off." Take your roller and begin at the top of the wall and roll it all the way to the bottom in a continuous stroke. This will remove any roller marks and leave you with a smooth, clean wall.

Faux Painting

TOOLS

- Measured mixing cup
- Paint tray and liner
- Rags
- Sea sponge
- Flogging brush
- Small bristle brush

One of the most popular ways to change the look and feel of a room is with faux painting. Faux painting combines color with texture to create a mood, enhance your furnishings, and give your room a designer look without the expense.

There are several faux finishing techniques to choose from. We've shown four of the most common here: dragging, flogging (sometimes called stippling), ragging, and sponging. Each of these techniques uses two colors to provide depth and a different way of applying the paint to create texture. One of the two colors goes directly on the wall; the other is mixed with a glaze and is applied with a brush, a rag, or a sponge. Alternatively, you can roll on the colored glaze and remove some of it with a brush, rag, or sponge. For example, you can sponge on a glaze, or sponge off a glaze—each creates a slightly different look.

Before you get started faux-painting, here are a couple of tips that will help create a successful finish. First, a clean, dry, dull surface is an essential foundation for painting. Wash your walls with mild soap and rinse thoroughly. Then remove loose paint, patch holes, and sand smooth. Remove dust with a vacuum or tack cloth. Next, mask ceilings, baseboards, and trim with tape. Then paint the wall with your desired basecoat color and allow it to dry completely—4 hours is good, but overnight is better.

As you begin applying the glaze, step back often to check out your work from a distance. This will help you see any uneven spots so can you maintain a consistently random pattern.

MIXING GLAZE

Most paint manufacturers that sell supplies for faux painting also offer measured mixing cups to make it easy to get the proper ratio of glaze to paint. This ratio is commonly 4 or 5 parts glaze to 1 part paint. You wouldn't think this would be enough paint, but the glaze will instantly take on the color of the paint as soon as you stir it. Alternatively, most home and paint centers sell inexpensive generic measured plastic cups for mixing paint.

DRAGGING

Dragging is a simple technique where you apply the glaze to the wall with a roller and then drag a clean brush over the surface.

Roll on glaze. Begin in one corner of the wall and roll your glaze coat on the entire height of your wall and approximately 3 feet wide (top photo). This will allow ample time to work the glaze before it begins to dry.

Drag with small brush. As soon as you've rolled on the glaze, lightly drag a dry brush down through the wet glaze in one continuous stroke from ceiling to floor (photo below right). Try to apply even pressure as you go and keep the tool at an angle to produce a streaked appearance. Wipe off excess glaze from your brush after each stroke to maintain a clean edge. Continue rolling and dragging until you've completed the wall, and then move on to the next one. Consider experimenting with alternating vertically and horizontally combed squares for a basket-weave effect, or create a plaid pattern by combing horizontally through your vertical stripes before they dry.

FLOGGING

Flogging is also referred to as stippling. With this technique, you apply the glaze to the wall by slapping or flogging the wall with a paint-loaded brush.

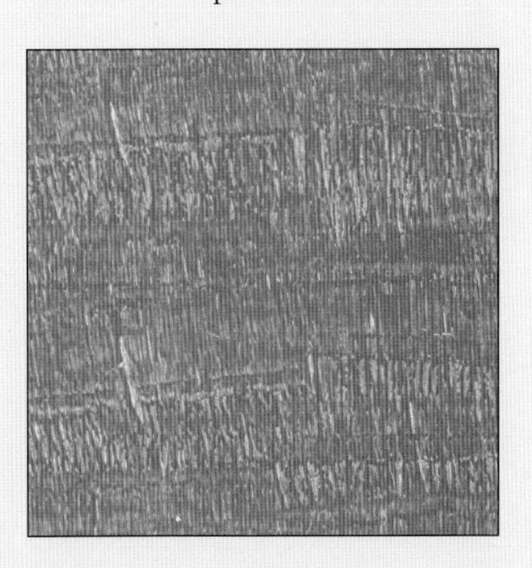

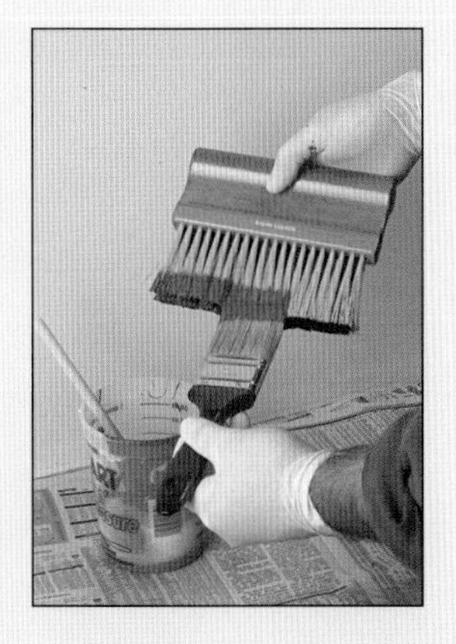

Load glaze on brush. After you've let the basecoat dry, apply the glaze to the tips of a wide flogging or wallpaper brush with another brush, as shown in the photo at near left.

Flog with large brush. Now flog, slap, or stipple the glaze onto the wall with the brush (bottom right photo). Stop frequently to reload the brush, and work on about a 3-foot-wide section at a time. Stippling is done by tapping the wall with the brush held almost perpendicular to the wall so that just the tips of the brush hairs strike the wall.

RAGGING

Rag-rolling is a simple technique with a stunning effect. It produces a delicate, fabric-like texture with a variegated appearance. The glaze can be applied or removed with the rag.

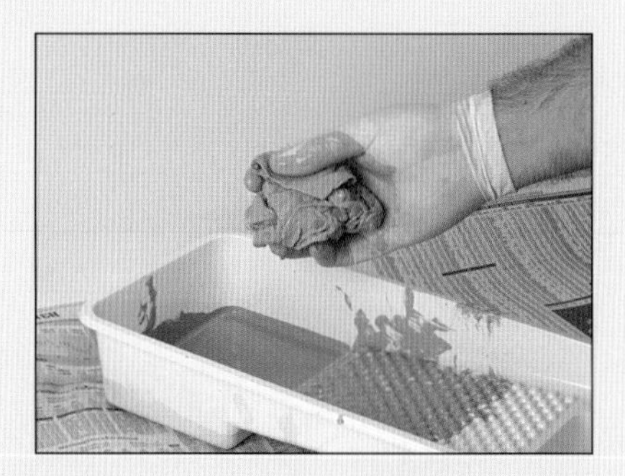

Load the rag. Soak a damp cotton rag with your glaze, and blot or wring out the excess (top left photo). The more glaze you leave on the rag, the bolder your effect will be. It's best to pour glaze into a paint tray for easier dipping and blotting.

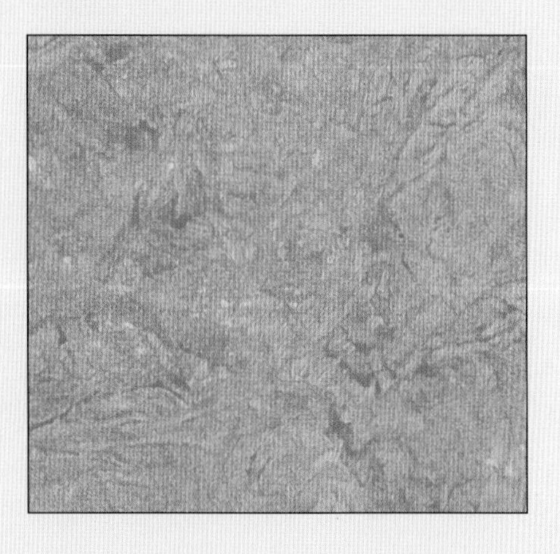

Pounce with rag. Next, roll your rag into a ball and then lightly dab it repeatedly on the wall, working in a roughly 2-foot square (right photo). This is called "pouncing." To produce varied textures, reshape the rag often and reload it as it dries out. Overlap each impression, and rotate your hand frequently to create a seamless look. You can also rag off the glaze coat: Roll on a solid 3-foot square of glaze; then dab with a damp rag to remove portions of the glaze to reveal your basecoat color.

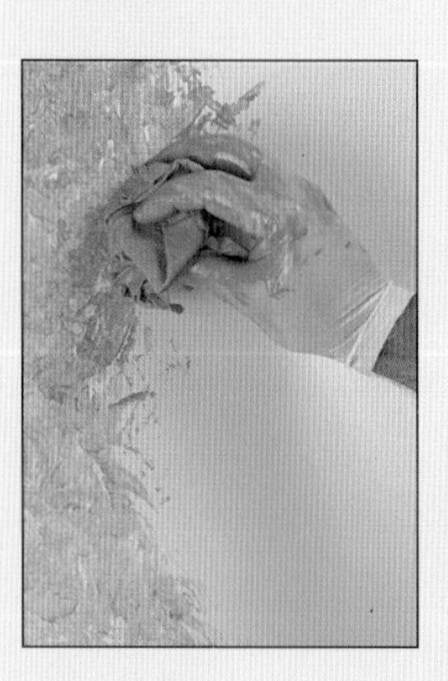

SPONGING

Sponging is a simple technique, yet it produces professional-looking results. The glaze is either put on or removed with a sponge. To create the varied texture, it's important to use a natural sea sponge instead of a man-made sponge, as these do not have the randomness in hole patterns that a natural sponge does.

Load the sponge. Wet your sponge with clean water and wring it out thoroughly. Then load the sponge either by dipping into the glaze and blotting off the excess with a paper towel, or by applying glaze to the sponge with a brush as shown in the photo at near left.

Pounce with sponge. Begin in an upper corner and gently pounce the sponge repeatedly against the wall (bottom right photo). Overlap each impression, and rotate your hand at the wrist with each dab for a random pattern. As your sponge becomes drier, reload and repeat, working in roughly 2-foot-square sections. For even more dimension, consider sponging on a second glaze coat color. Allow ample time for your first glaze coat to dry before you begin.

Stenciling

TOOLS

- Stencil
- Level or chalk line
- Laser level (optional)
- Dauber

Stenciling is an easy way to add a theme to a room. Patterns are varied and range from the Arts & Crafts motif shown here to animals, flowers, landscapes—you name it. Most stencil pattern templates are cut into flexible plastic sheets that clean up quickly. The paint is generally flat and usually involves two or more colors. The tool of choice for applying stencil paint is a foam dauber like the one shown in the top photo on page 146. Stenciling supplies can be found at most crafts stores.

Reference lines. Stenciling requires moving a pattern template around the perimeter of a room. For the pattern to look continuous, the template must be positioned level around the room as it's moved. This means you'll need some kind of a reference for positioning the template. You could snap a chalk line, but then you'd be faced with finding a way to remove blue chalk from your walls. Some stencilers draw a light pencil line to serve as a reference. The method we've found that works best is to use a laser level (bottom left photo). These are becomingly increasingly inexpensive and can be rented at most home and rental centers. The big advantage of a laser level is that it shoots a perfectly level line along a wall without leaving any marks.

Position the stencil. Position your stencil on the wall so that its bottom edge is aligned with your reference line. Then use painter's tape to secure it temporarily to the wall, as shown in the bottom right photo. Take care to ensure that the stencil lies flat on the wall; otherwise paint will sneak under it, ruining the pattern. Most stencils have a couple of small reference holes near the bottom edge. Lightly mark these with a pencil—you'll use these to align the stencil after you've finished painting the first pattern.

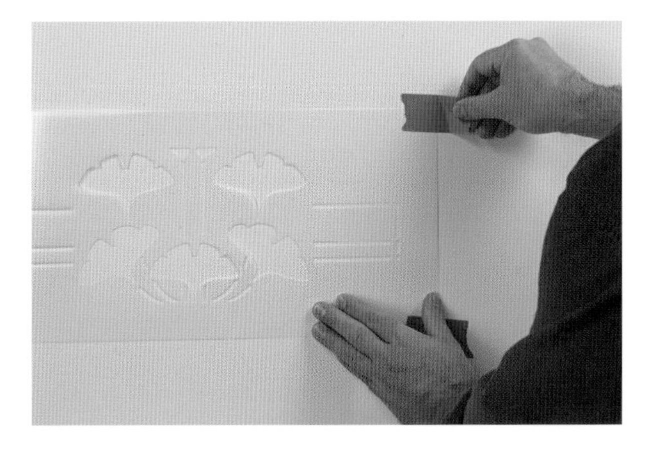

Apply first color. With the stencil in place, you can apply your first color. Pour a bit of paint into a small cup and dip the end of your foam dauber into it. Blot off the excess with a paper towel, and then apply paint to the desired portions of the stencil by gently tapping the end of the dauber on the wall as shown in the top photo. If necessary, use your other hand to press the stencil flat against the wall as you paint. Repeat this for all the similar paint sections.

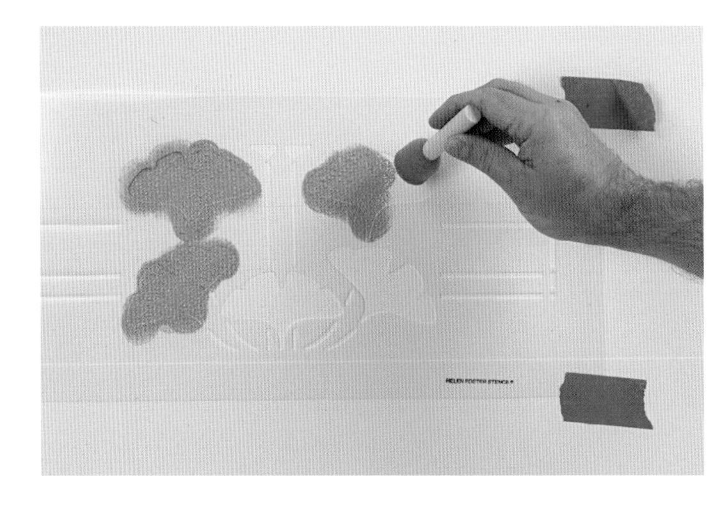

Apply second color. Clean off your dauber—or better yet, have a couple of these on hand—and apply the second color to the stencil (middle photo). Repeat for all similarly painted sections, and switch to another color if needed. Continue painting and switching colors until the entire pattern is painted.

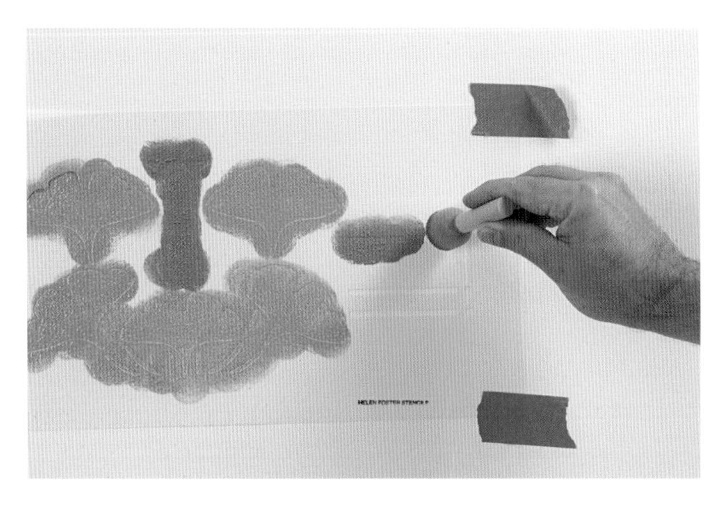

Move pattern and repeat. Now carefully peel off the painter's tape and gently lift the stencil away from the wall. Place the stencil on a flat surface, and wipe off both the front and the back of the stencil with clean paper towels. When the first pattern you painted has dried, move the stencil over. Take care to align the stencil with the reference lines and marks you made earlier, as shown in the bottom photo. Then tape it in place and paint the pattern. Repeat for the entire wall.

Stripping Wallpaper

TOOLS

- Garden sprayer
- Perforating tool
- Bucket and sponge

When old wallpaper needs to go, it's time to strip it off. How you strip it will depend on the wallpaper type and how it's glued to the wall. Many newer wallpapers are "strippable"; that is, they can literally just be peeled off the walls. Older, pasted-on wallpapers can be removed by breaking down the glue. This is done by first perforating the wallpaper (see below) and then spraying on a removal solution. If you are planning on repapering the walls, you can paper over the old wallpaper as long as it's in good condition, is firmly bonded to the wall, and is relatively smooth.

Perforate the paper. In most cases, you'll need to perforate the wallpaper so the solution can dissolve the wallpaper adhesive. To check this, wet the paper with a sponge. If it soaks in, you don't need to perforate. If it doesn't, the paper is coated and needs perforating. This entails punching tiny holes in the wallpaper with the aid of a perforating tool (often referred to by the brand name Paper Tiger). Just rub the tool on the wall in a circular motion as if you were washing it (top left photo).

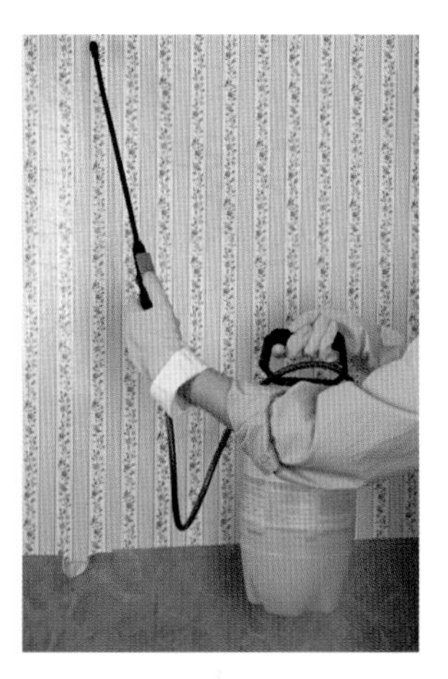

Spray on solution. There are a few things to do before you spray on the remover solution. Cover any furniture and the floor with drop cloths, seal electrical switches and receptacles with masking tape, and lay old towels at the base of the wall to collect runoff. The best tool for applying the solution is an ordinary garden sprayer. Follow the manufacturer's mixing instructions and fill the sprayer. Spray on generously to wet the paper (top right photo). Wait 15 minutes and spray on a second coat.

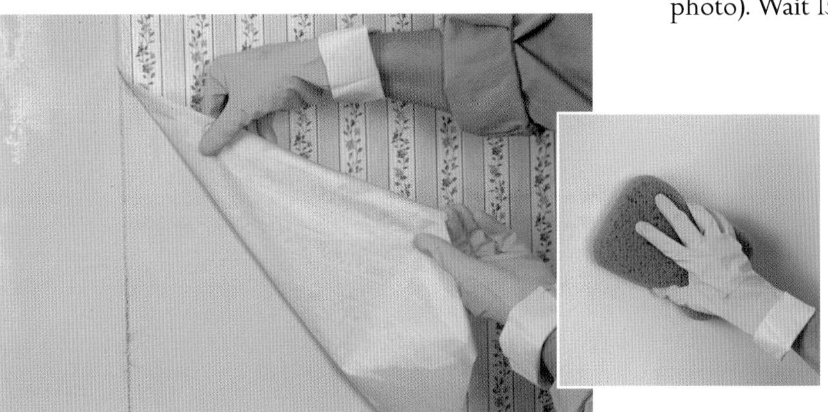

Wait and peel. When you've waited the recommended time, try to peel off the paper. If the solution has done its work, the paper will peel right off (bottom left photo). If it doesn't, apply additional coats as needed. When all the paper is removed, wash the wall with clean water (inset).

Wallpapering a Wall

TOOLS

- Tape measure
- Wallpaper tray
- Bucket and sponge
- Wallpaper brush
- Seam roller
- Level and straightedge
- Wide-blade putty knife
- Utility knife and scissors

If the walls in the room you're making over are in poor shape—dings, dents, and stains—wallpaper may be the way to go as it will hide all of these. Also, wallpaper is a great choice if you're looking to add design and texture to the walls. The number of patterns and textures available is staggering. Now, hanging wallpaper is more complicated than painting, but it's fairly straightforward and easy work—it just takes a bit longer. Also, keep wallpaper jobs simple by always using prepasted paper. The variety that requires paste is a real hassle to work with.

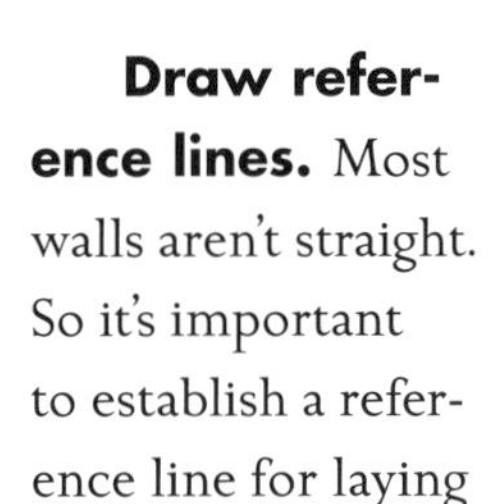

Wall prep. Even though you'll be covering up dings and dents, you'll still need to prepare the walls as you would for painting, except that you don't have to worry about hiding stains—the paper will do that. Once the room is ready, set up a workstation. A 2×4-foot piece of 3/4" plywood on a set of sawhorses works well (bottom left photo). Cover the plywood with a plastic drop cloth and have plenty of towels on hand for water spills.

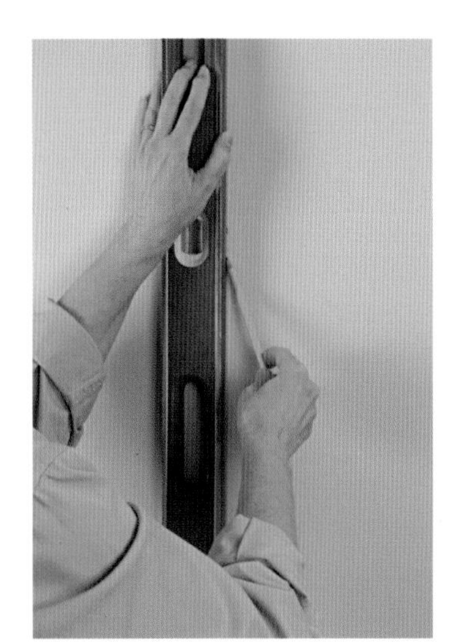

Draw reference lines. Most walls aren't straight. So it's important to establish a reference line for laying the first strip of wallpaper. Begin at the least conspicuous corner of the room, and press a 4-foot level up against the wall as shown in the far right photo above. Use a pencil to draw a plumb line. If you're planning on using different patterns for the top and bottom of the wall (as shown here), measure up the desired height and use a level to mark a reference line around the perimeter of the room.

Cut paper to length. Now measure from the top to the bottom of the wall and cut your first strip to this length plus 4" to 6" extra, as shown in the top right photo. You'll trim this to final length once the paper has been hung. For successive strips with a patterned paper, follow the manufacturer's measuring and cutting directions for how much extra to add for pattern-matching.

Wet the paper and book. With the strip cut to length, the next step is to wet the paper and book it (if necessary). Some wallpapers require some soak time before they're hung—check your directions for how long you should keep the wallpaper submerged in the tray. Other papers must be "booked" for a certain time to allow the paste to activate. This just means folding the strip back on itself so the paste sides come together (inset).

Hang paper and smooth it out. When you've waited for the paper to soak or book, grip the paper by the top edge and take it to the wall. Start at the ceiling and allow a 1" overlap. Align the strip with the reference line you drew earlier, and press it into the wall with the palms of your hand. Then use a brush or a sponge to smooth out the paper and remove any air pockets. Start at the top and use downward strokes, checking constantly to make sure the edge of the strip is still aligned with the pencil line. Brush air pockets out toward the edges. If you encounter a large wrinkle that can't be brushed out, peel off the strip and rehang it.

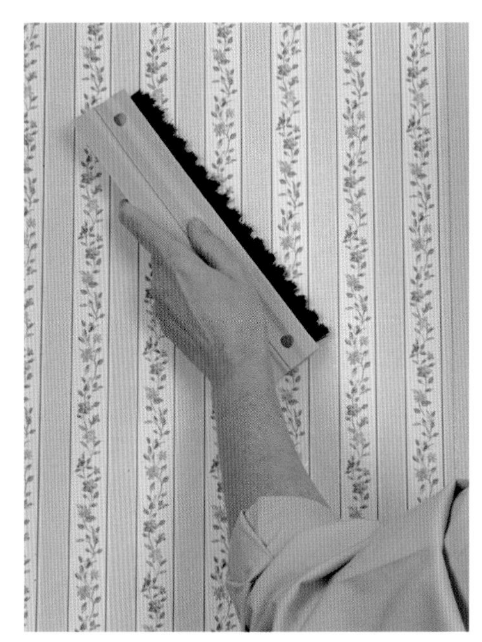

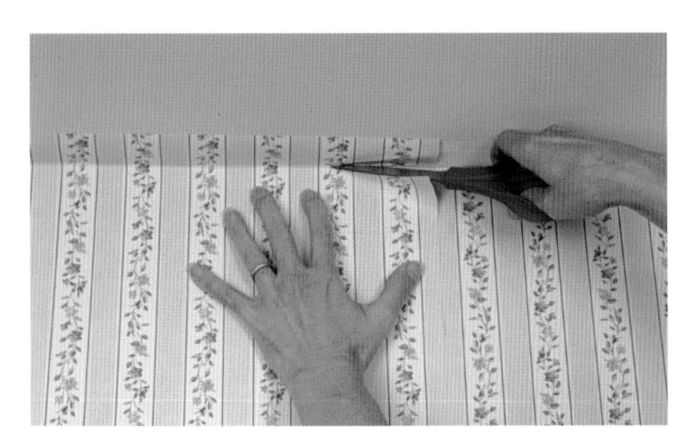

Trimming the strip to final length. To trim the paper to final length, first press the paper into the corner with a wide-blade putty knife. Then peel it back, cut it with scissors at the fold that you made with the knife, and press the paper back in place. To cut around electrical receptacles, first cut a small "X" with a utility knife. Then use scissors to cut out a rectangular area no larger than the box. Continue hanging strips until the walls are covered.

Roll the seams. The seams where the edges of wallpaper meet need a little extra attention to lie flat and stay flat. After you've hung all the paper, go back around the room and roll all the seams with a plastic seam roller, as shown in the photo at right. Don't press hard here: You're just trying to press the paper into the adhesive and wall to get a good bond.

SEPARATING PATTERNS WITH MOLDING

If your wallpapering plans call for different papers on the top and bottom of the wall, consider using molding to separate the two. The molding will cover any inconsistencies and add a nice finishing touch to the wall.

Level molding. To add a decorative molding, start by using a 4-foot level to mark a reference line where you'll align the bottom of the molding. Do this around the entire perimeter of the room.

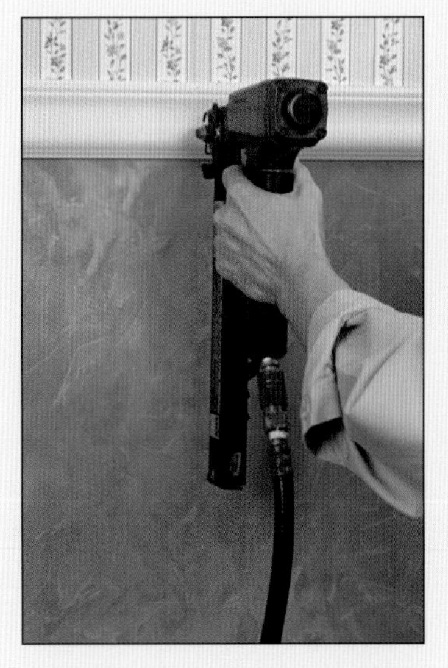

Attach painted molding. Before you attach the molding, it's best to paint it first. Then use a stud finder to locate and mark the wall studs. Attach the molding to the wall studs with brads (if you have access to an air nailer, this is the best tool for the job). Set the heads below the surface, and fill all nail holes with putty.

Wallpaper Border

TOOLS

- Wallpaper tray or bucket
- Sponge or wallpaper brush
- Utility knife or scissors
- Tape measure

A wallpaper border, whether at the top or midsection of a wall, is an excellent way to dress up a room. Borders let you easily and inexpensively add a theme to a room or simply tie all the design elements of the room together, as shown in the top photo. Unlike standard wallpaper, which requires a lot of cutting and careful positioning, the narrow depth of a border allows for fuss-free installation.

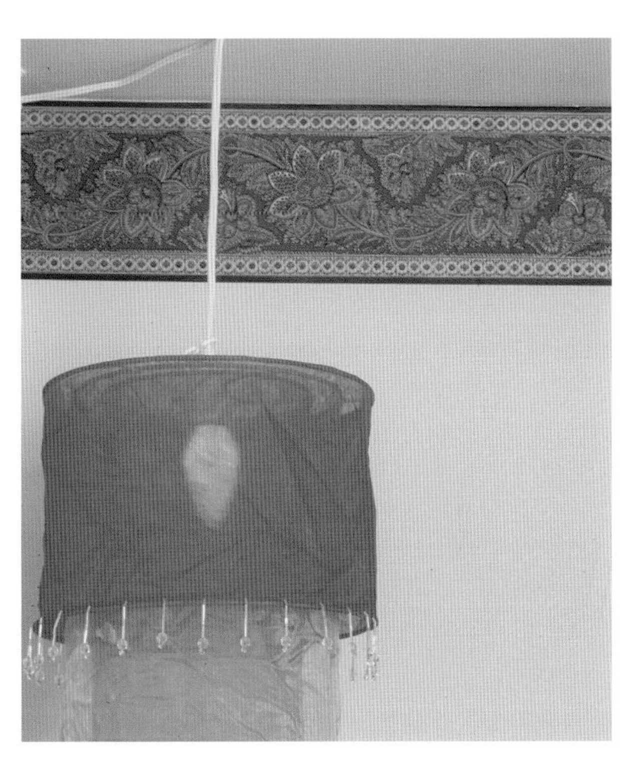

Wet the paper. To hang a wallpaper border, start by cutting a strip to fit the length of the wall. Then roll it up and submerge it in a bucket or a wallpaper tray. Hold it under the water the recommended time and then slowly pull it out, allowing the excess water to run back into the bucket (bottom left photo).

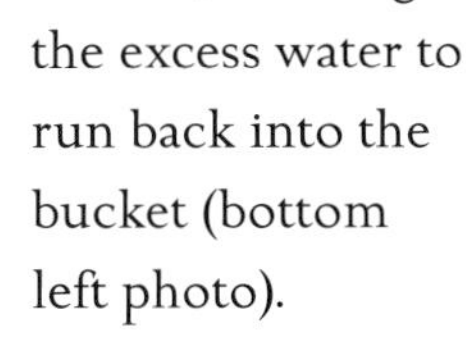

Book it if necessary. When you have pulled out the entire border, book it if the manufacturer recommends it. Booking is simply folding the border back onto itself so the pasted sides come together, as shown in the bottom right photo. Booking is used to allow the adhesive to activate without drying out. Let the border rest the recommended time. Then peel the ends apart and take the border over to the wall you're working on.

Apply the border. Press the border in place so the top edge is flush with the junction of the wall and the ceiling, as shown in the top left photo. If this junction is uneven, slide the border up or down until it's level and until there are no kinks or creases in the border. Because border strips are narrow and tend to be long, it's best to have a helper on hand to hold one end of the border as you hang it. Press the border in place with the palms of your hands or a wallpaper brush.

Sponge out air pockets. With the border in place, go back over it with a damp sponge to work out any air pockets. Start in the center of the border and work your way toward the ends, taking care to wipe away any excess paste that may squeeze out from under the border, as shown in the lower left photo. Rinse your sponge frequently to prevent paste from building up on the border or on your wall.

Overlap at corners. When you come to an inside corner, trim your first border so it runs onto the adjacent wall 1/2". Then hang the next border strip on the adjacent wall starting in the corner, taking care to match the pattern. Although this method takes more time than simply allowing a longer strip to continue around the corner, it guarantees that the paper will fit snugly into the corner (photo below). This prevents air pockets from forming, which frequently occurs when a longer strip is allowed to continue onto the adjacent wall.

Wainscoting

TOOLS

- Prybar
- Wide-blade putty knife
- Stud finder
- Level or laser level
- Circular or hand saw
- Hammer and nail set
- Air nailer (optional)

Wainscoting is short boards that are attached, usually vertically, to the lower half of a wall. This not only provides protection to the wall, but it also gives a room a rich finishing touch. In years past, installing wainscoting meant using wood panels that were held in place with rails and stiles—something that required advanced woodworking skills.

Fortunately, this project is much easier now because of new wainscoting products. These new wainscoting "systems" utilize fit-together panels that are machined on the ends to fit into matching base and cap moldings; see the drawing below. This makes installing wainscoting a simple process that can easily be accomplished in one weekend.

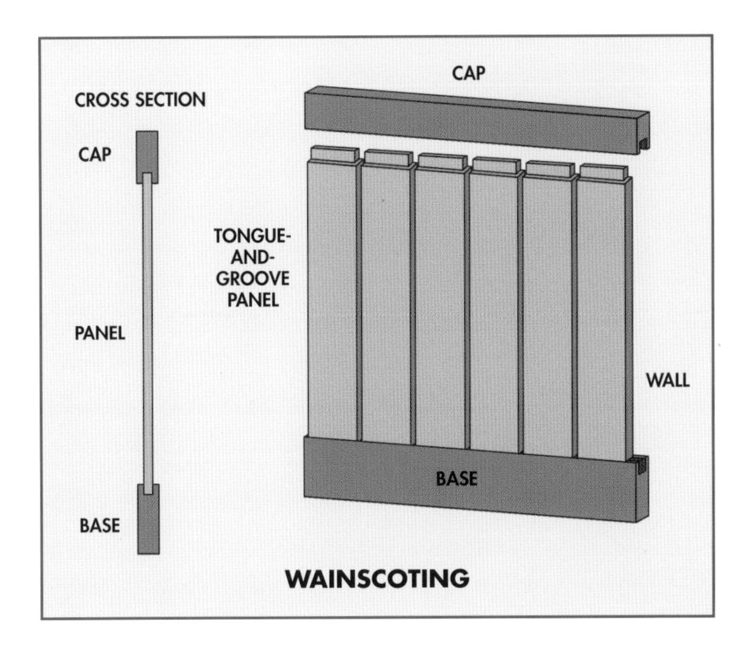

Prepare the room. To prepare a room for wainscoting, start by removing any receptacle and switch covers that will be affected by the wainscoting. Then, using a wide-blade putty knife to protect the wall, pry off the baseboard molding around the perimeter of the room with a prybar, as shown in the bottom photo.

Locate the wall studs. The next step is to locate the wall studs. These will be used to nail in place any panels that go over a stud, but more importantly, to attach the base and cap moldings securely to the wall. Use an electronic stud finder to locate these, and then mark each location with a pencil as shown in the top photo.

Install the base. With the room prepped, you can begin installing the wainscoting. Start by attaching the base molding to the wall at each of the marked stud locations, as shown in the middle photo. Check this with a level as you install it to make sure it creates a level foundation for the wainscoting panels. Cut the base as needed when you encounter corners, and work your way around the room.

Install first piece. When all the base molding is in place, you can add the panels. With most systems, these simply slip into a groove in the top edge of the base molding. Since the panels are tongue-and-grooved together and are also held in place with the cap molding, you don't need to try to affix each piece to the wall. Occasionally check the panels with a small level to make sure they're going in plumb (photo above); adjust as necessary.

Continue adding panels. Keep adding panels, attaching them to the wall whenever the panel sits over a wall stud, as shown in the top photo. Drive a nail through the panel and into the stud. If you want, you can run a small bead of construction adhesive behind each panel before placing it on the wall, but this shouldn't be necessary—and it'll make removal much more complicated. If you encounter any electrical receptacles or switches, mark and cut the panels as needed to wrap around the electrical box.

Install the cap molding. When all the panels are in place, add the cap molding. The bottom edge of this should be grooved (or rabbeted as shown in the drawing below) to fit over the panels. Set the molding in place and check it with a level before securing it to the wall studs with nails, as shown in the middle right photo. Continue adding cap molding until the wainscoting is complete. Then go around the room and fill in any nail holes with putty; sand flush when dry.

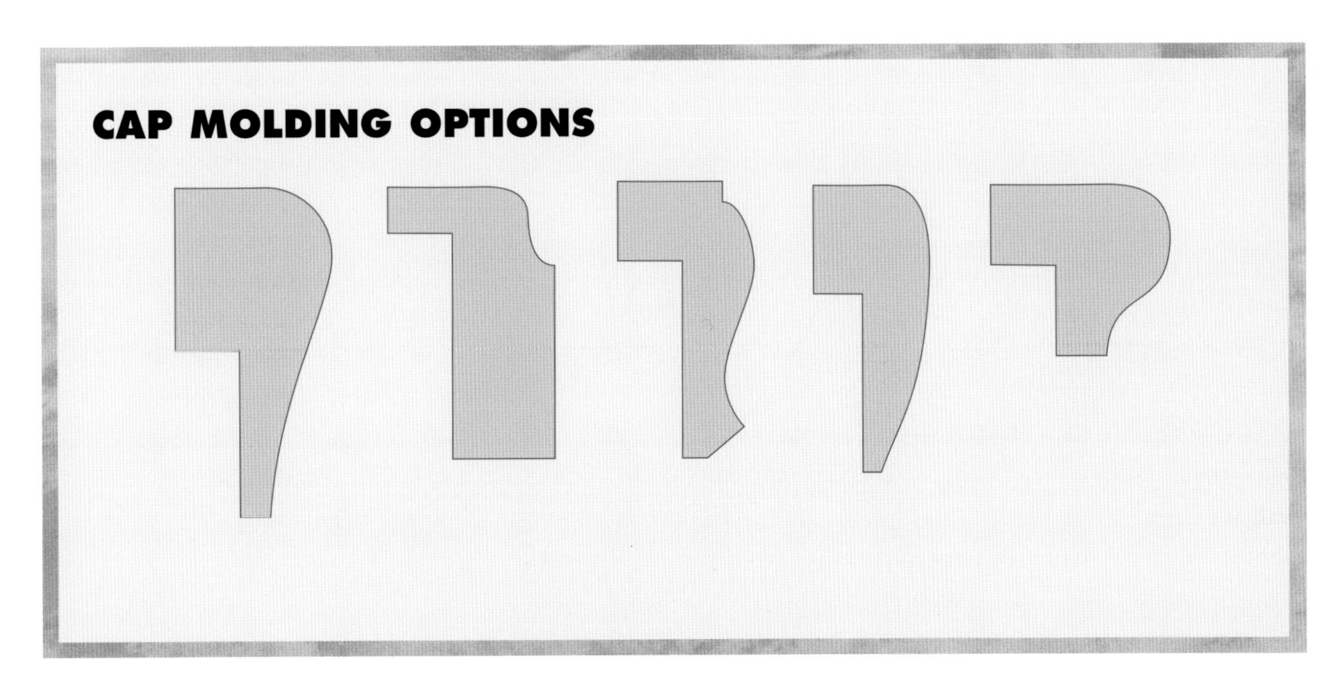

Installing Chair Rail

TOOLS

- Level and tape measure
- Chalk line and stud finder
- Putty knife
- Hand saw and miter box
- Power miter saw (optional)
- Hammer and nail set
- Air nailer (optional)

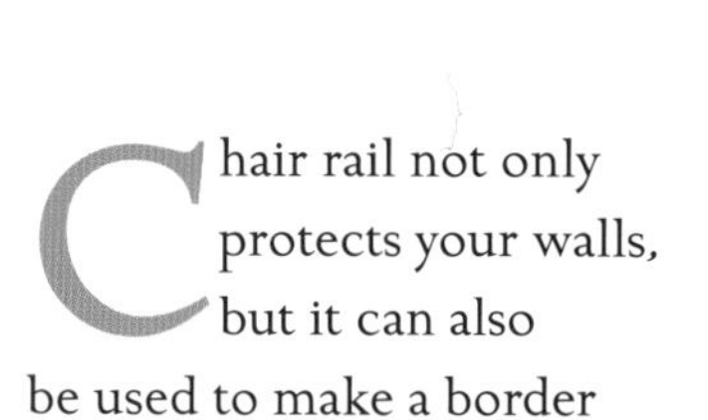

Chair rail not only protects your walls, but it can also be used to make a border between top and bottom wall expanses. Many homeowners like to dress the walls above and below the chair rail differently. So, you could paint the sections of the wall different colors, or wallpaper one section and paint the other. If you are planning to paint or wallpaper the room where you'll be installing the chair rail, do so now before installing the chair rail. You can purchase premade chair rail in a variety of shapes (see the drawing at right), or you can develop your own profile by building up the molding using several pieces; see the bottom drawing on page 157.

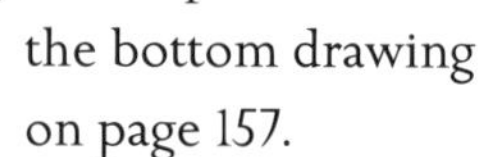

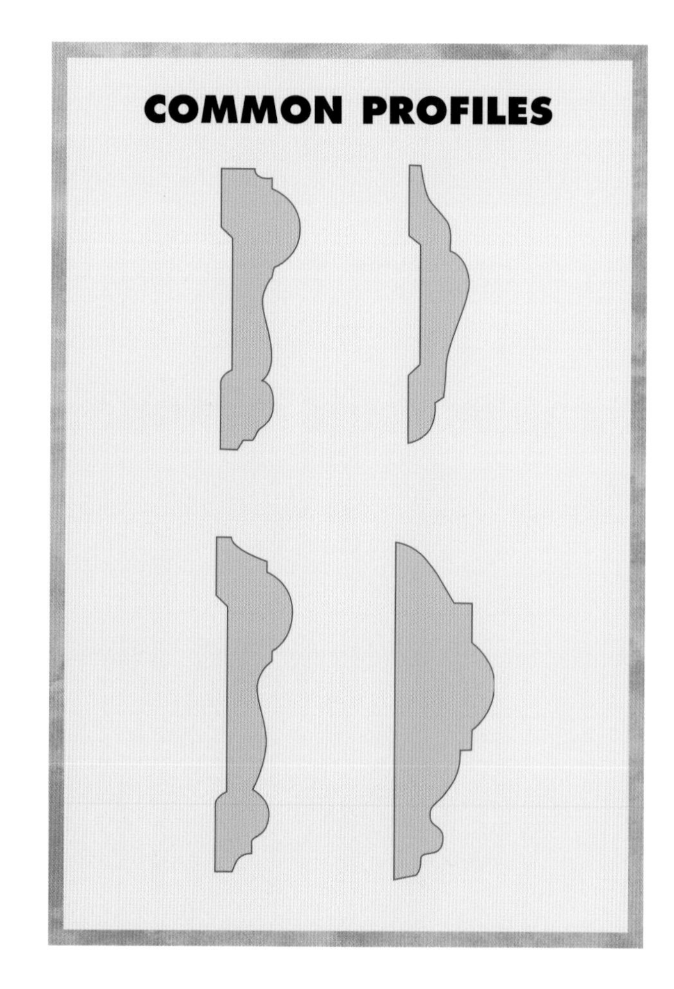

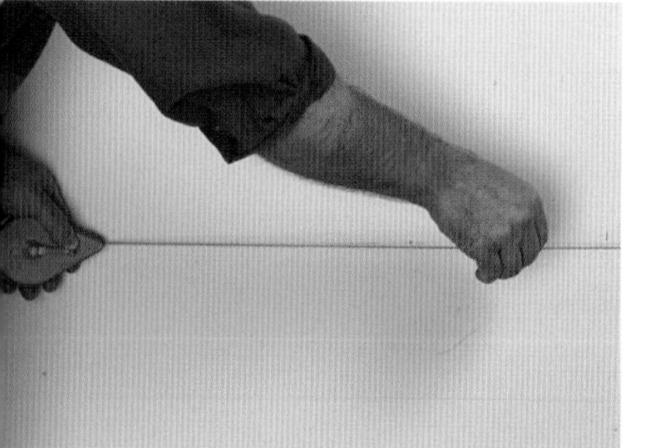

Locate and mark height. Chair rails are typically installed 32" to 36" above the floor. Measure this distance around the room and mark it by snapping a chalk line, as shown in the bottom photo.

Locate studs. After you've marked your reference line, use an electronic stud finder to locate the wall studs in the room, as shown in the top left photo. Use a pencil to mark each location. This is where you'll secure the chair rail to the wall.

Attach at studs. Cut your first piece of molding and position it so its bottom edge aligns with the chalk line you snapped earlier. Having a helper to hold the long strips of chair rail will make this job go a lot quicker. When aligned, secure the chair rail to the wall at each stud location with a 2"-long finish nail (an air nailer will make quick work of this job; these can be rented at most home centers and rental centers).

If you're running the chair rail around the room, you'll need to either miter or cope the ends to fit into the corners. When all the chair rail is in place, go back and conceal any nail holes with putty. Once dry, sand the putty smooth.

BUILT-UP MOLDINGS

½" CORE-BOX BIT
OR
¼" COVE BIT
⅛" ROUND-OVER
¾" HALF-ROUND
¼" × 1¼"
½" × 3" STOCK

¼" ROUNDOVER
¼" × 1¼"
¼" VEINING BIT
⅛" × ¾"
⅛" ROUND-OVER
½" × 3" STOCK

Joan Miró

WINDOWS & DOORS

Possibly the most fundamental makeover maneuver is to improve walls with paint or wallpaper. Within just hours, you can change the mood of a room, shrink or enlarge the visual space, hide flaws or stains, coordinate with your furnishings—and all at fairly low cost, with no more than average skills. No wonder it's the most popular home improvement around. And no wonder, too, that many homeowners mix and match surface treatments for more interesting effect. You might add wainscoting around the bottom half of a room, for example, and paper the top half—or sponge-paint the upper half and top it off with a wallpaper border. Alternatively, a chair rail can help break up a large wall surface and give you two different "canvases," above and below the rail, for your special effects. So next time, why not go beyond the fundamentals—after all, they're your walls, so make them over your way.

Acrylic Block Window

TOOLS

- Stud finder, level, and tape measure
- Circular, drywall, and reciprocating saws
- Framing square and chalk line
- Hammer and nail set
- Electric drill and bits
- Caulking gun
- Utility knife

If you want to bring in light while still preserving privacy, acrylic block windows are among the best ways to accomplish both goals. They are perfect for letting light into a dark room while still keeping the rooms separate. To install a block window, you'll need to build a rough opening in the wall to accept the unit. In most cases, this opening should be 1/2" to 3/4" wider and taller than the window you're installing. This leaves room to insert the window, then shim it level and plumb before fastening it to the framing (consult the manufacturer's instruction sheet for the recommended gap). For the most part, framing window openings in interior walls is fairly straightforward. Exterior walls, on the other hand, pose a challenge—you will, after all, be knocking a hole in the side of your home. Granted, this can be nerve-wracking, even for an experienced do-it-yourselfer, and may be best left to a window contractor.

Remove wall covering on one side of wall. In order to frame a rough opening for a window, you'll need to start by removing the interior wall covering to expose the existing framing so that you can modify it, as shown in the bottom left photo. See page 47 for more on framing windows.

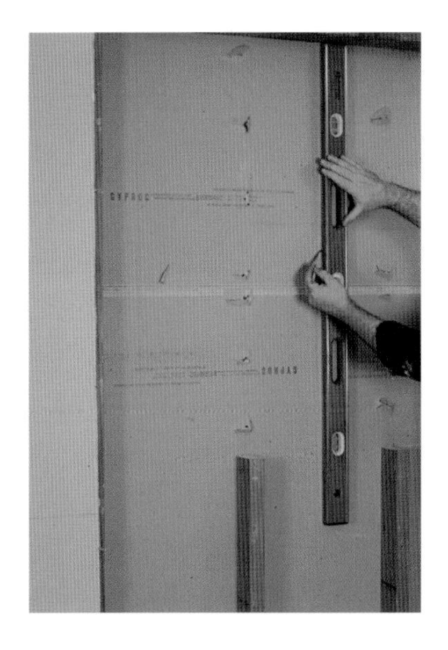

Remove necessary studs. If you need to remove more than one wall stud in any exterior wall or in an interior load-bearing wall to make way for a new rough opening, you'll need to build and install temporary supports to bear the load until the new framing is in place. With supports in place, cut any studs that need to be removed. A reciprocating saw will quickly zip through the studs and fits easily between them, as does a hand saw or "toolbox" saw. With leather gloves on for protection, grip each stud, bend it back toward you, and twist, as shown in the top left photo. In most cases, this will release the stud from the nails holding it in place. If not, lever it back and forth while twisting at the same time. Stubborn studs may need a prybar or crowbar to convince them to give up their grip.

Lay out window on wall. Once the studs are removed, carefully lay out the rough opening on the inside of the wall with a tape measure, level, and pencil, as shown in the top right photo.

Frame opening. Start framing the opening by cutting and installing the king studs that run between the sole plate and top plate. Then cut a pair of jack studs and nail these to the king studs. Next, measure the span between the king studs and cut the header components to length (typically two pieces of 2-by material with a layer of 1/2" plywood sandwiched in the middle); screw or nail them together. Next, position the header and toenail it to the jack and king studs. Finally, install cripple studs between the header and top plate and the windowsill and sole plate (middle photo). Face-nail one cripple stud to each king stud, and then space the remaining cripple studs 16" on center. Note: Now it's safe to remove any temporary supports.

Cut through opposite wall. With the rough opening framed, you can cut through the opposite wall. For interior walls, this can usually be done with a drywall saw, as shown in the bottom photo. For exterior walls, it's best to drive 16d nails through the exterior wall at each inside corner of the opening; then run a chalk line around the nails and snap the line to define the opening. Now you can cut through the exterior from the outside with a circular saw or reciprocating saw. Note: If your exterior is covered with vinyl or clapboard siding, it's best to remove this before cutting through. Then you can cut the siding to fit tight around the window once it's installed.

Test the fit. With the framing in place and the wall coverings removed on both sides, take the time to test the fit of the window, as shown in the top right photo. Make sure that there's the recommended clearance on all four sides for shimming. If you're installing the window in an exterior wall, you'll need to create a weatherproof seal around the opening. There are a number of self-adhesive and staple-on membranes designed specifically for this. They're made to slip under the siding and wrap around the framing of the rough opening. It's also a good idea to run a generous bead of silicone around the exterior perimeter of the rough opening before inserting the window.

Secure window via nailing flanges. If the window fits properly, slip it into the rough opening and shim it so it's level and plumb. Secure the window to the framing. For the window shown here, this is done on the exterior by driving nails through a nailing flange into the framing (bottom left photo). Other windows may attach differently.

Add the wall covering. All that's left is to install wall covering to conceal the framing. For interior walls this usually means installing drywall, as shown in the bottom right photo. If you installed the window in an exterior wall, reinstall the exterior siding by cutting it to fit snugly against the new window. Then run a generous bead of silicone around the perimeter of the window where it contacts the siding to create a watertight seal. Finally, cut trim to match your existing house trim and nail it in place. Set the nails, fill with putty, and paint to match.

Acrylic Door Insert

TOOLS

- Tape measure and straightedge
- Screwdriver
- Circular or saber saw
- Hammer and punch
- Drill and bits (optional)
- Hand saw (optional)
- Rubber mallet

Because acrylic block panels weigh so much less than glass and can be made with thinner profiles, they can actually be inserted into doors to allow light to travel through your home, flowing from room to room. The panel shown here is manufactured by Hy-Lite Products, Inc. (www.hy-lite.com). Panel inserts are available for both interior and exterior doors and come with either 6" or 8" blocks. Block color options include clear and green, and patterns can be wave, frosted wave, and cross rib. Trim choices include oak, pine, bright gold, bright bronze, bright copper, chrome, polished black, and white (shown here).

What makes these so easy to install is that the blocks are preassembled into a single unit. All you have to do is cut a matching hole in your door and attach the insert with the hardware provided. The panel insert is attached to a two-part keeper frame: One side is permanently attached to the panel; the other side screws in place, and the screws are concealed with a vinyl cover (see the drawing at right).

Remove door. To install an acrylic door insert, start by removing the door you'll be working on. Tap the hinge pins out with a hammer and a punch, and lift them out. Then lift off the door (top right photo) and set it on a pair of workhorses covered with an old blanket or towels to protect the door from scratches. Unpack the door insert from its shipping materials, pry off the vinyl screw covers, and set them aside. Then remove the screws holding the keeper frame sections in place; set these aside for use later.

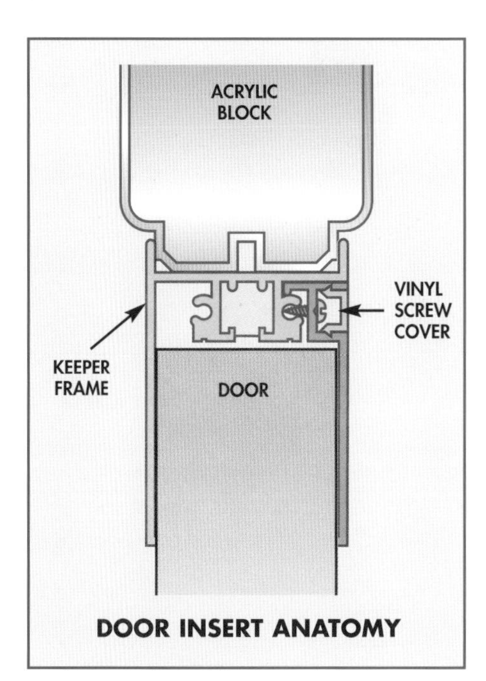

DOOR INSERT ANATOMY

Lay out opening on door. If the door you're working on is flat, measure down from the top edge and draw a horizontal line. Then measure the door from side to side and mark the center on the line you just drew. If your door insert came with a template, align the centerline on the template with the mark you just made and center the template from side to side on the door. Then trace around the template with a pencil. If your insert didn't come with a template, measure the insert. Then, starting at the centerpoint on the line you drew, lay out the insert shape on the door. A simple way to do this is to lay the insert centered on the door and run masking tape around its perimeter to define the opening, as shown in the top photo.

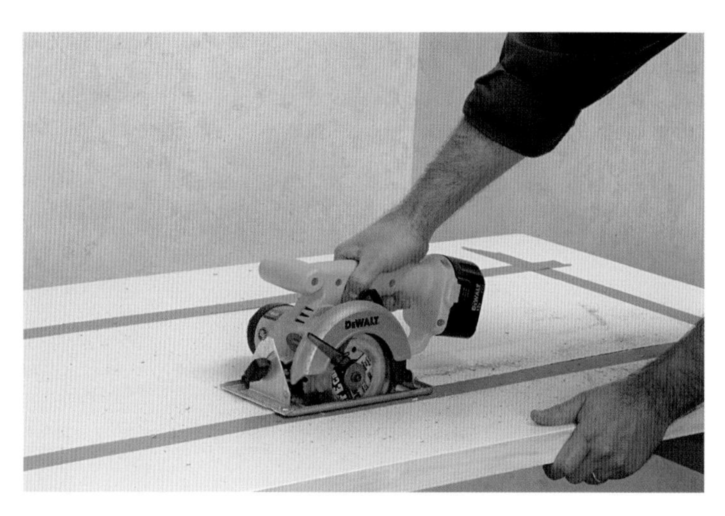

Cut out opening. Once the opening for the door insert is laid out, you can cut it. There are a number of ways to do this. One is to start by drilling 3/8" access holes in each corner and then use a saber saw to cut out the opening. Another method is to make a series of plunge cuts with a circular saw; a cordless trim saw like the one shown in the middle photo is perfect for this. In either case, you can protect the door surface from scratches by applying a layer of masking tape to the base of the saw before cutting the opening.

Finish cuts at corners (if necessary). If you used a circular saw to make the long cuts for the opening, you'll need to finish the cuts at the corners with a hand saw, as shown in the bottom photo. That's because the curved blade can't make a completely vertical cut, as is possible with a saber saw.

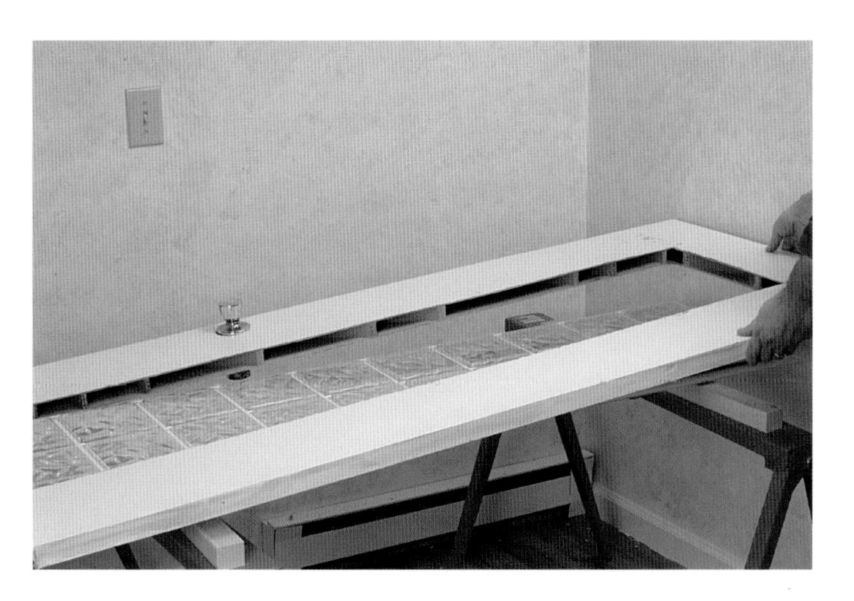

Position insert in opening. With the opening cut, set the door aside momentarily and position the door insert on the sawhorses with the removed keeper frame side up. Then carefully place the door over the insert as shown in the top photo. Align the door so the insert is centered in the opening from side to side and from top to bottom.

Secure with screws. Reinstall the keeper frame pieces, making sure to align the holes in the door insert (middle photo). Usually, the keeper pieces will need to go on the same side from which they were removed. Start with the top keeper piece and install the screws. Then proceed to the bottom piece and the sides.

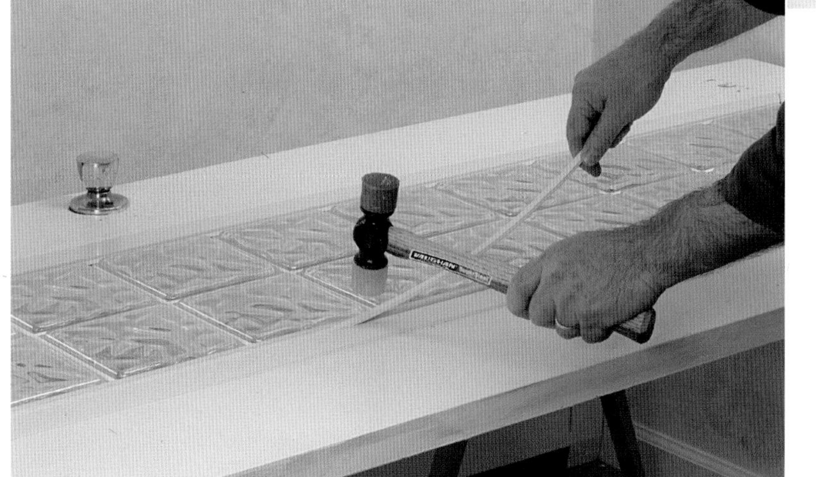

Tap on cover strip. Now that the door insert is secured in the door, you can add the vinyl strips that conceal the screws. These strips can be tapped into place using a soft-faced or rubber mallet as shown in the bottom photo. Finally, remount the door onto its hinges and tap in the hinge pins.

Removing a Door

TOOLS

- Hammer and cold chisel
- Wide-blade putty knives
- Reciprocating saw
- Screwdriver or driver/drill
- Cat's paw or prybar

If a new door is in your future, odds are you'll be replacing a door, not installing one where there previously wasn't a door—that rather ambitious project is generally best left to a professional. But replacing a door is a fairly simple task that can easily be accomplished by most homeowners. Measure your current door and purchase a replacement, keeping in mind which way the door opens and closes.

Pry off trim. The first step in removing a door is to pry off the existing trim on both sides of the door, as shown in the bottom left photo. How you do this will depend on whether or not you want to reuse the trim. If you're not planning on reusing it, a prybar like the one shown here will make quick work of the job. If, however, you want to salvage the trim, use a pair of wide-blade putty knives. Slip one knife, then the other, under the trim. The bottom knife will protect the wall covering while you gently pry off the trim with the other.

Remove hinge pins. Once the trim is removed, you can turn your attention to the door itself. Start by removing the hinge pins; it's usually best to start at the bottom hinge and work toward the top. Although most folks reach for a screwdriver and hammer to drive the pins out of the hinges, we recommend using a cold chisel and hammer instead, as shown in the top left photo. Some hinge pins can be extremely stubborn; the numerous hammer blows to a screwdriver will both mushroom the head and damage the tip.

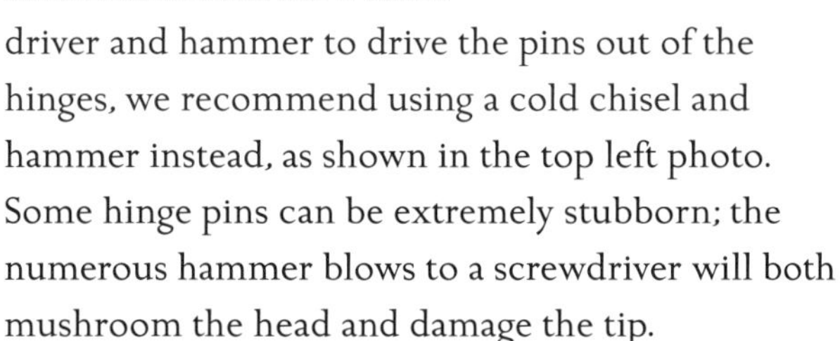

Remove door. When you've removed all of the hinge pins, you can detach the door. Swing the door open slightly to get a good grip, and lift the door up slightly and out—it should come away cleanly, as shown in the top right photo. If not, try pivoting either the top or bottom of the door away from the jamb to release it. Solid-core doors are surprisingly heavy, so consider having a helper on hand to detach and move the door.

Remove hinges. When most doors are installed, one screw on each hinge jamb is removed (usually the center one) and replaced with a longer screw. This longer screw will pass through the jamb and into the jack stud in the rough opening to firmly support the door. Instead of trying to cut through these screws in the next step, it's easier to remove them (top photo). If in doubt as to which hinge screws are the long ones, just remove them all.

Cut through nails and pull jamb nails. To release the door jamb from the frame opening, you'll need to cut through the nails that secure it to the framing members. The best tool for the job here is a reciprocating saw fitted with a demolition blade. Since these saws are powerful and can buck hard when they come in contact with a nail, it's important to press the cutting guide of the saw firmly against the wall as you make the cut, as shown in the photo at far left. An alternative to cutting the nails is to pry them out. You'll need a cat's paw for this, and a lot of patience (inset above).

Remove threshold and jamb. Once you've cut through all the nails, there's one more thing to do before you remove the jamb. If you're working on an exterior door, you'll need to unfasten the threshold from the subfloor; this usually entails removing a couple of screws. Now you should be able to pull the jamb out of the opening as shown in the bottom photo. Since you're likely to encounter nails that have been cut off, it's a good idea to protect your hands with leather gloves. Grip one of the side jambs firmly and give it a tug to pull it out.

Installing a New Door

TOOLS

- Hammer and nail set
- Caulking gun
- Staple gun (optional)
- Screwdriver
- Level and utility knife
- Driver/drill and bits

The impact of a new door on the look and feel of a room can be dramatic. For example, if you remove an exterior solid-core door with no windows and replace it with a new door that has windows (or cut art glass, as shown here), light will flood into the room, providing an entirely different ambiance. Before you install your new door, you'll need to first remove the old one; see pages 166–167 for step-by-step instructions on how to do this. If you're installing a new exterior door, the exterior brick molding may be preinstalled or you may have to attach it to the door jamb prior to installation. Brick molding is available precut and pre-primed. All you need do is mark a 1/8" reveal and nail the molding to the jamb.

Test the fit. Remove the packing materials from your new door and set it in the opening to check the fit as shown in the bottom photo. If the door does fit, check for clearance between the jambs and framing for the shims that you'll use later to level the door.

For exterior doors, apply a layer of roofing felt to the inside faces of the rough opening to protect them in case water ever seeps past the weather stripping or exterior caulking. Cut strips about 12" wide and work them under the siding, and then wrap them around to cover the framing members. Then staple the felt in place. Also, you'll want to install a drip cap above the door. A drip cap is a piece of extruded aluminum that's shaped like an "L." It's designed to slip under the siding, and a small lip on the front edge will direct water away from the door. Cut the drip cap to length, apply a bead of silicone caulk to the edge, and force it up between the siding and the roofing felt that you installed earlier.

Caulk the threshold. The final thing to do before installing an exterior door is to apply caulk between the threshold and the subfloor to keep out moisture. Use a high-quality silicone caulk and apply generously in a zigzag pattern, like the one shown in the top photo. Remember: It's a whole lot easier to wipe off excess caulk than it is to remove the door after it's been installed and apply more caulk when you discover that the threshold leaks.

Install the door. Now you can install the door. If it's an exterior door, consider adding a little bit more insurance against the elements—apply a bead of silicone caulk on the back side of the brick molding. This caulk will help fill any gaps between the brick molding and the roofing felt. Note: You'll also caulk around the brick molding later, once the door is completely installed. Lift the door up into position, taking care not to tear the roofing felt, and press it into the opening as shown in the middle photo.

Shim the door level and plumb. With the door in place, the next step is to add shims to level and plumb the door. Start by inserting shims behind each of the three hinges (bottom left photo), behind the opening for the plunger for the door lockset, and at the top and bottom of the latch side jamb. Also insert shims at the center and both ends of the head jamb. Insert the shims in pairs of opposing wedges, and adjust them until they solidly fill the gap between the jamb and the framing members.

Check for level and adjust. Next, hold a level up against one of the side jambs and check it for plumb (bottom right photo). Adjust the position of the shims until the jamb is plumb. Then move to the other side jamb and repeat the process. Finally, hold your level up against the head jamb to make sure it's level. If any of these are off, the door won't open or close properly. Take your time here and double-check everything one more time before proceeding to the next step.

Secure jamb to frame. When you're satisfied that the door is level and plumb, you can secure it to the door jamb (top photo). Your best bet here is a 2 1/2"- to 3"-long casing nail; use galvanized nails for exterior doors. Make sure to drive the nail through the jamb only where the shims are. The idea here is to drive the nail though the jamb and the shims into the framing members. This way the jamb will be fully supported. As you nail the jambs in place, check for plumb again with a level and adjust the shims as necessary.

Remove the retaining bracket. Although the door is firmly secured at this point, there are a few more things to do before it's really rock-solid. The first thing is to install long hinge screws. In order to access the hinge screws, the door must be opened. All manufacturers of prehung doors install some sort of hardware to keep the door closed until it's installed. This may be as simple as a nail driven through the jamb and into the door, or as fancy as a retaining bracket (like the one shown below). In either case, remove it so you can open the door.

Install long hinge screws. Most prehung doors come with three long hinge screws that are designed to pull the door jamb firmly into the framing members. The door hinges may or may not have an empty hole waiting for these. If not, you'll need to remove one screw from each jamb hinge and replace it with a longer screw. If your door didn't come with these, use 3"-long galvanized deck screws and drive one into each hinge, as shown in the bottom right photo.

Anchor brick molding. If you're installing an exterior door, now's the time to drive nails through the exterior brick molding and into the framing members (top left photo). Use hot-dipped galvanized casing nails, 2 1/2" to 3" in length. Drive the nails through the face of the brick molding and into the framing member about every 12" or so. Then go back and countersink each nail with a nail set and fill the holes with an exterior-grade putty.

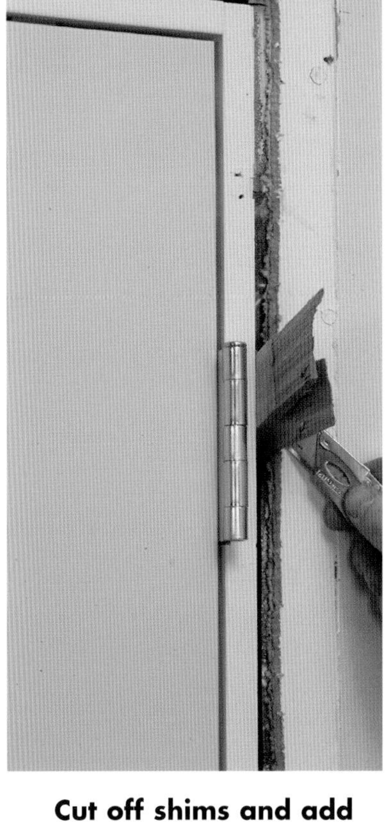

Caulk exterior. There's one more thing to do on exterior doors before moving inside, and that's to apply a bead of caulk around the perimeter of the brick molding as shown in the bottom photo. Use a high-quality paintable silicone caulk and apply a generous bead where the brick molding meets the siding. Fill in any gaps as needed with the caulk, and then go back over the caulk with a wet fingertip to smooth it out.

Cut off shims and add trim. On the inside of the door, cut off any protruding shims with a sharp utility knife as, shown in the top right photo. Then you can apply door trim. Finally, install the lockset of your choice and test the operation of the door. If all went well, it should open and close smoothly without binding and create a solid seal against the elements.

Installing Blinds

TOOLS

- Tape measure
- Driver/drill and bits
- Awl and screwdriver

For a simple way to add both light and privacy to a room, install some blinds. Mini-blinds like the ones shown here come in a wide variety of sizes and colors. They're available to fit most standard windows and are available in vinyl, aluminum, and wood; they can be either light-filtering or room-darkening. Blinds can be installed inside or outside the window frame. Inside mounting tends to provide more of a custom look, but outside mounting generally gives better light control.

To determine the size blinds you'll need, measure the opening. When mounting inside the frame, measure the width between the points where brackets will be placed—top, middle, and bottom. Record the narrowest of these measurements. Measure the length from the top inside casing to the sill. At least 1" of flat surface is needed on the inside casing to attach the brackets. For blinds mounted outside the frame, measure the overall width of the area to be covered. This measurement should overlap the window by at least 1 1/2" on each side and at least 3" above the window down to the bottom sill.

Locate the mounting brackets. Mini-blinds typically attach to the window frame via a pair of plastic or metal brackets designed to accept the top section of the blind. To locate these brackets on the inside of the frame, butt one bracket up against the side of the frame and use an awl to mark the mounting hole locations (bottom left photo). Simply insert the awl through the mounting hole and press to make a depression in the frame. You'll mark the other bracket location once you've installed the first bracket—this ensures that the blind will fit between the brackets.

Drill the mounting holes. With the mounting holes marked, they can now be drilled. Fit the recommended-sized drill bit in your drill, and drill through the window frame at each mounting hole location (bottom right photo).

Install the blinds. With both brackets in place, you can install the blinds. Simply slide one end into each bracket as shown in the top right photo. If the fit is too loose or too snug, remove the blinds and loosen the mounting screws on one bracket so they're friction-tight. Wiggle the bracket as needed and then retighten the screws. Check the blind again and repeat for the other bracket if this doesn't take care of the problem.

Attach the brackets. Now you can attach the mounting brackets. Use the screws provided and attach the mounting bracket to the window frame as shown in the top left photo. Next, temporarily place one end of the blinds in the bracket you just mounted and slip the other bracket over its opposite end. Hold the loose bracket in place against the window frame and mark its position with a pencil. Remove the blind, reposition the loose bracket so it's aligned with the mark you just made, and use an awl to mark the mounting hole locations. Drill these holes and then mount the bracket with the screws provided.

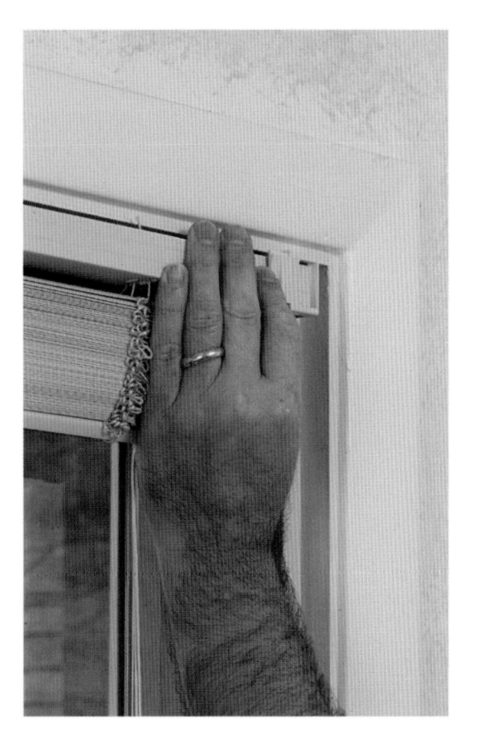

Add the caps. Most mini-blinds are held in place via a pair of caps that fit into the mounting brackets. These may be plastic or metal, and slide into grooves in the top and bottom front faces of the brackets. Simply slide them in place to secure the blinds as shown in the bottom photo.

Mounting Curtain Rods

TOOLS

- Electronic stud finder
- Tape measure
- Driver/drill and bits
- Screwdriver
- Level

Almost any room you make over will probably require new window treatments—often involving installing new rods to hold curtains. Unfortunately, many homeowners don't know how to mount rods securely because they aren't aware of the underlying framing that often makes this a very simple job. All windows are framed in a similar manner: A horizontal framing member called a header is installed to assume the load of the wall studs that were removed to create the window opening; see the drawing at right.

The header is supported by jack studs (also referred to as trimmer studs) that are attached to full-length wall studs known as king studs. The shorter studs that run between the header and the double top plate, or from the underside of the rough sill of a window to the sole plate, are called cripple studs. And these framing members are the best thing to screw into when mounting curtain rods. Hollow-wall fasteners aren't needed as long as you stay within the bounds of the framing.

Locate studs and header. The first step to mounting a curtain rod is to locate the framing members. You know already that they wrap around the opening, so locating them with an electronic stud finder is usually fairly simple, as shown in the top right photo. The question will be the size of the header. For exterior walls and load-bearing walls, the header will be 6" or wider; on non-load-bearing interior walls, the header may simply be a 2×4 on edge.

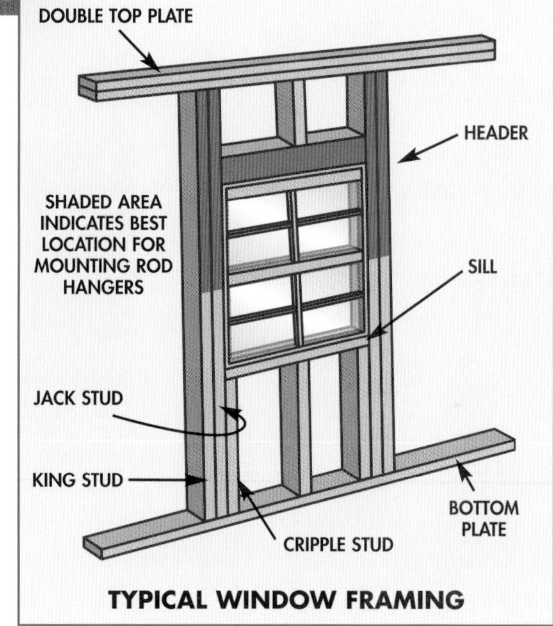

TYPICAL WINDOW FRAMING

Locate and drill bracket-mounting holes. Once you've located the framing members, measure down the desired height from the ceiling and position a bracket (inset). Mark the mounting hole locations with a pencil or awl, and remove the bracket. Fit the appropriate-sized bit for the mounting screws in the drill, and drill the mounting holes into the framing members as shown in the top left photo.

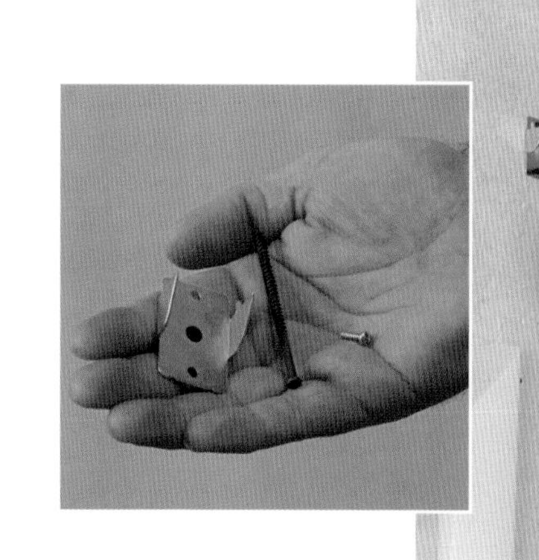

Attach the brackets. Now you can attach the mounting brackets. Unfortunately, the screws that are provided for most brackets aren't long enough to reach the framing members. A 1 1/2"- to 2"-long trim-head screw (like the one shown in the center inset photo) works best. Hold the bracket in place and drive screws into the framing members as shown in the far right photo.

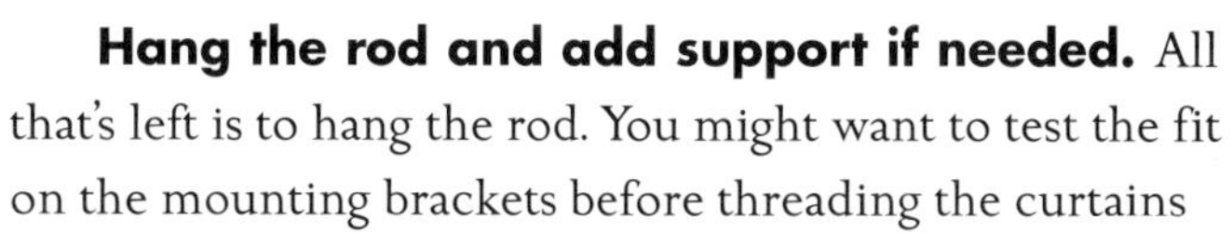

Hang the rod and add support if needed. All that's left is to hang the rod. You might want to test the fit on the mounting brackets before threading the curtains onto the rods. For rods that span wide expanses, you'll likely need a center support hook. Check with a level to make sure the rod isn't sagging, and mark the position for the hook (inset). Drill a pilot hole into the header and thread the hook into the hole. Slip the curtain rod onto the hook, and you're done.

WELCOME

LIVING SPACES ELECTRICAL

Don't let the chapter heading scare you off: Most of the projects here require just a modest skill level, and will help bring upgraded lighting to your makeover room. Yes, major electrical work is best left to a licensed contractor, but the tasks here can be done (with care, please) by just about anyone who can work a screwdriver and a circuit tester.

Would you like to add a dimmer switch to an existing light? Bring recessed lighting or track lighting to a room? Spotlight your collectibles with subtle, under-cabinet lighting? You'll see how to do all these jobs in this section. Since lighting can do so much for a room—show off a special feature, hide a design deficit, set a mood—it's well worth the time to top off your makeover with one of these projects. Illuminating your handiwork will bring that final "ta-daa!" to your moneysmart makeover.

Surface-Mount Wiring

TOOLS

- Driver/drill and bits
- Tape measure and level
- Hammer
- Wire stripper
- Diagonal cutters
- Screwdriver
- Hacksaw

Want to add a receptacle or a ceiling light and switch but hesitate at the thought of cutting holes in your walls? Consider surface-mount wiring. Surface-mount wiring attaches directly to an existing wall or ceiling; it's available in either metal or plastic. Although the metal type will stand up longer over time, it isn't as easy to work with as the plastic. Both types are paintable, and when painted the same color as the wall, will almost disappear.

To use surface-mount wiring, you'll first need to "tap" into an existing line. Then it's simply a matter of running lengths of metal or plastic channel or "raceway" to the desired location. Raceway is available in a variety of precut lengths, or you can cut it to a custom length with a hacksaw. Connectors, elbows, and boxes complete the run. Then all that's left is to run wire and hook up the new fixtures.

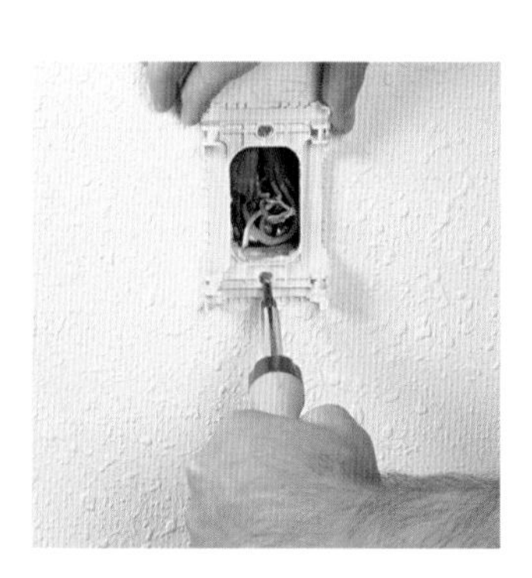

Convert existing box. Find the receptacle that's closest to where you want your new wiring. Turn off power to the receptacle at the breaker or fuse panel. Remove the old cover plate and receptacle. Then attach a "starter" box to the electrical box (bottom left photo). A starter box has a large rectangular hole in the plate that attaches to the box; this allows the wiring to pass into the new box.

Install raceway and boxes. The next step is to measure and cut lengths of raceway to reach the destination of the new box. Press-fit connectors and inside and outside elbows make this an easy task. Just make sure to subtract the length of the connector from the raceway before you cut it to length. Attach the raceway to the wall by screwing directly into studs, or drill holes for plastic anchors (top photo). Just like the raceway, surface-mount boxes are also attached to the wall either by screwing into studs or with plastic anchors. To use plastic anchors, position the back plate of the box where you want it and make a mark through the mounting holes in the back. Then drill holes, insert the plastic anchors, and screw the back plate to the wall.

Run wiring. Running wire through surface-mount raceways is simple. All you do is cut the wire to length plus 6" extra on each end for your electrical connections. Then place it in the raceway and thread the ends into the boxes, as shown in the bottom right photo. Most surface-mount systems come with snap-in flexible plastic clips that fit inside the track to hold the wiring in place.

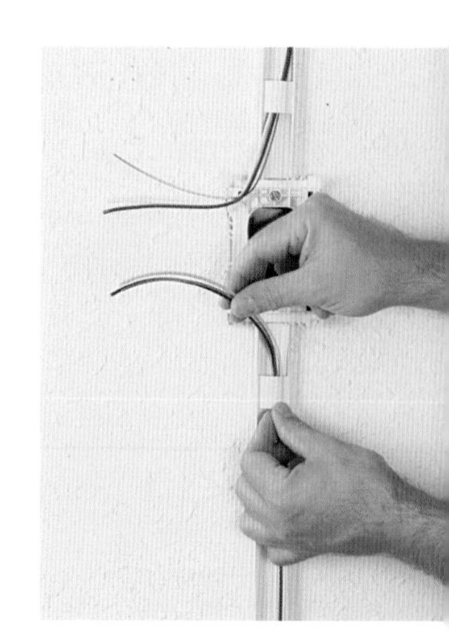

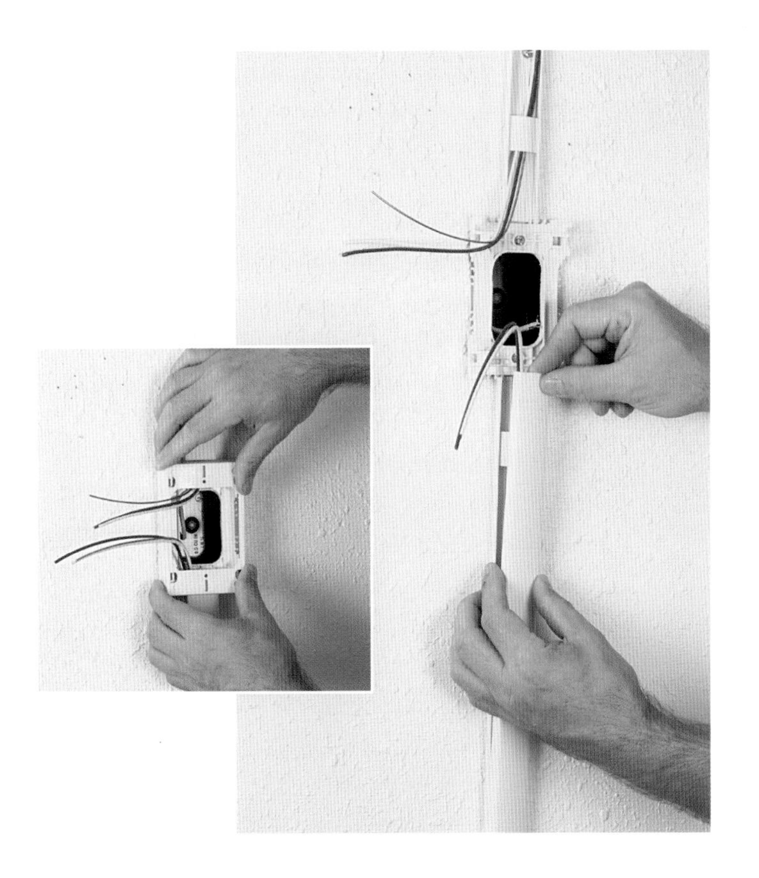

Install raceway covers and box covers. With the wiring in place, you can install the covers onto the raceway to conceal and protect the wiring. Both the metal and plastic varieties simply snap onto the raceway (top left photos). After you've installed all the covers on the raceways, you can add the covers to the electrical boxes. Here again, these simply snap into place.

Make electrical connections. Strip the ends of the wires you've run as needed to make your electrical connections. Use wire nuts to connect wires; when done, push the wiring back into the surface-mount boxes as shown in the top right photo. If you're installing receptacles or switches, you'll want to wire these now, too.

Add cover plates. Finally, you can add any cover plates to the surface-mount boxes, as shown in the bottom photo. If you've installed metal raceways, you may need to secure the raceways to the wall with metal straps that fit over the raceway. In most cases, you'll need to secure these to the wall with plastic anchors. Now you can restore power and test the new wiring.

Installing a Dimmer Switch

TOOLS

- Circuit tester
- Screwdriver
- Wire stripper
- Linesman's pliers

Did you know that you could change the mood in a room with lighting without replacing the fixture? Just install a dimmer switch to vary a light fixture's brightness. This is a quick and easy job; the only challenge that may arise is getting the larger-body dimmer switch to fit inside the existing electrical box. (In some cases, you'll need to add a box extender to get everything to fit; these can be found wherever electrical supplies are sold.) Besides, since most dimmer switches generate a small amount of heat, they should never be shoehorned into a small box.

Dimmer switches come in many styles. The most common are the toggle-type, which resemble a standard switch; dial-type (shown here), where rotating the dial varies brightness and the on/off function (or it can be the push-to-turn-on-or-off variety); and the slide-action style, which often has an illuminated face. Although most dimmer switches are designed to replace single-pole switches, three-way dimmer switches are also available.

Remove the old switch. Turn off the power and tag the main service panel. Remove the cover plate screw and cover plate. Test for power with a neon circuit tester by placing one probe on the metal box or ground wire and then touching the other probe to each screw—the lamp should not light. Remove the switch mounting screws, gently pull out the switch (bottom left photo), then disconnect each of the wires with a screwdriver (inset).

Wire the dimmer switch. Since many dimmer switches use wire leads for connections instead of screw terminals, straighten the wire ends with pliers. Connect the dimmer wires to the circuit wires with wire nuts, as shown in the photo at right (usually provided with the switch). These wires are interchangeable so you can connect them to either wire. Alternatively, connect the existing wiring to the screw terminals of the switch with a screwdriver.

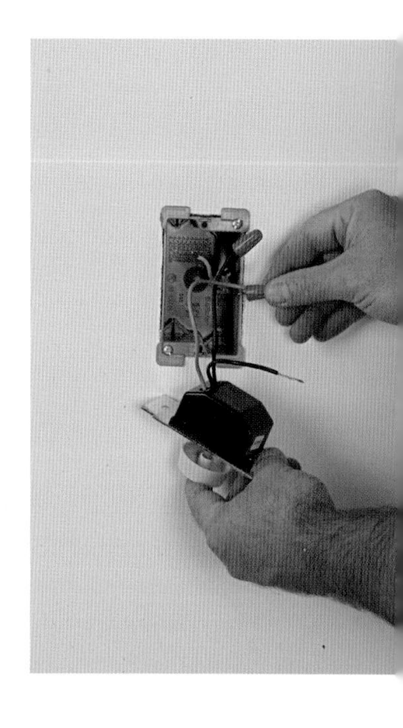

Install the dimmer switch. Finally, push the dimmer switch into the electrical box. Install the mounting screws (bottom photo) and cover plate, and restore the power and test.

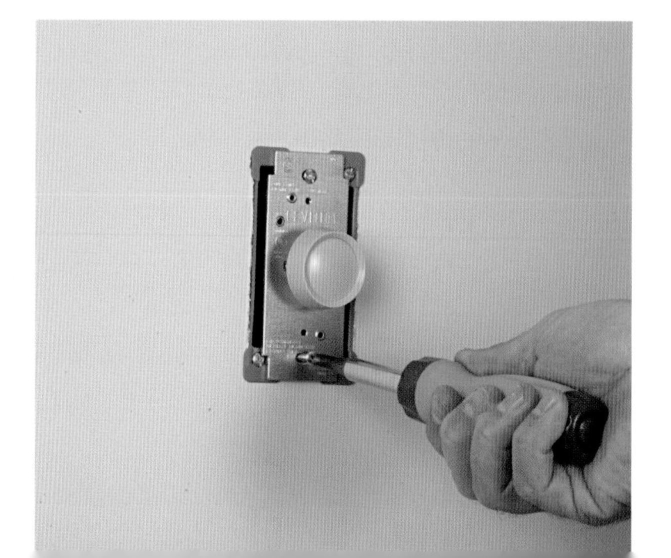

Installing Recessed Lighting

TOOLS

- Stud finder and screwdriver
- Diagonal cutters
- Wire stripper
- Drywall saw
- Needle-nose pliers
- Compass (optional)

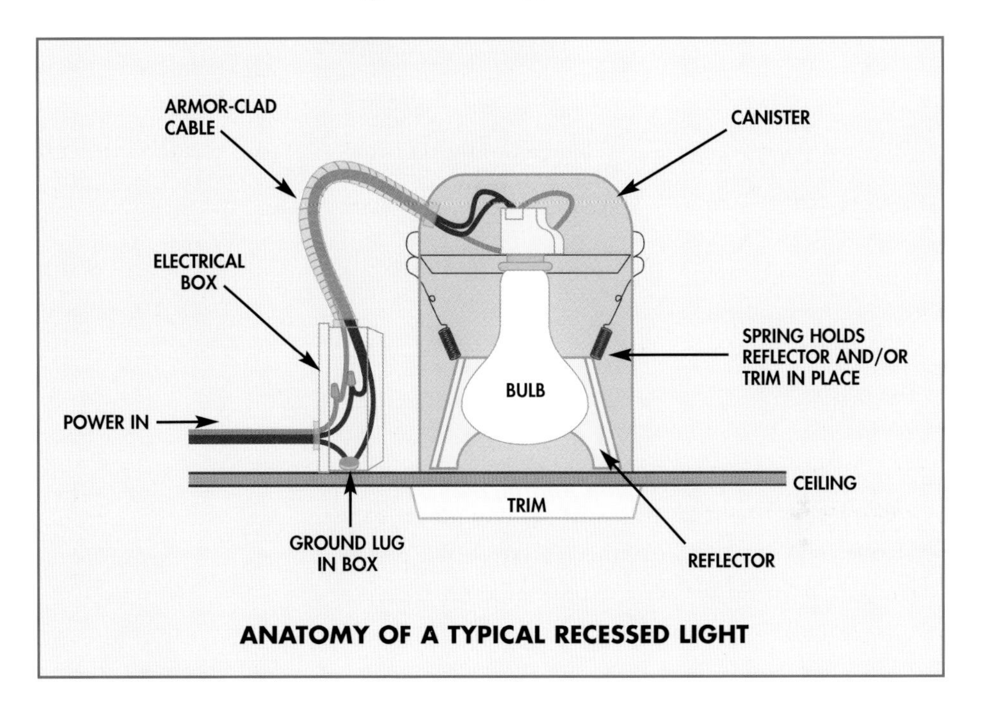

ANATOMY OF A TYPICAL RECESSED LIGHT

Recessed lights are easy to install, they let you put light exactly where you need it, and, because they're recessed into the ceiling, they give the impression of higher ceilings. They are also so unobtrusive that they won't clash or interfere with other design elements in the room. Recessed lights are designed to be mounted in one of three situations: in suspended ceilings, in new construction, and the one that applies most to makeovers, in remodel work. Recessed lights are either single units or two-piece units consisting of a mounting frame and a light; see the drawing above right.

The first step in installing a recessed light is to identify where you want the light. Then locate the ceiling joists with a stud finder as shown in the bottom left photo. If you have easy access to the ceiling from above, you can secure the fixture to the joists. When access is restricted, you'll use the remodel clips provided with the light.

If possible, locate the light between joists to provide plenty of clearance during installation. Mark the hole for the light on the ceiling, either using the template provided (as shown in the bottom right photo) or with a compass set to the recommended radius.

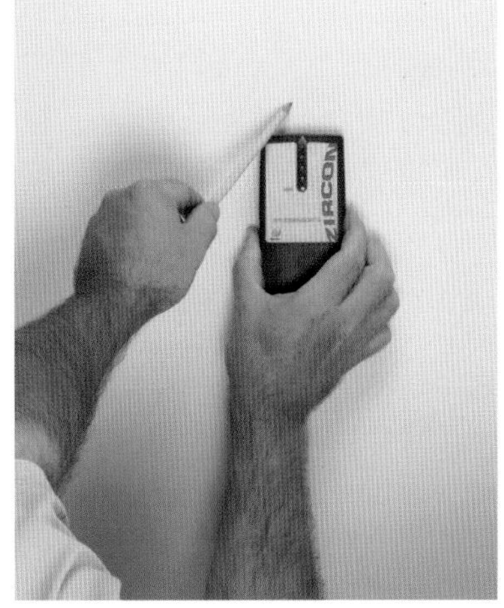

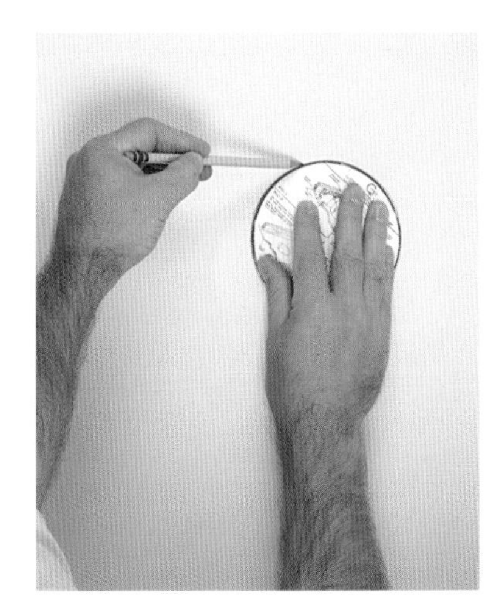

Cut out hole. After you've marked the hole in the ceiling, use a drywall saw or a reciprocating saw to cut the opening for the light, as shown in the top photo. Clear out any insulation to make room for the fixture. If your light is a two-piece model, separate the parts as directed and drop the can through the frame. Then push the frame through the hole in the ceiling and attach it to the ceiling with the remodel clips provided.

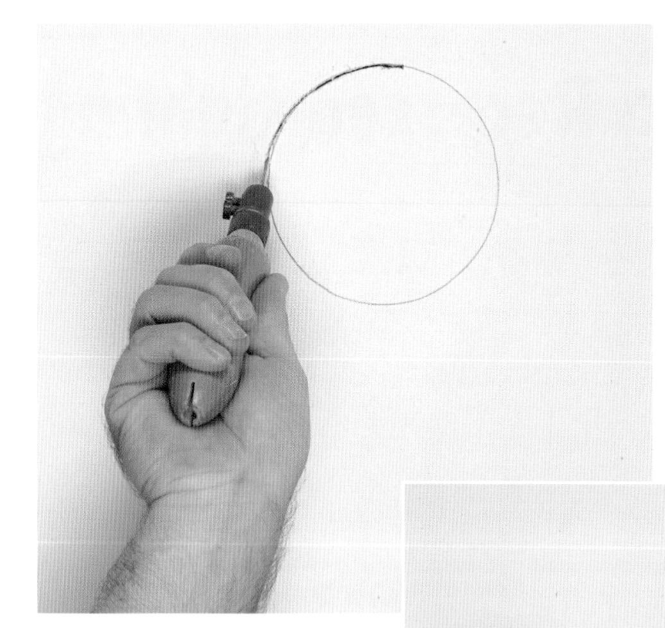

Wire the fixture. Now you can run power to the light; the simplest way to do this is to route the power cable of the old overhead light to the new location. This way the existing light switch can control the lights. If this isn't possible, run new lines or have them installed by an electrician. Note: If your ceiling is insulated, as most are, make sure to purchase lights that are rated to come in contact with insulation. When you've got the power cable routed to the light, follow the manufacturer's directions to wire the fixture as shown in the middle photo.

Insert light in ceiling. With the fixture wired, the next step is to insert it through the hole and up into the ceiling, as shown in the bottom photo. For two-piece units, insert the light fixture through the frame you mounted earlier.

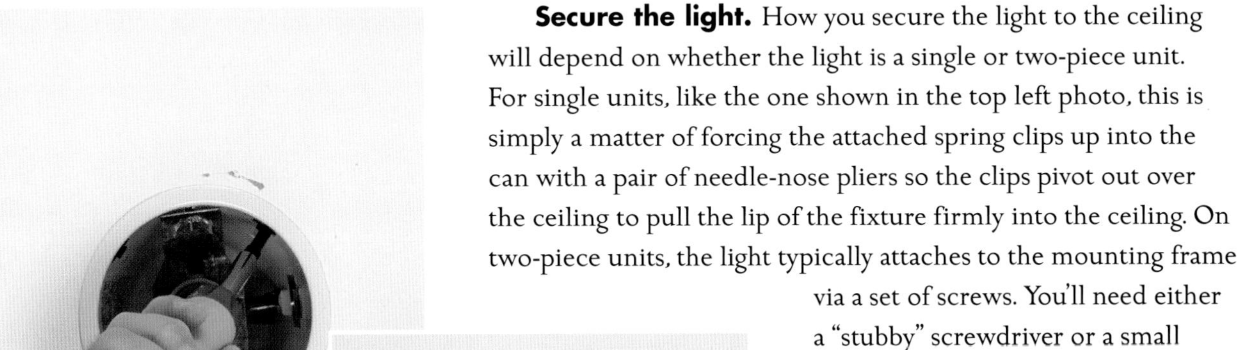

Secure the light. How you secure the light to the ceiling will depend on whether the light is a single or two-piece unit. For single units, like the one shown in the top left photo, this is simply a matter of forcing the attached spring clips up into the can with a pair of needle-nose pliers so the clips pivot out over the ceiling to pull the lip of the fixture firmly into the ceiling. On two-piece units, the light typically attaches to the mounting frame via a set of screws. You'll need either a "stubby" screwdriver or a small socket wrench to tighten these, as space inside the can is cramped.

Install the lamp. On some recessed lights, the bulb holder may need to be threaded into a socket up inside the light. If the light you are installing is like this, install the bulb holder now, as shown in the middle photo. Then screw in the recommended lightbulb.

Add trim. All that's left is to add the decorative trim to the fixture. There are many different ways trim is held in place. On some models, the trim is simply pushed up into the fixture and spring clips hold it in place, as shown in the bottom photo. Other lights use long springs that must be hooked onto tabs up inside the fixture to secure the trim. After you've added the trim, restore power and test.

Installing Track Lighting

TOOLS

- Screwdriver and level
- Driver/drill with bits
- Wire stripper
- Diagonal cutters
- Circuit tester

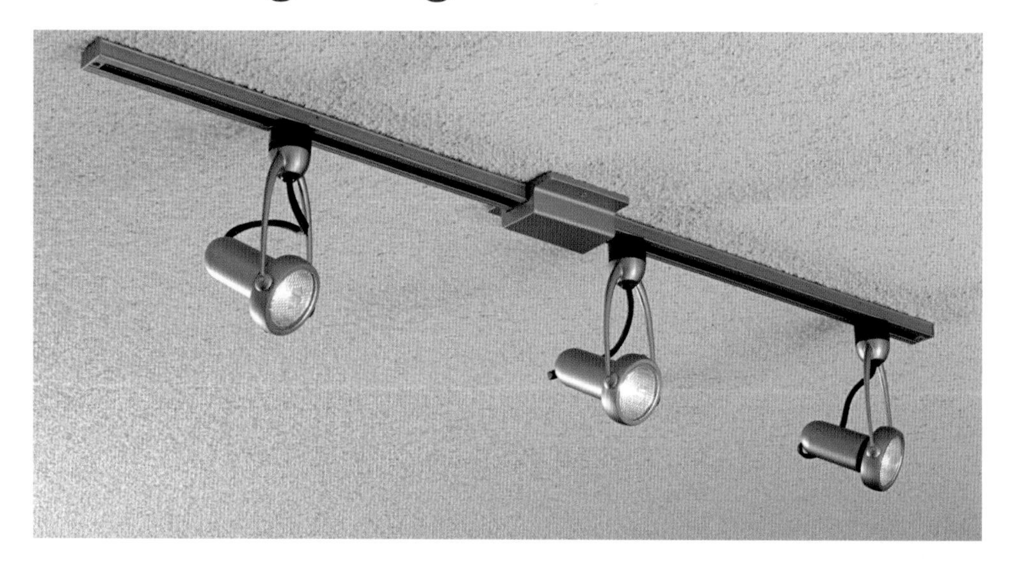

Track lighting is a great way to provide customizable accent lighting in your home; individual lamps snap into a track anywhere along its length to spotlight different areas of the room or special wall treatments. You can either replace an existing fixture with track lighting or have a new electrical box installed to add lighting to a new area in your home.

With the design choices available today, the lighting itself can complement the look of any room, or offer an intriguing but subtle contrast to your décor. From sleek contemporary metals to art-glass antique styles, track lighting now looks right at home anywhere.

Lay out centerline. To install track lighting, start by turning off power to the existing fixture. Remove the old fixture (if applicable), and check the wires for power with a circuit tester before disconnecting them. Then remove the wire nuts and unscrew the old mounting plate. Next, draw a centerline for the track so it's centered on the electrical box from side to side and from end to end. A 4-foot level works great for this, as shown in the bottom left photo.

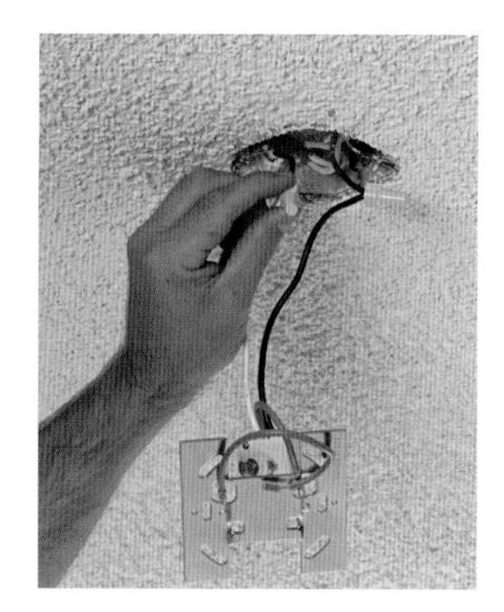

Connect the wiring. Connect the wiring on the connector housing to the circuit wires, following the manufacturer's directions, with wire nuts: black to black, white to white, and green to ground (bottom right photo).

Attach connector housing to box. Next, carefully tuck all the wires up into the electrical box and screw the connector housing to the box as shown in the top left photo. As usual, how the plate attaches to the box will vary from fixture to fixture.

Install track and attach cover plate. Now you can align the track with the reference line you drew earlier and insert the track into the connector housing. Next, mark through the track onto the ceiling for plastic anchors or toggle bolts. Remove the track and drill the holes for the anchors. Then hold the track in position and screw it to the ceiling (top right photo). Note: Some units (like the one shown here) have a pair of setscrews on the connector housing to grip the track as well. Once the track is secured, place the cover plate over the track and fasten it to the connector housing with the screws provided (inset above).

Add fixtures. To complete the installation, unpack the individual light fixtures and install them in the track in the desired locations, as shown in the bottom photo. In most cases, a connector on the end of each lamp fits into the track and then is rotated to snap it in place and make electrical contact with the track. Finally, add bulbs, restore power, and test. Adjust the fixtures to get the desired lighting effect.

Under-Cabinet Lighting

TOOLS

- Screwdriver
- Awl
- Electric drill and bits
- Hammer (optional)

If you've installed cabinets as part of a makeover or you simply want to illuminate a countertop, consider installing under-cabinet lighting. Under-cabinet lighting can be as simple as installing a single strip light underneath the overhead cabinets, or as complex as adding a series of puck lights, either as task lighting or as an accent.

Locate best position for light. Though you can mount an under-cabinet light anywhere under a cabinet, most manufacturers recommend locating the strip as close to the front of the cabinet as possible to create the best coverage (bottom left photo).

Mark mounting holes. When you've determined the best position for the light, locate and mark the holes for the mounting hardware. Many lighting manufacturers provide a template for this. Position the template where you want the light. Then, using a awl, press through the template at the hole locations to make a depression on the underside of the cabinet (bottom right photo).

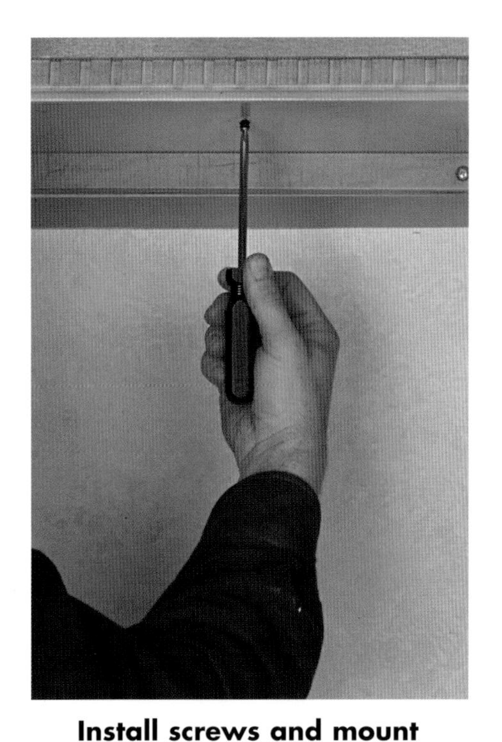

Install screws and mount light. Using the recommended-sized bit, drill pilot holes for the screws (provided with most lights) into the underside of the cabinet. Then drive the screws into the bottom of the cabinet with a screwdriver (above).

Mount the light. Mate the keyhole-shaped slots in the underside of the light fixture with the screws you just installed, and slide the fixture over in the slots in the fixture to lock it in place (above). Most under-cabinet fixtures are designed to plug into a wall receptacle. Halogen fixtures typically require adding a low-voltage transformer that plugs into a standard receptacle.

CONCEALMENT STRIPS

If the under-cabinet lights you've mounted are visible at eye level, install a concealment strip to hide the strip and prevent glare, as shown in the photo at right. This strip is just a 1" to 2" strip of wood or molding nailed to the front edge and finished to match the cabinet.

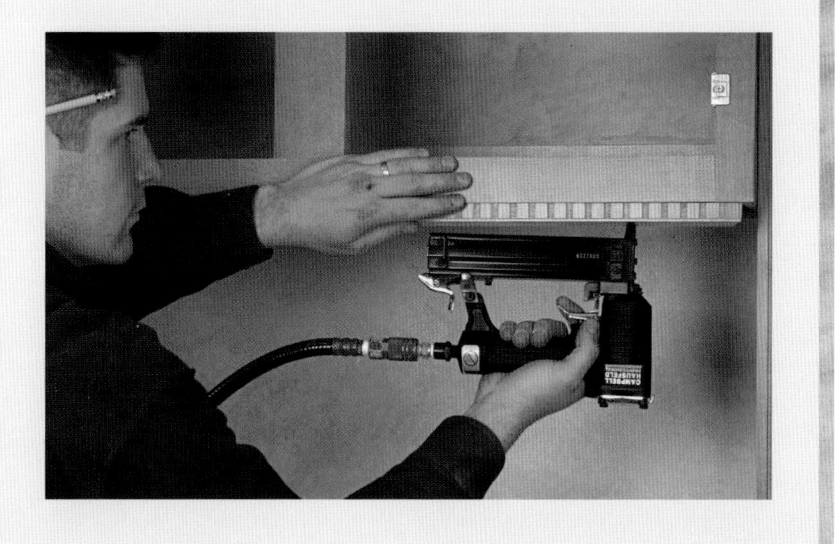

Installing Overhead Lighting

TOOLS

- Screwdriver
- Putty knife
- Wire stripper
- Diagonal cutters
- Circuit tester

It's easy to replace an incandescent light fixture to give a room a new look. There are, however, a couple of things to keep in mind. First, make sure the new lighting fixture will fit and that it doesn't hang too low. Second, the ceiling-mounted electrical box must be able to handle the weight of the new fixture. Fixtures that weigh under 50 pounds can be supported by just the box. If the fixture weighs more than that, most building codes require that the box be attached to framing members. Regardless of the type of fixture you're installing, pay close attention to the maximum allowable wattage for the bulbs. Light fixtures do generate heat. Using bulbs rated higher than the fixture is rated for can cause plastic parts to melt, metal parts to overheat, and eventually lead to a fire.

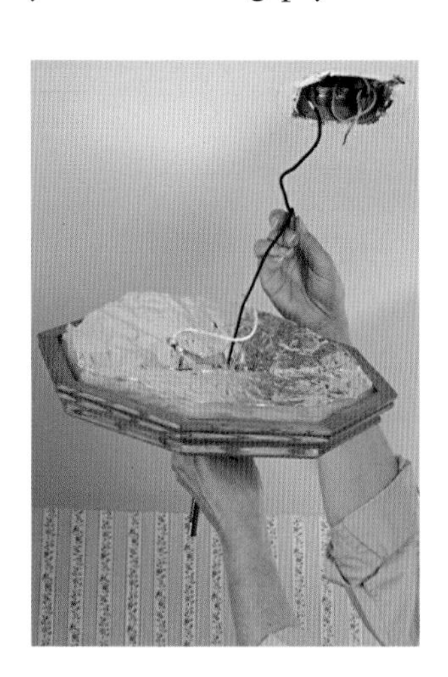

Remove old fixture. Start by turning off the power to the fixture and tagging the service panel. Then remove the diffuser and the bulb(s). Next, unscrew the retaining nut that holds that holds the decorative cover plate onto the electrical box. If the old fixture doesn't come off easily, run the blade of a utility knife or putty knife around the edges of the cover plate to free it from old caulk or paint. Before disconnecting the wires, test to make sure there's no power. If the fixture is heavy, consider making a simple hook out of an old coat hanger to hang the fixture from the box while you work. Once you're sure the power is off, unscrew the wire nuts, separate the wires, and set the old fixture aside (photo above left).

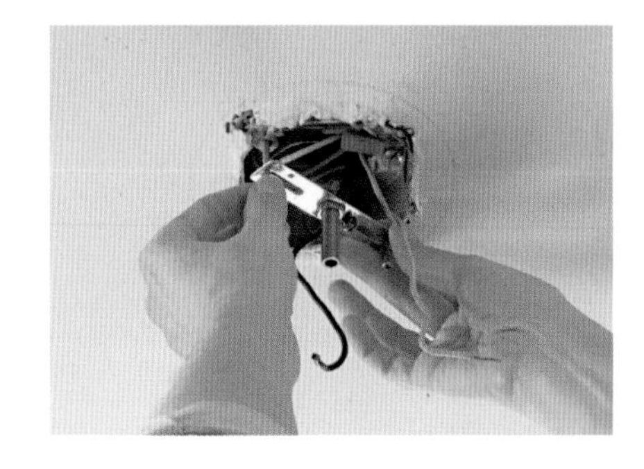

Attach mounting strap. Prior to 1959, incandescent light fixtures were often mounted directly to an electrical box. Electrical code now requires the fixture be mounted to a flat metal bar called a mounting strap or plate that is secured to the box (bottom photo). Most new fixtures include a mounting strap (or you can buy a "universal" mounting strap at your local hardware store). Fasten the strap to the box with the screws provided.

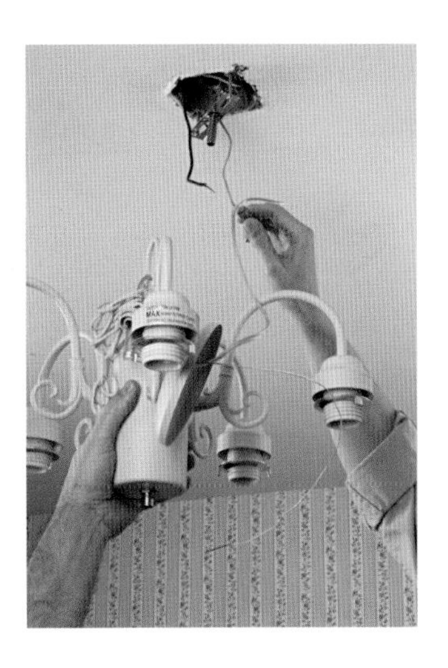

Wire new fixture. Before you install the new fixture, inspect the wires coming out of the box. If the insulation is cracked or the ends are nicked or tarnished, cut the ends off and strip off 1/2" of the insulation from the end with a wire stripper. Now you can attach the new fixture wires to the circuit wires with wire nuts that are supplied with the new fixture, as shown in the top left photo.

Attach fixture. Next, attach the fixture to the mounting plate with the hardware provided (top right photo). If you're planning on installing a medallion (see the sidebar below), do it before you attach the fixture. Then screw in the appropriate bulbs and attach the diffuser. The diffuser is typically held in place with a decorative cap or retaining nut. Tighten this friction-tight and no more—overtightening can crack the diffuser.

INSTALLING A MEDALLION

A common problem when replacing an overhead fixture is that the base plate of the new fixture is smaller than the old one. This can leave an unsightly portion of the ceiling exposed. You could patch and paint this area, but a more elegant solution is to install a medallion. Not only will this cover up the problem area, but it will also add a distinctive touch to both the ceiling and the new light fixture. The medallion shown here is manufactured by Style Solutions (www.stylesolutionsinc.com) and is made from urethane foam, so it's lightweight and easy to install.

Paint if desired. Urethane foam takes paint readily, so if you'd like to add some color, paint the medallion now when it's easiest, before mounting it to the ceiling.

Apply adhesive. Because it's so light and offers such a large gluing surface, a urethane medallion can be secured to the ceiling just by applying a bead of high-quality urethane adhesive to its back.

Press in place. To install the medallion, simply press it in place over the electrical box. Apply a couple of strips of tape to keep it in place until the adhesive sets up.

Index

METRIC EQUIVALENCY CHART

Inches to millimeters and centimeters

inches	mm	cm	inches	cm	inches	cm
1/8	3	0.3	9	22.9	30	76.2
1/4	6	0.6	10	25.4	31	78.7
3/8	10	1.0	11	27.9	32	81.3
1/2	13	1.3	12	30.5	33	83.8
5/8	16	1.6	13	33.0	34	86.4
3/4	19	1.9	14	35.6	35	88.9
7/8	22	2.2	15	38.1	36	91.4
1	25	2.5	16	40.6	37	94.0
1 1/4	32	3.2	17	43.2	38	96.5
1 1/2	38	3.8	18	45.7	39	99.1
1 3/4	44	4.4	19	48.3	40	101.6
2	51	5.1	20	50.8	41	104.1
2 1/2	64	6.4	21	53.3	42	106.7
3	76	7.6	22	55.9	43	109.2
3 1/2	89	8.9	23	58.4	44	111.8
4	102	10.2	24	61.0	45	114.3
4 1/2	114	11.4	25	63.5	46	116.8
5	127	12.7	26	66.0	47	119.4
6	152	15.2	27	68.6	48	121.9
7	178	17.8	28	71.1	49	124.5
8	203	20.3	29	73.7	50	127.0

mm = millimeters   cm = centimeters

Photo credits

Photos courtesy of Andersen Windows (www.andersenwindows.com): page 21 (top left), page 30, page 31.

Photos courtesy of Armstrong (www.armstrong.com): page 8 (top), page 12 (bottom), page 17 (top/middle), page 23 (bottom), page 26 (top right), page 34 (top/bottom), page 35 (all), page 124, page 130 (both bottom).

Photos courtesy of Croscill Inc. (www.croscill.com): page 22 (top left), page 38 (top right).

Photos courtesy of FSC Wallcoverings (www.fschumacher.com): page 11 (bottom left), page 14 (top), page 22 (bottom), page 38 (top left/bottom), page 138.

Photos courtesy of KraftMaid Cabinetry (www.kraftmaid.com): page 20 (top/bottom), page 29 (top/bottom), page 36 (all).

Photos courtesy of Lane Home Furnishings (www.lanefurniture.com): page 9 (middle), page 11 (top/bottom right), page 12 (top right), page 14 (middle), page 15 (bottom), page 22 (top right).

Photos courtesy of Mohawk Industries (www.mohawkind.com): page 4, page 6, page 8 (bottom), page 26 (top left), page 27 (all), page 176.

Photos courtesy of ODL (www.odl.com): page 19 (bottom), page 32, page 33 (top/bottom).

Photos courtesy of Progressive Lighting (www.progressive-lighting.com): page 39 (all).

Photos courtesy of Rocky Mountain Hardware (www.rockymountainhardware.com): page 24.

Photos courtesy of Solatube International (www.solatube.com): page 135 (all).

Photos courtesy of Timberlake Cabinet Company (www.timberlake.com): page 9 (bottom), page 14 (bottom), page 15 (top), page 20 (middle), page 28 (bottom), page 29 (middle), page 37 (all), page 90.

Photos courtesy of Wilsonart International (www.wilsonart.com): page 1, page 3, page 12 (middle), page 18 (top), page 21 (bottom left/right), page 26 (middle/bottom), page 64, page 158.